SEVEN RIVERS
TO CROSS
A Mostly British Council Life

Bruce Nightingale

Bruce Nightingale (signature)

The Radcliffe Press
London · New York

For Diana
in gratitude for sharing
so much

Published in 1996 by
Radcliffe Press
An imprint of I.B.Tauris & Co Ltd
Victoria House
Bloomsbury Square
London WC1B 4DZ

175 Fifth Avenue
New York
NY 10010

In the United States of America
and Canada distributed by
St Martin's Press
175 Fifth Avenue
New York
NY 10010

A full CIP record for this book is available from the British Library

A full CIP record for this book is available from the Library of Congress

ISBN 1–86064–131–8
Library of Congress Catalog card number: available

Copy-edited and laser-set by Selro Publishing Services, Oxford
Printed and bound in Great Britain by WBC Ltd, Bridgend, Mid Glamorgan

Contents

Contents

Contents

Contents

Maps and Illustrations

1 Home-made punt on Cam. BN punting with (back to camera) Roderick Fisher, Mary Elspeth Milford and (facing camera) Erica Greenwood and Peter Greig, 8 June 1954
2 Alhaji Ahmed Tijjani Malumfashi, senior livestock superintendent, Northern Nigeria, 1958
3 Diana at catering resthouse in Zaria, Nigeria, March 1960
4 Rehearsing Bach in St Michael's CCAP, Blantyre, April 1968
5 Concert in Tokyo Bunka Kaikan, with consort of viols from Ueno Gakuen Music College, September 1971
6 Sunday morning at Royal Selangor Flying Club, 25 July 1976
7 Biblioteca Britanica, Bucharest, 1979
8 Rohia monastery, northwestern Romania, April 1981
9 Sir Richard Francis at the helm in Gulf of Finland, June 1988
10 New offices and library in Dianapuisto, Helsinki, March 1988
11 Book presentation to president of Addis Ababa University, Comrade Dr Abiy Kifle, 15 December 1988
12 Annual staff lunch party in Addis Ababa, on day of EPRDF takeover, 27 May 1991

Acronyms

AB	able-bodied seaman
ABRSM	Associated Board of the Royal Schools of Music
ADG	Assistant Director-General
ADO	assistant district officer
AGM	annual general meeting
ALERT	All-Africa Leprosy Research/Rehabilitation and Training
ARIA	State Impresario Agency of Romania
ASB	Admiralty Selection Board
BAC	British Aerospace Corporation
BAFTA	British Academy of Film and Television Arts
BBC	British Broadcasting Corporation
BBFC	British Board of Film Censors
BETS	British English Teaching Scheme
BFI	British Film Institute
BFTPA	British Film and Television Producers' Association
BISFA	British Industrial and Scientific Film Association
BOAC	British Overseas Airways Corporation
BOTB	British Overseas Trade Board
BUFTC	British Universities' Film and Television Council
CBSO	City of Birmingham Symphony Orchestra
CCAP	Church of Central Africa Presbyterian
CEPES	Centre européen pour éducation supérieure

COI	Consolidated Operas Incorporated/Central Office of Information
CRD	cultural relations department (of the FCO)
CUMC	Cambridge University Musical Club
CUMS	Cambridge University Music Society
CUSO	Canadian University Services Overseas
DES	Department of Education and Science
DHSS	Department of Health and Social Security
DIY	do-it-yourself
DO	district officer
EC	European Community
ECO	English Chamber Orchestra
ELTO	English language teaching officer
ENT	ear, nose and throat
EPLF	Eritrean People's Liberation Front
EPRDF	Ethiopian People's Revolutionary Democratic Front
ESC	education, science and culture
FCO	Foreign and Commonwealth Office
FTVAC	Films, Television and Video Advisory Committee
GCSE	General Certificate of Secondary Education
GP14	general-purpose 14-foot sailing dinghy
HM	Her Majesty('s)
HMA	Her Majesty's Ambassador
HMS	Her (*or* His) Majesty's Ship
HMV	His Master's Voice
HQ	headquarters
IBA	Independent Broadcasting Authority
IBM	International Business Machines
ICA	Institute of Contemporary Arts
ICI	Imperial Chemical Industries
ICL	International Computers Limited
ILCA	International Livestock Centre for Africa
IUC	Inter-University Council (for Higher Education Overseas)
IVS	International Voluntary Service

KEEP	Kiyosato Experimental Educational Project
KELT	Key English Language Teaching
KLM	Koninklijke Luchtvaart Maatschappij NV (Royal Dutch Airlines)
LEPRA	Leprosy Relief Association
LFF	London Film Festival
LIFS	London International Film School
LMH	Lady Margaret Hall
LMMM	London Multi Media Market
MBA	Master of Business Administration
MBC	Malawi Broadcasting Corporation
MBE	Member of the Order of the British Empire
MTA	Marine Transport Authority
MV	motor vessel
NA	Native Authority/Native Administration
NATO	North Atlantic Treaty Organization
NFA	National Film Archive
NFT	National Film Theatre
NGO	non-governmental organization
NHK	Nihon Hoso Kyokai (Japanese Broadcasting Corporation)
NPFF	National Panel for Film Festivals
NPO	New Philharmonia Orchestra
NYO	National Youth Orchestra
OAU	Organization of African Unity
ODA	Overseas Development Administration
OLQ	officer-like quality
OS	Ordinary Seaman
OU	Open University
PECDAIC	political, economic, commercial, defence, aid, information and consular
PILC	Programme of Inservice Training for Language Centres
QFI	qualified flying instructor
RAF	Royal Air Force
RMS	Royal Mail Steamer
RN	Royal Navy

RNAS	Royal Naval Air Service
SCO	Scottish Chamber Orchestra
SDO	senior district officer
SHAPE	Supreme Headquarters Allied Powers Europe
SKOP	a Finnish bank
SS	steamship
SSVC	Services Sound and Vision Corporation
STOL	short takeoff and landing aircraft
TAROM	Romanian Air Transport
TLC	tender loving care
TONA	touring officer, northern area
TOSA	touring officer, southern area
TSS	turbine steamship
UAC	United Africa Company
UC3	underwater control third class
UDI	Unilateral Declaration of Independence
UN	United Nations
UNA	United Nations Association
Unesco	United Nations Educational, Scientific, and Cultural Organization
USIS	United States Information Service
VIP	very important person
VSO	Voluntary Service Overseas
WIDER	World Institute for Development Economics Research
WOC	World Orthopaedic Concern

Glossary

addis megeb bet	new eating house, or restaurant (*Amharic*)
alkali	local Muslim judge (*Hausa*)
Ato	Mr (*Amharic*)
beit-el-mal	house of money, or treasury (*Hausa*)
di'o	district officer (*Hausa*)
etsu	Nupe equivalent of Emir (*Hausa*)
Gaimusho	Ministry of Foreign Affairs (*Japanese*)
glögi	mulled sweet wine (*Finnish*)
hiragana	syllabary for normal words (*Japanese*)
jangali	cattle tax (*Hausa*)
joulu	yuletide/December/Christmas (*Finnish*)
Kabuki	a type of theatre (*Japanese*)
kakaki	eight-foot ceremonial trumpet (*Hausa*)
kakemono	wall-hanging scroll painting (*Japanese*)
kana	the two phonetic syllabaries, *hiragana* and *katakana* (*Japanese*)
kanji	adaptation of Chinese-style ideographs (*Japanese*)
katakana	syllabary for transliterated foreign words (*Japanese*)
korkeakoulu	technical university (lit. highschool) (*Finnish*)
koto	traditional stringed instrument (*Japanese*)
lamido	Fulani equivalent of emir (*Hausa*)
maliki	one variety of Muslim law (*Hausa*)
Maskal	Finding of the True Cross (*Amharic*)
meishi	name card (*Japanese*)
Monbusho	Ministry of Education (*Japanese*)

mulkin kai	self-government (*Hausa*)
Noh	a type of drama (*Japanese*)
padang	field/central open area of a village (*Malay*)
parador	high-class country hotel (*Spanish*)
pikku joulu	little yuletide, mid-November (*Finnish*)
promotio	academic investiture (*Finnish*)
rivitalo	row house/terraced condominium (*Finnish*)
romaji	romanized method of writing (*Japanese*)
rumfa	market shelter/grass hut (*Hausa*)
salla	Muslim feast day (*Hausa*)
Salvarea	Romanian ambulance
sardauna	traditional ruler of Sokoto (*Hausa*)
shakuhachi	traditional bamboo flute (*Japanese*)
Timkat	Epiphany (*Amharic*)
tsuica	plum brandy (*Romanian*)
Vappu	May Day celebrating end of winter (*Finnish*)
vierasvenesatama	guest-boat harbour (*Finnish*)
Wzo	Mrs (*Amharic*)

Acknowledgements

I am indebted to many former colleagues for commenting favourably on several short anecdotal pieces and for encouraging me to take up the challenge of writing a book-length treatment of the ups and downs of life and work, chiefly within the British Council context.

Sensitivity to possible accusations of pretentious self-importance — who would want to read anything of this sort? — made me reluctant at first, but the widespread ignorance of the worthwhileness of this particular form of winning friends and influencing people, and at the modest middle-ranking level here described, reinforced the need to make the effort. Furthermore, the Radcliffe Press recognized that there was a gap in their list which could well be filled in this way, and I am grateful to Dr Lester Crook who persuaded me that only an autobiographical framework could elucidate the stresses and strains, the pleasures and rewards, of such a way of life.

It would be wrong to name the individuals who have been mentors, guides, colleagues and friends in diverse circumstances and often in remote places; they will recognize themselves in the text and should not be implicated in its many shortcomings. Some of the detail may be thought superfluous, but whereas too much can be boring too little may fail to create an atmosphere. An account that aims to be favourable and that promises to avoid controversial axe-grinding must nevertheless offer a 'warts and all' picture, so there is no pretence that British Council work was all intellectual enjoyment — much of it had to be mundane and sometimes tedious.

Acknowledgements

I wish to thank my editor, Mrs Selina Cohen, for her meticulous attention to detail, and it is no mere formality to acknowledge the forbearance of my wife, to whom the book is dedicated and who put up with the postponement of many domestic tasks during the writing.

Totnes, April 1996

Foreword
by Sir John Hanson KCMG CBE
Director-General of the British Council

Far more people in Britain are aware of the BBC World
Service than they are of the British Council. Yet both organizations are crucial for Britain's reputation abroad. The
World Service is strong in the air; the British Council is strong on
the ground. And that is where the British Council is known best —
on the ground, overseas, working in more than a hundred countries, where the Council brings countless thousands of people into
crucial long-term contact with Britain.

That is the organization Bruce Nightingale joined in 1965,
drawn by the same motivation as I was two years earlier, and as
generations of colleagues have been before and since. Britain is
one of just a handful of countries with the capability to support its
overseas interests through its cultural and educational resources,
through the international role of the English language, by welcoming foreign students into its universities, by the excellence of its
arts, through the networks of contacts built on professional and
scientific links between Britain and the world. The British Council
takes the lead for Britain in all this work. It is a high octane
mixture. Some people join the Council to work for progress and
development in Africa and Asia. Others lean towards European
cooperation or reconstruction in east and central Europe. All are
pulled by the excitement of contact with foreign cultures and
foreign languages — and people of diverse backgrounds and
beliefs. Underlying all their activities is an unshakeable belief in

the importance of mutual understanding in an uncertain, but inter-dependent, world.

Excitement brings its dangers as well as its rewards. Bruce Nightingale's account of life in Addis Ababa in the final throes of civil war, when the Mengistu regime fell, is mirrored in the experi-ences of Council staff who have been caught up variously in the Nigerian civil war, the Iranian revolution, the Iraq hostage episode and a variety of wars, earthquakes and other disasters across the face of the planet. At its very worst, two council staff were mur-dered by terrorists on an Athens street in 1983. In recent months the Council has been forced to pull its staff at short notice out of Yemen and Algeria. They will certainly have left with reluctance. No one cheerfully abandons ties that have grown over decades and which matter in people's lives.

So perhaps it is not surprising that the story of this book is not so much a Council career as a way of life. Or a family business: from Nigeria, through Malawi and places east and west to Ethiopia, for Bruce and Diana Nightingale and their family it was a joint venture of equal commitment. The British Council, like all international organizations involved in communication, must exploit every aspect of media technology and the Internet. But there is no substitute for person-to-person exchange and the trust and confidence that human contact engenders. Britain's engage-ment in the world would be catastrophically the less without it.

January 1996

PART I

The First Age, 1932–65:
Seeking the Right Road

1

Rural Childhood
and Urban Schooling

M y father was director of music of Dauntsey's School for 25 years, from 1928 to 1953. The school is situated on the northern edge of Salisbury Plain, six miles south of Devizes, in the centre of a group of five villages — West and Market Lavington, Great and Little Cheverell, and Littleton Panel. This environment changed radically in the period before, during and after the Second World War, but at the time of my birth in 1932 the countryside was undisturbed; very occasional motor traffic, horses rather than tractors on the farms, elm trees, a working blacksmith in the village, bicycles quite popular, and regular congregations in the churches. The army was in evidence during manœuvres from time to time, otherwise contact with the world at large was restricted to travel by the steam trains of the Great Western Railway, either up to Paddington or down to Bristol and the west. The Cornish Riviera express whistled through Lavington station once a day.

Devizes moonraker and Wiltshire wurzel
My mother gave birth to all five children in the same nursing home in Devizes in sight of the Moonrakers' Pond. First me, then two sisters before the war, followed by two more sisters in 1942 and 1944. We all claim to be less stupid than we may seem, a claim based on the story of the Devizes smugglers who hid their

contraband in the pond. When asked by the excise men to explain their nocturnally observed attempts at raking it to the surface, they feigned the simple-minded belief that the moon's reflection on the surface of the water indicated the presence of great riches for which they were fishing. A shrug of incredulity, and the investigators gave up.

By 1939 my parents had moved out of the Glebe House of All Saints, West Lavington, and built a fine new family house of modern design just outside Little Cheverell. It stood in an acre of ground — formerly allotments, but rather sandy and in need of manure — which, as war approached, was vigorously developed for the cultivation not only of fruit and vegetables but also for the support of livestock, including goats, rabbits, hens, ducks and bees. Encouraged by her brothers in the army — neither of whom, alas, would survive the war — our mother was determined to be able to feed us in the event of invasion and disaster. Meanwhile my schooling, and that of my sisters, was in the capable hands of Miss Florence Holiday's 'dame school', the county elementary school in the village being generally avoided by the small minority of middle-class, professional parents in the district. We had little idea of how 'rough' that might have been, but the consensus of the masters of Dauntsey's School and their wives was probably correct. The three Rs came to me readily from the age of four and a half onwards, but my vivid memories at around the age of six can be regarded with hindsight as significant, in that the BBC Schools Radio Service offered nature study and travel talks on certain afternoons. They held my attention very closely.

My father's concern to teach me the piano from the age of five was not effective, but we did better with singing, and this led him to think of a choir school as the next step. In the spring of 1939 for three months (including my seventh birthday) a serious illness kept me in bed; it was septicaemia derived from an infected finger, and caused great anxiety.

Yet later in the year we visited Christ Church, Oxford, where Sir Thomas Armstrong was organist and choirmaster, and known to my father from his Royal College of Music days. Did he think my voice promising enough? Evidently so, but my mother did not like the look of the choir school, so early in 1940 attention was switched to Windsor where St George's Chapel in the castle needed choristers.

As on subsequent occasions, the competition was said to be stiff, and the tests were conducted by Dr Harris (later Sir William) in his house in the lower ward of the castle. There was no expectation that eight-year-old boys would be able to read music, but the reading aloud of an unseen psalm was the first hurdle, after which my party piece of John Goss's well-known setting of H. F. Lyte's hymn 'Praise my soul the King of Heaven' impressed the selectors sufficiently to award me a choristership. The value was a proportion of the boarding fees at St George's School, but an elaborate list of costly uniform had to be bought from the designated suppliers in London.

Windsor in wartime
An unforgettable date — 1 May 1940 — was my first day away from home, and the beginning of several months of agonizing unhappiness at a time when parents had enough to worry about without a homesick child threatening (emptily) to run away. There was an epidemic of chickenpox and the weather was very hot, so exacerbating the feelings of a child whose emotions were a tangle of incredulity that loving parents could wittingly have consigned him to such incarceration. The sudden plunge from an idyllic home environment, ruled by love, into an incomprehensibly alien daily routine and discipline, ruled by fear and compulsion — that was the one experience 'never to be inflicted on any child of mine'! Alas for such resolutions — all three of my daughters have subsequently been through the same version of hell. Yet girls' prep schools in the 1970s were civilized compared with the marked barbarity of the tradition-bound boys' boarding establishments of my time. Even so, the benefits were not inconsiderable.

First, we were very well taught — maths, Latin and French, with an occasional glance at English, geography and history — by staff who for a variety of reasons had not been called up for the war. Secondly, the musical discipline involved a combination of mental and physical exertion which stimulated a range of capabilities of long-term value, such as concentration, stamina, patience and teamwork. Thirdly, by a subtle form of indoctrination we were half convinced that we were engaged in work, not just of service to the Almighty, but in 'work of national importance'.

The Dean and Chapter made no concessions to Hitler. In spite of some parental concern that disruption of sleep by air-raid warnings, uncertain diet and other irregularities were damaging our health — and there were two serious flu epidemics — the authorities of St George's Chapel took pride in their unique determination to maintain two choral services a day. Matins at 9.15 a.m. meant a boys' practice at 8.30 and evensong at 5.00 p.m. a practice at 4.15 — a total of three hours singing daily (more on Sundays) except Wednesdays, which was our day off.

What effect did all this have on lessons and sport, and more sensitive matters such as religion? One economy measure in recognition of the realities of the war had been agreed by the Dean and Chapter; that was a reduction in the number of choristers from 24 to 18. In the school there were another 20 boys known as supers (i.e. supernumeraries, presumably) who paid full fees, and a similar number of dayboys, a total of about 60. In academic achievement and on the games field the choir was fully competitive with the supers and dayboys. The energy expended in choral training and performance evidently made a paradoxically positive contribution. But the intense exposure to Anglican liturgy, music, reading and prayer did produce a premature religiosity in some boys, including me. At one extreme this was punctured with the normal onset of adolescence (as in my case), and at the other it led to a lifelong devotion to established Christianity — with most boys taking a middle course.

In some quarters it was firmly believed that Windsor Castle was spared the blitzkrieg because Hitler fancied living in it, but no chances were being taken, especially as members of the Royal Family were often in residence. There was a battery of Bofors anti-aircraft guns deployed on the Brocas, just across the Thames. When the siren warned of an air raid and the guns opened up, it was a source of childish pride for me to know that my Uncle Tony, an officer in the Royal Artillery, was in charge of our defences.

The organist and choirmaster was universally (and mostly with affection) known as Doc H. He had a round, usually jolly face with a few wisps of hair across an otherwise bald head. Our note learning and voice training was normally conducted in a benign atmosphere, and certainly enjoyed by most of us with the musical sensitivity required for the technical challenge. From time to time, however, we suffered from a 'batey [bad-tempered] practice'. Once there was a disastrous breakdown in the middle of an unaccompanied anthem, and Doc H, who had been listening in agony, leant out from the organ loft and said in a stage whisper — 'Boys, boys, you've let me down!' In the vestry after that service, the Dean, Bishop Hamilton, said, 'It is a relief to know you are human after all.'

On Saturday mornings there was a full practice with the lay clerks (the alto, tenor and bass singers) in the choir stalls of the chapel rather than in the separate practice room where we normally rehearsed. Behind the choir on each side were the stalls of the Knights of the Garter, and over each stall hung a heraldic banner. One Saturday morning, as we were finishing the practice, workmen came with a ladder and took down the banner of the Emperor of Japan who had been deprived of his garter following the infamous attack on Pearl Harbor (December 1941). The banner was laid on the chancel floor and we stood in a circle to admire the gold chrysanthemum on its scarlet ground. Suddenly Doc H said 'Come on, boys, let's stamp on it' — and we did, solemnly and ceremoniously, leaving footmarks all over it. Were they still there when the banner was revived for the Emperor's reinstatement 30 years later?

The Princesses Elizabeth and Margaret Rose were teenagers at this time and Doc H was involved in their musical education. For the first eight choristers this entailed the privilege of four boys on alternate Monday afternoons attending the red drawing room of the castle to join the royals in singing part songs and madrigals. The rest of the group consisted of senior Eton boys, some Grenadier Guards officers from the garrison, and a few 'wobbly sopranos' (as we arrogantly thought) from the Windsor and Eton Choral Society. Possibly in recognition of this 'service', we received at the school from the Princesses a much appreciated supplement to our food supplies — part of a consignment of Argentinian honey sent to them by loyal British subjects far away.

Royal christenings took place in the private chapel of the castle, and there were no fewer than three major funerals in St George's during the war — the Duke of Kent, Princess Beatrice and the Duke of Connaught. The first of these required the choir to be re-assembled in the middle of the summer holidays and was none too easy with telephones 'reserved' for military use. Other effects of the war included the keeping of hens in the chapter garden adjacent to the school, and the reversal of use of rooms in our building. Desks and blackboards were moved upstairs to the dormitories and we slept downstairs in the classrooms, ready at the sound of an imminent danger bell (activated in the round tower lookout of the castle) to rush down to the cellars.

Becoming head chorister in January 1945 forced me to begin keeping a diary (a habit that has remained ever since) in order to record mundane details, such as which boy's turn it was to go to tea with which canon, or to sing with the princesses, or to have time off, or to help with the washing-up. Rather more significant events of that year included Victory in Europe and Victory in Japan celebrations, the general election 'landslide' to Labour and, more personally, my winning a music scholarship to Clifton College, Bristol. My treble voice began to show signs of deteriorating in the autumn, but lessons on the cello had been quite fruitful for several years, so presumably the selectors detected adequate musicianship.

A fourth term as head chorister (and head prefect) saw me helping a new headmaster to pick up the threads, and within a week of Easter 1946 my journeys to Bristol began.

Bristol after the blitz

The experience of transfer from the top of one school to the bottom, or even middle forms, of another is good preparation for being posted to, or finding for oneself, a new job. At least the hurdle of homesickness was no obstacle now, yet my first term in Oakeley's House (since converted luxuriously for the intake of girls) was as ill-starred as my first in Windsor. Scarlet fever rather than chickenpox was epidemic, and after only four weeks the sanatorium took me in for a full month (there was talk of a dreaded isolation hospital somewhere) and then home for the rest of the term.

Hence my four years of annual cycle did not begin properly until the autumn of 1946, at the age of 14½, with the later consequence of a curtailed period in the sixth form. Yet Bosham creek in Chichester harbour, where my maternal grandmother lived, offered ideal recuperation, and the second postwar summer holiday there enabled me to 'go solo' in sailing dinghies. Even so, Clifton's director of music, Douglas Fox, had extracted a promise from my father to send me for a week on a schools' orchestra course in Sherborne, which entailed a reluctant break in the joy of messing about in boats.

What was an independent school of this sort like in the late 1940s? Above all, the ethos was strict discipline, enforced with a variety of sanctions, based in houses for sleeping, games and private study, and on the school as a whole for classroom work in forms and sets. Call-over in the house before breakfast, 9.00 a.m. chapel for all (punctuality and attendance checked), then an almost continuous timetable ending with another call-over and house prayers at bedtime. Respect for the system, for others and for oneself was effectively instilled provided you conformed, and if you failed to be tidy, punctual and properly dressed more than three times in one term the head of house would get approval from the housemaster to administer a relatively mild form of corporal punishment. It was the indignity rather than the pain of three whacks with a cane that 'braced up' the offender. Reinforcing this regime was a hierarchical framework with fags at the bottom and sixths at the top, which encouraged a progressive increase in the capacity and desire to organize and take responsibility for the lives of those in the layer beneath. My stint as head fag involved making a rota of petty duties and ensuring they were carried out by my peers. Progress up the house hierarchy kept more or less in step with academic progress up the school.

Only a few long-serving masters will have observed the evolution of this system to what it has become 45 years later, transformed by a shift in social and educational norms, yet still flourishing and achieving high quality in all fields.

My life as a music scholar, however, was abnormal. For all of us there was 'work' and there was 'games', and the life of many was dominated by rugger in the winter terms and cricket in the summer, with an elaborate and inexorable series of inter-house competitions (culminating in 'cock house' matches) and school matches for the very proficient. For me 'work' had to include music, and this resulted not only in a distortion of the normal curriculum but also in a whole series of extra obligations in terms of performing — in house competitions, in school concerts or in Bristol at large. Clifton's musical reputation was high and vigorously maintained under the leadership of Dr Douglas Fox, but he found me a bit odd; never before had there been one among his flock who could not — and seemed incapable of learning to — play the piano. Happily, after a couple of years my broken treble became a serviceable tenor, so singing lessons were allowed instead of those painful sessions at the keyboard. Stranger still, however, was one who wanted to specialize in science. This really was a problem, and needed discussion between my parents and my housemaster to resolve it.

Among the masters there were many strong personalities and several inspiring teachers. 'Work' was based on Latin as the form subject and C. F. Taylor inspired most of us to learn that, and very much more, supremely well. It was to my lasting benefit to be in his fifth form for my school certificate (now GCSE) year, since he effectively lit the torch of intellectual curiosity in my adolescent mind. But he could be scathing, and once said memorably to a less-awakened friend, as much in despair and self-criticism as anger, through clenched teeth, 'Do you know, boy, sometimes I despise your mentality!'

As a counterpoise there was also inspired teaching of maths by P. C. Unwin who opened my eyes to the power of the practical applications of trigonometry, statics and dynamics in his sprightly manner of asking — 'Will it slide or will it topple?' Physics-with-chemistry was also well taught, as was history, and my exam results were surprisingly good. So what should my future course be? Parental puzzlement was relieved by the consultation already mentioned, but would this lead to university entrance? Not easily, since my academic level was only moderate; but how about the back door? Would not my chances of a choral award to Cambridge be high? Yes, but the major ones were at King's or St John's, and at neither was it possible for their choral scholars to read any science subject because laboratory times clashed with chapel duties. So it came about that after one year of maths, physics and chemistry (and music, of course) my studies switched to history, English (and music) for my final year in the school, which included the privilege of being taught by J. L. Thorn.

Meanwhile 'games' (compulsory rugger and cricket) demanded some energy, and my contribution as a wing three-quarter to victory in several inter-house matches was by no means ignominious; but once above a certain level in the system one was allowed to opt for athletics or hockey in winter; and in the summer my escape from everlasting cricket was rowing one year and tennis the next. The overriding priority remained, however, to perform on my cello in the first two years and/or to sing in my last two years, taking a prominent part — usually solo — in the house singing competition, a music club members' chamber concert, the Christmas concert, the orchestral concert, the speech day concert, and the house instrumental competition — plus the occasional choral society performances in Bristol cathedral or St Mary Redcliffe church. It is hard to credit some of the flattering reports in *The Cliftonian* at the time. Humiliation was not far off.

Two final points about my schooling should be covered. One major outside commitment was the National Youth Orchestra (NYO), the brainchild of Miss Ruth Railton who toured all the schools of Britain auditioning likely candidates in 1947. She consigned me to the seventh desk of the cellos, and my pride in being a founder member survives, in spite of only scraping in. The first course under Dr Reginald Jacques was in Bath in April 1948, and my subsequent attendance was in alternate school holidays. He also conducted the third, in Liverpool, in January 1949: but by the time of the fifth course in Leeds in August, under Walter Susskind, my attention was beginning to focus exclusively on the paramount need to get into Cambridge by singing, so that was my last NYO attendance. (Some 35 years later my third daughter Jessica enjoyed several courses in the viola section.)

Secondly, although my eventual success in being awarded a choral scholarship to King's College, Cambridge, in the competition of March 1950 (thanks to an appropriate background, some lessons from Miss Madge Thomas and a bit of skilful coaching by Dr Fox) opened a wonderful and exciting prospect, my personal

11

development had not kept pace in other respects. At the age of 18 such non-musical capabilities normally expected of a product of my sort of school had been sadly neglected. My relatively high profile had fostered the illusion of being an effective person. That was not so, as will become clear in the next chapter. Two unhappy decisions help to explain it; first, although it was normally compulsory for all boys to spend Monday afternoons 'playing soldiers' in the Combined Cadet Force (or Corps), my parents were in a postwar pacifist frame of mind, and my housemaster was persuaded to allow me to be a pseudo-pacifist and be excused the corps in the interest of extra music time. And the second 'turning point' occurred towards the end of my first year when a perspicacious house tutor recommended that an Outward Bound course would do me good. How right he was, but family finances could not manage the cost of that as well as the Sherborne school orchestra course to which a music scholar had to be committed.

Should music be master or servant? About this time began my awareness of a love–hate relationship that lasts to this day.

2

Two Years
Before the Mast

The decision to allow me to opt out of 'playing soldiers' in the school corps was inspired partly in the knowledge that conscription at the age of 18 was still a national requirement so that some sort of military training would be inevitable. Why, therefore, waste time doing it at school? In retrospect, however, there is little doubt that my lack of basic familiarity with the elements of man management and leadership in a 'combat' organization was to prove a serious handicap. Furthermore, there was a deep-seated family assumption that the navy was preferable to the army; my father had flown seaplanes and flying boats in the Royal Naval Air Service (RNAS) in the First World War, in spite of his father and grandfather having been Church of England clergymen; and my maternal grandfather (and other forebears) had been naval officers. The RNAS was absorbed into the RAF between the wars, but became the Fleet Air Arm in the Second World War, and in 1950 it was possible for national servicemen to become naval pilots and navigators.

Postwar conscription for national service
In almost total ignorance of the wide gap between the likely requirements and my personal capacities at that time, it was duly arranged during my last term at Clifton for me to enrol in the

13

Royal Naval Volunteer Reserve on HMS *Flying Fox* in Bristol, being the only way a conscript could be sure of allocation to the navy rather than the otherwise automatic assignment to army recruitment. It was permissible to defer national service for higher education, and King's had said when making the award that my choral scholarship would be valid either in the current year or not until 1952, depending on another man's exam result. Simultaneously, the Korean War had caused the period of conscription to be increased from 18 months to two years; King's found they did not need me until October 1952, it was not possible to wait for the next Fleet Air Arm entry competition, and my 'joining up' became urgent so that two years could be completed in time for Cambridge.

The unforgettable date of 9 October 1950 marked my joining 'the mob' at Victoria barracks (now demolished) in Portsmouth, and the beginning of a long period of adjustment, or readjustment, to the real relationship of my own deficient personality to the adult world. As was reasonable, recruits with an 'educated' background were put into a class of NS/CW candidates, or national service ratings (ordinary seamen) who, at the end of a mere three weeks of initial foot drill, rifle drill (square-bashing) and simulated mess-deck life, would be presented to an Admiralty selection board (ASB) for 'commission and warrant' training. The class leaders (one of them a de Rothschild) had both been cadet officers in the naval sections of their school corps, and the rest of my companions had similarly appropriate experience. It did not take long for me to be regarded as the odd man out, yet the instructor petty officer was admirably fair and encouraging, and my struggle to catch up fast was not entirely fruitless.

On the day of reckoning the ASB passed all but three of the class: two were deferred (Tom Chadwick and Trevor Davies — why should their names be remembered?) and my failure was solitary. The board had been unable to detect any OLQs (officer-like qualities) in me and, as for 'power of command', there had been little hope of acquiring it in so short a time. Most of the class went off to become national service upper yardsmen, while my 'draft chit' consigned me with Tom and Trevor to basic seamanship training in Devonport aboard HMS *Indefatigable*, one of the biggest aircraft carriers afloat, with double hanger decks converted from aircraft handling to trainee mess decks.

Seaborne indoctrination

This setback (as hinted in the last chapter) was my first serious failure in a life which had hitherto been one of steady progression. It was a salutary shock, yet it should not have surprised me on any dispassionate estimate of my prospects. It disturbed me enough to stimulate a determination to seek for means of self-improvement, and within a few weeks this resulted in my enrolment in a correspondence course with the Pelman Institute. Clearly, a vague and romantic interest in seafaring, coupled with some practical knowledge of handling sailing boats, and a craze for making warship models in prep-school days, was an absurdly slender basis for any aspiration to advancement in a short-term naval career. My family had readily admitted that there might never be any prospect of 'getting my feet under the wardroom table', yet there was no appreciation — such as impressed me in years to come — that not to have attained commissioned rank during national service was a quite significant shortcoming. Would it have been easier in the army? Not necessarily, and in any case the dye was cast, so the challenge was to make the best of it.

Self-reliance was not the problem; that had been learnt very early as a boarding-school survival technique. What needed bolstering was my self-confidence. Far from displaying the expected characteristics of an ex-public schoolboy, my appearance was timid and my demeanour ineffectual. My participation in team games had been undistinguished, and the recent concentration on singing could hardly have been less relevant. Fortunately, the applied psychology of Pelmanism, spread over the ensuing 11 months, helped to indicate the way forward. At the same time my mastery of lower deck language and customs improved daily, and even a little previous understanding of big ships was useful.

Indefatigable as a training ship was grossly untypical of normal naval life. No other mess decks anywhere could be like the cavernous, open-plan areas of floating aircraft hangars. Banks of steel lockers constituted the only boundaries between the various classes, and there were frequent disputes requiring resolution by the petty officers in charge. The flight deck was handy, of course, as a parade ground. At the risk of becoming extremely cynical it soon became my habit to compile a catalogue of 'naval absurdities', and the earliest of these was the task of sweeping rainwater uphill on the flight deck.

After a month in Devonport, *Indefatigable* spent another month in Portland, the open space of Weymouth Bay being good for learning boat work, both pulling and sailing whalers and cutters. On 30 January 1951 the ship sailed for Gibraltar and the process of seeing the world began. The motion at the extremities of a big ship pitching in an Atlantic swell is similar to repeatedly going up and down several storeys in the lift of a tall building, so seasickness took its toll of many raw trainees. The classrooms for formal instruction were well forward in our vessel, and my memory of taking my turn to vomit out of the scuttle (not 'porthole', please) remains vivid. Once across Biscay, however, there was a wonderful new experience — a warm wind.

The first 'run ashore' in Gibraltar was a revelation to one who had been prevented by the war and its aftermath from the trips to the continent which all schoolchildren now do. The Main Street (so called) was lined with stores displaying unimaginable 'goodies', and as rationing was still in force in Britain my first duty was to send home the biggest food parcel my pay packet could afford. Even more interesting was a day trip by coach to Cadiz, organized by the Free Church chaplain, and exposing us to cheap food and drink in Franco's Spain.

It was an odd coincidence that Mark Bridgman, who was to marry my eldest sister Sheelagh seven years later, had joined the navy in Portsmouth on the same day as me; but in contrast to my two-year commitment he had signed on for 12, seriously determined to work his way up. The physical courage and mental stamina to achieve this has earned my admiration ever since, and life in an adjacent training class of *Indefatigable* gave me ample opportunity to observe his early struggles, which were in due course deservedly successful. His rugger-playing background and boat wisdom helped, but sheer guts were essential. Our common motto has remained 'Them wot's keen gets fell'd in previous!'

For recreational purposes *Indefatigable* carried several Royal

Naval Sailing Association 14-foot sailing dinghies — tubby, and with a typically unmodernized gunter-lug rig, but providing an adequate excuse for Mark and me to crew each other and win some races in the harbour. Together we collected a sailing prize from the Rear-Admiral. In early March the ship returned to Portland, the training courses were complete, and by the end of the month my draft chit had consigned me to Royal Naval barracks Devonport to join the pool of 'gash hands' — the daily slave market for detailing — and for Easter leave.

From dry dock to the North Atlantic
HMS *Cumberland* was a county-class heavy cruiser, originally designed to carry eight-inch guns, but now totally disarmed and colloquially known as a 'three-funnelled bastard'. She was being refitted to become a boffins' vessel, or a floating test-bed for the Royal Naval Scientific Service. My draft to *Cumberland* found her in dry dock and my duty was to man the telephone exchange on a watch-keeping basis. This was not a good beginning to naval life proper, but had to be endured for several months. We moved out of the dock into the basin, then into the river, and eventually into Plymouth Sound, progressively carrying out victualling, fuelling, compass-swinging and turning trials. By the end of May we had completed stabilizer trials and full power trials, had endured a commander-in-chief's inspection, and moved to Portland for more sea trials. All summer we were in and out of Portsmouth and Spithead, and also spent a memorable week in the Firth of Clyde, doing the measured mile off the Isle of Arran.

Meanwhile, the watch-keeping routine had enabled me to take 'seven beller' leaves, that is, 24 hours off expiring at 11.30 a.m., and one of these was spent in London at the Festival of Britain. Others were spent with my family in Bosham when within range. But my escape from the telephone exchange and return to ordinary seaman's duties came in time for 'painting ship' in preparation for the Mediterranean. *Cumberland* sailed via Gibraltar for Malta where six weeks of gunnery trials, using the boffins' latest equipment, culminated in the scoring of a direct hit by a 4.5-inch shell on an air-towed target.

By this time it had become apparent that the ship was a sadly unhappy one, manned largely by reservists who had been recalled from their civilian occupations because of the war in Korea. They would have been content on a fighting ship in the Far East, but doing 'research' was not convincing. The symptoms were theft on board, misbehaviour ashore and record numbers of 'defaulters' to be punished. Little of this affected my enjoyment of boat party duty, manning the motor cutters and learning to operate the 'kitchen' or 'bucket' steering gear, and (being once more a watch-keeper) enjoying seven-bell leave to explore the many artistic and historic attractions of the Maltese island. Fairly hot autumn days were followed by wonderfully fresh nights, and it was permitted to sling hammocks in the open, my favourite 'billet' under the stars being between two guard-rail stanchions. We wore tropical rig (white shorts and sandals), drank the official 'limers' issue (lime juice against scurvy) and acted on the order 'out wind-scoops' to increase air circulation below decks. Most weekends the ship was moored in Dockyard Creek of Grand Harbour, Valetta, and a series of letters home is preserved, giving my thoughts on all these novelties. They included local celebrations of the two great sieges — of 1565 and 1943 — and visits ashore as a 'culture vulture' in uniform, not just in the city but by bus and on foot into the centre of the island — to the medieval citadel of Mdina, for example. A Canadian sailor encountered in the Roman villa there was heard to remark 'Gee, I wish we could have seen all this *before* schooling!'

Significant beyond recognition at the time was my first discovery of the British Council. Its institute in Valetta had a reading room, which accepted servicemen and later allowed me a ticket for the Commonwealth premier screening of *The Lady with a Lamp*, with Anna Neagle as Florence Nightingale.

Letters home also reported trouble with a tropical ulcer on my leg, which confined me to the sickbay for some time; the ship's call in Algiers for two days in late October; and a fiasco of incompetent handling when berthing on the detached mole in Gibraltar. Throughout this period there was always a good supply of Penguin or Pelican books in my oilskin pocket, especially all the classics' series to date and all the plays of G. B. Shaw; but *Teach Yourself Portuguese* took precedence for a while in preparation

18

for four fascinating days in Lisbon, after which we steamed off into the Atlantic, chasing patches of heavy weather in order to test our multi-finned stabilizers to the limit. Blissful unconcern followed from my now having reliable sea legs.

Early December saw us back in our base of Devonport with Christmas leave granted and all 'Guzz ratings' in high spirits — including me with another draft chit pending.

Underwater (torpedo and antisubmarine) special training
The authorities were understandably reluctant to invest much in short-service conscripts, but early in my second year my need to escape the unqualified 'mob' of 'hands' devoted to little more than incessant cleaning and painting led me to apply for a 15-week underwater control course, such as would ensure postings to small, in preference to large, ships — and would provide a qualification, however lowly. This meant the spring of 1952 partly in HMS *Defiance*, a wooden-walled hulk moored in the Tamar river, and partly in HMS *Osprey*, the shore base on Portland Bill, together with days at sea in Castle-class frigates and Z-class destroyers chasing 'exercise' submarines by the asdic (Anti-Submarine Detection Investigation Committee) method. Asdics (since renamed sonar) involved listening to the echo pitch of an ultrasonic transmission through water, relying on the Doppler effect to estimate the speed of approach or otherwise. My performance, employing my sensitive musical ear, in hunting and locating the submarine 'quarry' so impressed the instructing staff that one of them asked me about officer training; but my response had to be that it was too late, even if by then some of the desirable 'class leader' attributes had emerged.

Meanwhile, my runs ashore were based on my Uncle Bill's house in Plympton and the Plymouth Arts Centre, or the Pelly family's house in Chickerell and the White Ensign Club of Weymouth. *Defiance* was a happy ship (in contrast to *Cumberland*); she had a few 14-foot dinghies attached, and best of all a 50-square-metre 'windfall' yacht (war prize from the Kiel Canal area) called *Sea Swallow* for which my crewing was appreciated in inter-service races on Wednesdays and Saturdays. Most significant for the future, however, were my several visits by bus to musical events in

Dartington Hall, which, by a string of chance meetings, led within a year to my father being invited to join the staff and the move of my family from Wiltshire to Devon.

The daily tot of rum, both ashore and afloat, was issued when 'Up Spirits' was piped at noon, and all ratings were classified as 'grog', 'temperance' or 'under age'. On my twentieth birthday my designation was duly changed from under age to grog — just for the hell of it. Then, in mid-May, with 18 months' service completed, my status was raised from ordinary (OS) to able-bodied (AB) seaman, my pay increased from 5/– (25p) to 10/– (50p) a day, and my rating as UC3 (underwater control third class) recognized. Finally, in mid-September, came my discharge back to civilian life — 'time expired'.

3

Cambridge and Oxford

T he transition from the lowest form of life in the navy to the privileged life of a gentleman undergraduate (not student, please) was tremendously liberating. A vista of at least three years of intense activity — musical, intellectual and social — lay ahead, and was the more exciting for having been postponed for two years.

The duties of a King's choral scholar
The first term as a choral scholar was testing by any standards. The worldwide reputation of King's College chapel choir was largely the work of Boris Ord, the organist and director of music. His achievement rested on perfectionist rehearsals and daily performances of the Anglican cathedral repertoire by a rigorously selected and hypersensitive team of 16 boys and 12 men. Furthermore, the choir had to be under constant retraining, for the generational turnover was about five years for the boys and three years for the men. The routine of 4.15 choir practice and 5.30 evensong took almost three hours out of every day, more on Sundays, and as a 'fresher' one had to do preliminary homework.

John Marvin was my fellow tenor, guide, mentor and friend throughout this ordeal of initiation, which included meticulous 'pointing' of the psalms, greater musical precision than most people could have previously experienced, reading plainsong notation (for the Wednesday men-only services) and close attention to intonation (essential in a building with a five-second reverberation). There was also some note learning of new music, even if Windsor and Clifton had provided limited familiarity. John was a model of patience, as was Bill Oxenbury who shared digs with me in 6 Corn Exchange Street (since demolished) and who had come up at the same time with an alto choral scholarship after army service. The pressure eased after the first term, but not until the full liturgical cycle of a year and its appropriate music had been mastered could one afford to do less homework.

The effects of all this on life in college and on the university education we sought were not unlike those of the beneficial stimuli described in Chapter 1. In choir practices, Boris Ord's disciplined rehearsal technique, which was timed to the minute, has inspired many emulators. But it was strictly authoritarian, and on one occasion when the senior alto made a remark that was interpreted as an insubordinate attempt at 'arguing the toss', Boris responded with 'If you want to be rude, my boy, I can be ruder.'

As for the risk of religiosity, one elderly lady was overheard in the front court one day, having emerged from evensong, saying to her companion, 'Isn't it wonderful to think of all those young men preparing for the Church?' Little did she know — although some were reading for the music tripos, most of us were reading English, history, law, geography or economics, that is arts/humanities generally, but none was tackling theology or moral sciences.

Essays, lectures and supervisions in history

John Saltmarsh was my first supervisor. There was never a kindlier person. He was an expert not only on medieval economic history in general but also on the fabric of the chapel and the long process of its construction — nearly a century from 1446 to 1538. His conducted tours of the building, including visits to the roof and the timbered space above the stone vault, were famous; and his favourite comment, in his characteristically singsong voice, was 'Each of the 22 pinnacles cost £6. 13s. 4d.' He knew the details of the unusually complete building accounts so well, and knew also the appropriate factor by which to multiply the figures for conversion to present-day costs, that his estimates were used by the college for insurance purposes.

Knowing that my capacity for academic writing had been rusting away for two years, he suggested first a general essay on 'The Mediterranean'. And, at the end of my first year, in the light of my nervousness about the four papers which constituted 'the Mays', or the preliminary exam for Part I of the history tripos, he said to me, 'Never mind, old boy, just go in and have a bash,' which proved excellent advice, because my marks were better then than in later years, in spite of the many distractions. One sort of distraction was familiar — the constant pressure from musicians in other colleges and the university at large to participate in their concerts either as tenor or, more often, playing cello continuo. The other sort of distraction was a novelty — for me, anyway; that of feminine company from Newnham, Girton and New Hall, both at lectures and joining in so much of the music making.

My other main supervisor was Christopher Morris, who dealt with the constitutional and philosophical aspects, and whose series of lectures on the history of political thought inspired me with considerable enthusiasm. This led in due course to my request to transfer to economics, which would require a fourth year and needed negotiation by the senior tutor, Patrick Wilkinson. He was a man of extraordinary sagacity who seemed invariably to know the right thing for me better than myself. He had been in on the choral scholarship selection procedure in March 1950, and had warned me off wanting to read law. The final hurdle had been to perform my party piece ('Waft her, angels, to the skies' from Handel's *Jephtha*) in the chapel. Sensing that my chances had been consolidated, he walked me down the ante-chapel and asked about my thoughts on what to read. My response mentioned both history and law, whereupon he said, 'We think that a year of law is enough to dry up anyone, so you should in any case read something else first.'

Subsequently he was instrumental in helping me from the supplementary exhibition fund, in nominating me for a travel grant, in convincing the state scholarship administrators to support me for the extra year (not in the choir), in recognizing that British Council work would suit me and, finally, in arranging for New College, Oxford, to accept me as affiliated during my year under Colonial Office sponsorship. But that is to look too far ahead.

Social excitements of the first May Week

Reverting to the spring of 1953, it should be mentioned that the age range in the college at this time was wider than normal on account of the continuation of conscription, some doing their national service before coming up and some after graduation. So those in residence could be in their late teens or mid-twenties — and older if doing research. The result was a very broad choice of friends, except that a choral scholar had 11 'colleagues' perforce at the start; but a spread of five years of undergraduate intake caused happy coincidences which would not otherwise have occurred. For example, Ben Elliott, who is now vicar of Mere, was two years my junior but came up at the same time and we studied together. Geoffrey Hardyman, my contemporary in Clifton, was in Clare College next door, and Tony Jacobs in Queens' the other side. A group of five 'medics' became friends through Peter Greig who shared digs with me. Mark Lowe (also of Clifton), Robin Milner, Nick Steinitz and Colin Tilney all came up in 1954 and our friendships have survived. My Clifton musical network included the organ scholars both of Clare (Keith Warner) and of Corpus Christi (Alan Vening), and later Richard Popplewell in King's itself. Then there was a handful of college hockey players and, later, oarsmen and squash players — but vigorous exercise does funny things to the vocal chords and had to be avoided before choir practices.

Some of us had girlfriends, but all liaisons were subject to pre-permissive social mores. Ben agonized with me over who to invite to the May Ball, which we viewed as the climax of the year; and when my invitation was accepted by Jane Pelly, to come all the way from Weymouth, some dancing lessons had to be squeezed into the last few weeks of term. Provost Sheppard liked to preside over the ball for some of the night from the alcove of the college hall, but one had to avoid catching his eye for fear of being 'blessed', a procedure open to misinterpretation by one's partner. There were bands, and champagne, and elegant clothes; sitting out areas and midnight walks in the streets of Cambridge; and — being determined to do everything properly — punting in the June dawn to Grantchester for breakfast. That took a lot of forgetting, and it combined with May Week concerts of all sorts to produce a

24

degree of nervous exhaustion which did not pass unnoticed by my parents on my return home to Wiltshire. Two weeks' 'reserve training' aboard the destroyer HMS *Zephyr* brought me down to earth pretty smartly.

The long vac term, Edinburgh and the Border Country
Boris Ord expected most of his protégés to support, if needed, the university madrigal society, which he conducted and which was especially known for singing on the river under King's Bridge during May Week. In this year it also performed *A Garland for the Queen*, a set of ten new part songs commissioned by the Arts Council, in the Royal Festival Hall on the eve of the coronation, 1 June. The society was also invited to take part in the Edinburgh Festival, so providing John Marvin and me with an excuse to plan a short walking tour.

The long vac term runs for six weeks from early July to mid-August, and is a peculiar Cambridge habit, much despised by Oxford people as strangely barbarian. The choir was compelled to be in residence, but for all others it was voluntary, so the college did not expect payment of its dues from us. Events during this period included the annual cricket match between the choral scholars and the choir school at Fenners, the university ground; sometimes a recording session; and the annual ritual known as Boris's Lammas Day Breakfast (1 August) — the biggest brunch imaginable, served in hall to the privileged few. This year, too, a few driving lessons to polish up the skilled but unofficial tuition of my father produced the desired result of passing my driving test.

A short interlude in Bosham with my family included a first cruise in the Solent area as skipper of the small, four-ton gaff-rigged sloop my parents had acquired a couple of years earlier. With my two elder sisters we went from Chichester harbour across to Wooton Creek, up the Beaulieu river, round to Porchester and Fareham Creek, up the Hamble river to Bursledon, and finally over to Cowes and up the Medina river — all in ten days of very unsettled weather.

Robin Locke was a mathematics don of Caius College, a keen clarinettist, a regular member of the Chelsea Opera Group orchestra, and a pillar of Bernard Robinson's Music Camp, then still at

Bothampstead Farm near Newbury. He offered me a lift in his car driving to Edinburgh, provided we could rendezvous at the camp. This was to be my first acquaintance with an institution of great significance, as will become apparent in later chapters.

The highlight of the festival was Glyndebourne's production of Mozart's *Idomeneo*, remembered for a beautifully matched set of soloists; and, being first-time visitors, we felt compelled to tour the sights. The Borders beckoned, however, and our plan to use Scottish youth hostels in easy stages involved stocking our rucksacks with food for supper and breakfast each day, so some initial shopping was necessary. We reached our first night stop ahead of schedule in the early afternoon, and were greeted with 'Ye'll nae git in till four o'clock' — a rule of the system that had escaped our reading. Blessed with fine weather all week, our route included the abbeys of Melrose, Dryburgh and Jedburgh, with a final climb over the Cheviot Hills into Northumberland.

Ian Stephens held a fellowship of King's on what seemed to be a 'without portfolio' basis. He was a rare polymath with a first in both natural sciences and history, and had been editor of the Calcutta *Statesman* at the time of the partition of India. His fund of useful introductions for footloose and globetrotting undergraduates was inexhaustible and, in his usual generous manner, he had given John and me strong encouragement to call on his old friend Charles Bosanquet, later vice-chancellor of Newcastle University. We duly presented ourselves at his home, Rock Moor near Alnick, and were swept in with 'I know what chaps in your condition need — a bottle of whisky and a bath!' — which was followed by a sumptuous supper and a lively evening with his family.

My parents' move from Dauntsey's School to Dartington Hall had been completed and there was just time to visit the new family home in Devon before returning to Cambridge.

Second-year sagas

One sad inconvenience was the clash of two attractive activities on Saturday evenings; the Cambridge University Musical Club (CUMC) members performed chamber concerts for themselves in the music faculty rooms and, on three occasions each term, a college group known as Consolidated Operas Incorporated (COI) presented to itself unrehearsed readings of the Gilbert and Sullivan corpus. (CUMC is different from CUMS which did big choral works in public.) As a cellist my contribution to the club was regular, but some light relief from the seriousness of chapel was very desirable, and the Gilbert and Sullivan readings were suitably light-hearted. Much of the enjoyment came from the mixed company, and my moment came in *The Gondoliers* when singing opposite a voluptuous red-headed Girtonian 'To Gianetta I was mated, I can prove it in a trice; 'tho' her charms are overrated, yet I own she's rather nice.'

This particular encounter led nowhere, but my association with Erica Greenwood, who was Tony Jacob's fellow flautist in the CUMS orchestra, was to last the whole year. Few musicians in the university avoided involvement in the Lent term production of Vaughan Williams's *The Pilgrim's Progress*, fully staged in the Guildhall, and conducted by Boris Ord (and, after an accident halfway through the week, by Alan Percival). Called a morality rather than an opera, it had been first produced by Covent Garden in 1951. Our 1954 version, with John Noble in the title role, became the basis of HMV's 1972 recording. (My part was the small one of celestial messenger.)

At home for the Easter vacation, my project to build a punt gathered pace. To ensure its transportability from Devon to the Cam river, my design envisaged a central 'box' section of ten feet with the tapered ends of four foot each being bolted on through watertight bulkheads. Materials were mahogany planks, oak bends, marine-quality plywood, resin glue and some 400 brass screws.

My long-suffering family tolerated the construction, which 'overflowed' into the kitchen and had to leave the house through a window. The vessel came up by road as intended, we varnished it in Lady Rachel Matthew's garage on Millington Road, it was launched at Fen Causeway bridge and completed its maiden voyage downstream to King's Backs on 8 June (see photograph). The senior tutor's permission had been obtained to moor it, but he had said 'You do realize you can't work in a punt, don't you?'

How transparent was my immature enthusiasm for such distractions! Meanwhile, another saga was the formation of a choir eight to row in the May bumps as King's fifth boat. Outings began in late April with Bill Oxenbury coxing and David Calcutt as stroke. Any tendency to glance in the direction of the occasional lady supporter on the towpath, and Bill would yell — 'Eyes in the boat!' An hour and a half on successive Saturday afternoons was scarcely sufficient, but we 'rowed over' on the first two days and nearly scored an over-bump on the second, yet got bumped by Corpus Christi on the third and over-bumped by Caius on the last.

Small wonder that my efforts to answer the examiners' questions in the six three-hour papers of the history tripos Part I resulted in a third-class marking. It was no surprise, but was suitably sobering.

The Rupert and Albert Brooke Memorial Fund

Early in the year Patrick Wilkinson had surprised me with the news that the college had decided to award me a travel grant of £35 (worth about £1400 now?) for use in the summer. The fund had been established by the Trustees of Mrs Brooke's will in 1930 in memory of her two much-admired sons, lost in 1914 and 1915. The awards had become known as 'good-chapmanship grants', and were clearly intended to broaden horizons.

Apart from one or two naval ports my ignorance of Europe was profound, so planning the best use of the grant — for a grand tour — became yet another distraction from 'proper study', especially since what evolved was a motorized expedition with girlfriend Erica, her brother Roger and my second sister Jenny. The first task was to buy a cheap but reliable car. This created the usual parental anxiety, but we settled on a 1937 Ford 8 (with 1950 engine) from a Cambridge garage. Second, came estimated route, timing and cost; and third, logistics and equipment for camping.

In five weeks we covered 3000 miles on roads that were very much postwar and a sore trial for a heavily laden vehicle, not infrequently 'touching bottom' when negotiating pavé and potholes. But my care, maintenance and 'nursing' paid off, and the lessons learnt were invaluable for many later expeditions — to Turkey two years later, to Austria in the winter of 1956/7, and four journeys across Europe to or from Romania between 1978 and 1981. For me the price of enlightenment was exhaustion.

28

Detail would be out of place but several principles emerged. For example, as time actually on the move is wasted, maximum sightseeing is achieved by eating before stopping. When camping, however, it is best to pack up and move off for an hour or so before breakfasting, and it is important to reach the next camp site in daylight. Do not rely on only one, possibly sleepy or ill, driver in the party. Try to avoid moving every day; two nights in one place followed by a longer travelling day is better. More obviously, perhaps, there must be agreement on the overriding interests among the party and an agreed method of controlling the 'kitty' expenditure.

Third-year excitements, economics and Shetland

The switch from history to economics was inspired by my realization of the need to sort out how to earn my living, other than by teaching or through music, both such options being ruled out for good reason. Economics offered the prospect of understanding how the world worked in the present and possible future, rather than the past. But Part II of the tripos was known to be a bit tough and to require two years. Would my choral scholarship be extended for a fourth year? My preference was to give it up, first because the quality of my tenor voice did not find great favour (rightly so, until many years later), and second because my relations with Boris Ord and Hugh Maclean (the organ scholar) were a bit cool; and third, to be honest, because of a degree of disenchantment with the chapel and all it stood for, which was curiously at variance with many of the dons of an agnostic persuasion on the high table. Happily the senior tutor's explanation to the ministry convinced them that the state should make up the difference in my maintenance for a fourth year not in the choir.

The strong tradition of economics in King's sprang from Maynard Keynes and continued through Pigou and Kahn. It was my privilege to have Eric Hobsbawm teaching economic history, Nicholas Kaldor teaching principles, and Harry Johnson teaching international trade. Others, particularly Robin Marris and Noel Annan, inspired and supervised my fourth year.

Meanwhile, the inexorable choral routine continued and, in this third year, it was my turn to introduce Peter Bingham, the new tenor colleague, to the mysteries and conventions. Another encounter with the British Council occurred early in 1955 when we gathered in London to see the playback of our televised carol service of the previous Christmas. Then, in the Easter vacation, the whole choir undertook a two-week tour of Switzerland. My room-share companion was Nicholas Steinitz, who later made a similar switch from history to economics but, unlike me, he did become a professional economist in the civil service. Travel was by ferry and train, the itinerary being far more leisurely than it would be now-adays by air. Five concerts only was considered sufficient and allowed plenty of time for visits in Basle, Berne, Geneva, Zurich and Kreutzlingen, a small place on the Bodensee.

By this time my circle of friends had widened considerably and the 'dating' of several girlfriends was a regular habit. Three in particular engaged my attention more than casually, but in no way exclusively. Avis Rombulow-Pearce was reading classics in Newnham, sang soprano, and her brother Christopher was in the agricultural service in Tanganyika; Jenefer Wiltshire was reading economics in Girton and was a wonderfully sensitive accompanist in a wide range of *Lieder* and other songs; and Mary Elspeth Milford, eldest daughter of Canon T. R. Milford (a founder of Oxfam) was reading English in Newnham and played the violin. Each of these friends, during the spring and summer of 1955, came with me for a few days to Bosham to stay with my ever-welcoming maternal grandmother, for a breath of sea air and an introduction to dinghy sailing — always refreshing after the confines of 'work' in Cambridge.

The preliminary exam in economics, like that in history, consisted of only four papers, and my efforts were given a lower second class — not too discouraging for a new subject and at least an improvement on the third in history. The long vac term was enlivened this year by a visit by the Duke of Edinburgh, a pageant in St John's, and two recording sessions. It finished with my last day in the choir and the prospect of a very different existence.

Robert Anderson was a research student in Egyptology and his brother John a medical student who subsequently specialized in ophthalmology. They played cello and violin respectively and came from a Shetland crofting family. They kept their connections

fresh by arranging musical house parties in Burravoe Manor on
the island of Yell, and Mary Elspeth was invited with me to join
them and David Cairns and Lenore Reynell in late August. We
were in Dartington with our own house party for a week of the
summer school, and the journey by my old Ford 8 from Devon to
Mid Yell took six days — no motorways then and maximum
speed 40 miles per hour. The whole experience remains vivid to
this day and proved to be a most memorable holiday. Overnight
stops northwards were mostly with Milford family friends, and on
reaching Aberdeen on the fourth evening we stayed with Dennis
and Mary Munby. The car was left with them and we took the
overnight boat to Lerwick as deck passengers — distinctly cold
and uncomfortable. A bus, a ferry and another bus brought us to
Burravoe by lunch time.

String quartet playing was the basic activity and the environment of treeless landscape, clear air, clear sea, birds, sheep and
stone walls was ideal. We caught mackerel, transported peat,
watched weaving and visited the Andersons' aunt, Mrs Thomasina
Spence. We prepared a sailing boat for a coastal voyage but were
frustrated by a gale and walked instead.

The journey southward was much more comfortable, involving
two nights at sea to enable the ship to call at Kirkwall, capital of
the Orkneys, where there is a fine Norman-style cathedral, and
then two days on the road from Aberdeen via Edinburgh to the
Milford family home in Lincoln.

The rest of September was devoted to my second and last stint
of reserve training, based on HMS *Osprey* in Portland but on
board the *Carisbrooke Castle* doing antisubmarine exercises for
most of the two weeks.

Fourth-year freedom to explore: jobs and Turkey
Roderick Fisher was also 'of the year 1952' and, having graduated
in zoology, was now embarking on research in entomology for a
Ph.D. We had agreed to share digs in 9 King's Parade, right opposite our porter's lodge; but in terms of accommodation my straw
was the shortest, so after one term it seemed wiser to move round
to 5 St Mary's Chambers. Among my neighbours there was
Murray Sanderson, over from Oxford to do the one-year overseas

31

service course in preparation for working in Kenya — the reverse of my move in the following year. As will be seen, much of his advice proved invaluable, and we kept in touch for many years.

Freedom from choral duties of so many hours a week offered scope to explore much that had previously been denied by clashes of timing. This included the consolidation of many musical friendships in the 'secular' world, especially the members of the Chelsea Opera Group, which performed on Sunday afternoons, and the network of Music Camp enthusiasts; but the priority was economics and the world of whatever work might lie ahead. A variously sponsored series of visits enabled me to be suitably awestruck by the blast furnaces of Stewart and Lloyds' steel works and rolling mills in Corby, to be mildly deafened by the looms of a Courtauld's factory, to be impressed by the Breckland conservation methods on Lord Iveagh's estate at Elveden, to watch Lyons of Cadby Hall produce swiss rolls by the mile, and to witness an auction at Sotheby's.

Help in exploring the non-ecclesiastical repertoire for the voice came from Colin Tilney, now an authority on early keyboard music and a world-class performer, and from Michael Bruno who enjoyed accompanying me on the piano, as did (for my cello) Norman Routledge, a maths don of King's and later Eton housemaster. Early in 1956 the college suffered two serious bereavements; first the suicide of Ivor Ramsay, the Dean, and then a few months later the sudden death of Provost Glanville after only a short time in office.

The search for an understanding of international institutions led me to join the Cambridge University United Nations Association, and its ten-day visit to Paris in the Easter vacation. This included guided tours of Unesco and the Organization for European Economic Cooperation (where an ex-King's economist, Jake Wright, was working) and visits to NATO headquarters (then in the Palais de Chaillot, but later moved to Brussels) and SHAPE — plus, of course, any number of unscheduled excursions to museums, and one particularly memorable sound, that of the Russian Orthodox Church choir on Palm Sunday morning.

Meanwhile, the University Appointments Board had helpfully arranged interviews in London for me with the Finance Corporation for Industry and with a firm of stockbrokers, but in mid-May an undergraduate of rare perspicacity, John Pilgrim, had arranged a meeting, which was addressed by an official from the Colonial Office, attempting to explain the apparent failures of British policy in Kenya and in Cyprus, which had been suffering from the Mau Mau and Makarios respectively. Several of us resolved there and then that the right thing to do was to go and see what was happening on the ground — hence, for me, a seminal occasion.

In taking stock of possible jobs my conclusion had been that my nature was that of an animal that did not thrive in captivity, so at this stage a desk in London was ruled out and some degree of out-door life took precedence. Horizons had been widened and globe-trotting was a family tendency. In spite of a general shrinkage of the British Empire, and preparation for independence in most territories, the Secretary of State for the Colonies still needed to recruit administrators, especially for East and West Africa. My father wrote, 'We do not think you ought to bury yourself in Africa,' to which my rather callous reply was 'People who go to Africa nowadays are not buried there.'

There was truth in both statements; parental anxiety was natural, yet 'the white man's grave' had been largely conquered by modern medicine. So in one afternoon — 28 June 1956 — selection boards both in the Colonial Office and in the British Council grilled me, probing character and motivation as closely as possible. The upshot was the offer of an appointment in Northern Nigeria from the first but silence until too late from the second.

A month before that, however, with the economics tripos Part II exams written (and yielding a decent lower second) the final flings of a fourth May Week included the usual plethora of parties and concerts, and a crazy May Ball escapade in the company of Janet Roseveare and Colin Tilney and his partner. We tired of Cambridge in the early hours, went to London for breakfast, then to Oxford for punting and a party in Somerville College (my shaving secretly in an all-women's college seemed remarkable at the time), followed by a late train home via Bletchley. Janet was reading classics at Newnham and her brother David Roseveare, a keen clarinettist, mathematics at Trinity. The network of friendships included Kate Palmer, a botanist, and Peter Miller, an entomologist, so connecting with my friend Roderick Fisher (see above). A plot was hatched to renovate an old Canadian army truck and mount a bug-hunting expedition to the Taurus mountains of southern Turkey.

My involvement in this project, as the only non-scientist, was possible because the Colonial Office expected me to attend their course for the next academic year in Oxford. This meant the opportunity to enjoy a long vacation without the previous long vac term obligations. The third entomologist was David Smith; and James Bogle, an engineer, with Michael Message, a medical student, made the party up to six — definitely the limit for the size of vehicle. That we never reached our prime objective is a story in itself, but we were on the road for seven weeks, from mid-July to early September, and achieved many secondary purposes. Planning and equipping this expedition could have benefited more from my advice, based on my 1954 experience, but the discussions took place during my preoccupation with exams.

The principal episodes can be briefly covered. The route assumed camping all the way, and took us initially through France, Switzerland and Italy into Yugoslavia. After 11 days of gentle progress down the Dalmatian coast we found we had misinterpreted our transit visas, so that on trying to exit towards Bulgaria we were put under open arrest for the night in the station yard of Dmitrovgrad. Tried the next morning before a people's court, we were fined for spending 11 days in the country when our visas were for a transit of only three. With some justification, they regarded us with suspicion as possible spies because we had (unwittingly in fact) passed by every naval establishment on their coast. Curiously, however, the summer of 1956 was the beginning of a short thaw in West–East relations, and Tito's Yugoslavia was trying to be kind to tourists, so the protest we registered with the British embassy in Belgrade made possible the recovery of our films and cameras. The Bulgarians gave no trouble, but our vehicle and its contents were the object of intense interest because hitherto land transit by foreigners had not been allowed. Both in Sofia and in Plovdiv small crowds surrounded us whenever we stopped. Once in Turkey and over the Bosphorus into Anatolia there was much evidence of strategic road building, then in its early stages, as part of the American determination to support NATO's right flank.

Somewhere we encountered Eric Williams of *Wooden Horse* fame. When asked what he was doing he limited his response to 'Oh, just buggering about in the Balkans'.

In Ankara we enjoyed the generous, casual and quite undeserved hospitality of an American couple, Ed and Margaret Turner, who worked for Unesco. After advising on a camping place they insisted on providing baths, washing our clothes and cooking the biggest breakfast imaginable. Pressing on south to Tuz Golu, the big salt lake (dried up in August), we took stock of our money and supplies and reckoned it necessary to turn for home, leaving the Taurus mountains beyond our grasp.

For me this journey provided three main revelations — the recognition of east European backwardness, to be experienced at close quarters in Romania two decades later; the significance of the old boundary between Habsburg (Christian) and Ottoman (Muslim) communities in the middle of Yugoslavia, not to mention the residues of Italian, German and partisan warfare; and a first encounter (apart from Algiers in the navy) with the world of Muslim culture, soon to become familiar in Nigeria and later in Malaysia.

South Parks Road and New College, Oxford
Before sending in my application to the Colonial Office, my father's first cousin, Ted Nightingale (ex-Sudan political service and resident in Kenya), had advised a preference for Tanganyika as being likely to 'last longer' from a career point of view, but it became evident that the selectors had certain conceptions about the character of recruits suitable for East or West African work, and that Northern Nigeria would be better for me. This meant learning Hausa and a smattering of other relevant subjects on the Devonshire 'A' course in Oxford. (Swahili was taught in Cambridge.) This, and the 'B' course for experienced administrators, was based at the Overseas Service Club in South Parks Road, but each member was affiliated to one of the colleges. On account of the *amicabilis concordia* which linked two pairs of

institutions — Eton and King's with Winchester and New College — it had fortunately been a relatively easy matter to arrange my affiliation. The most significant personal change at this time was financial independence at last; a reasonably generous tax-free monthly allowance paid in advance.

My digs for one term were at 91 Woodstock Road in an odd ménage run by three elderly ladies, two of whom were first cousins of my father — Helen (Nell) Nightingale (sister to Ted) and Seton Lee — of whom much more in 1970. Their insistence on providing dinner for their 'young gentlemen' lodgers on a regular basis proved inconvenient and obliged me to move to 2 Winchester Road in the new year.

The full complement of some 60 earnest young overseas civil servants of many races constituted both courses and included the last five Britons ever to be appointed as assistant district officers (ADOs) in Nigeria — together with Amuda Gobir from Ilorin and M. D. Yusufu from Katsina. It was very helpful to have course 'B' participants along with us, and two already serving in Northern Nigeria became particular friends — Ivor Stanbrook, later a barrister and Conservative MP, and Tony Davidson, who eventually joined the British Council.

Trekking on horseback was going to be a regular requirement so my bicycle took me out to a Hinksey riding school about twice a week for the first term. This did indeed prove a wise investment since the mounts available later were all stallions and would have readily detected any nervousness. Next in order of practical usefulness were the language lessons, but we also had instruction in field engineering and in car maintenance, and were examined in late April in anthropology, imperial history, tropical agriculture and forestry, and development economics. Further exams in late June covered Islam, central and local government, the law of evidence and both written and oral Hausa. Memories associated with these studies include 'sitting at the feet' of Margery Perham (the acknowledged authority on Lugard and indirect rule) in Nuffield College, and lectures on race relations from Professor Kirkwood at Queen Elizabeth House.

Meanwhile, in the autumn of 1956 the Anglo-French débâcle in Suez and the suppression of the Hungarians by Soviet tanks had hit the headlines. Refugees poured into camps in Austria and, by Christmas time, relief operations were in full swing. David Ouvry in Oxford knew of a UNA convoy of coaches being planned, and he persuaded Colin Tilney from King's, Paul Spicer and me to drive an old two and a half-ton Austin ambulance, owned by the Friends Meeting House in Mansfield, and to rendezvous with the convoy in Salzburg. Thus began my third 'camping' trip into Europe in two years, but this time in winter — a foretaste of subzero temperatures to be experienced 20 years later. Peter Wiles in New College saw no objection, but H. P. W. Murray, in charge of the Devonshire courses, warned me to be sure to get back.

By December there was a steady stream of aircraft and vehicles going east with relief supplies and returning west with refugees, but distribution to some of the more remote camps was not easy, so our relatively small truck could have been useful. We spent two days in the International Red Cross depot in Vienna sorting and loading 12 tons of supplies into two railway wagons, seven for Linz and five for Graz, and then set off through the first snowfall, having to buy snow chains to overcome a tricky pass. Alas, the weather combined with holidays for the Austrian railway workers to delay the wagons, so the plan to unload the Graz one and to distribute from there was frustrated. Good company and hospitality for three Christmas nights in the Schloss St Martin near Graz made up for this disappointment, and we did nonetheless manage to deliver goodies to five various camps *en route*, before heading homewards, crossing the Channel on 31 December.

Back in Oxford for Hilary term, in spite of the serious business of preparation for life in Nigeria, a modicum of music making was inescapable. The New College chapel choir under Meredith Davies found my voice useful occasionally, as did the Egglesfield Singers under Bernard Rose, and my connections with Cambridge music continued via the Chelsea Opera Group visits. Chamber concerts with the Oxford University Musical Club and Union in the Holywell Music Room and with friends in New College were also enjoyable. My most congenial friends in college were second-year historians such as Andrew Quicke and Sandy Murray (also flautist) who encouraged me with introductions to girlfriends in Somerville and Lady Margaret Hall.

The 1957 Easter vacation included a few days observing the West London stipendiary magistrate in action, followed by two weeks of attachment to local government, arranged conveniently for me to be in Chichester with the city council, the rural district council and West Sussex county council. This was followed immediately in the first week of April by the wedding of my eldest sister Sheelagh and Mark Bridgman in Bosham church (where my parents were married, and later my other three sisters), made especially memorable by the manning of a captain's gig by Mark's fellow naval officers to convey the bridal party from the quay by the church up the creek to the Old Schools for the reception. Not long after this Caroline Scott, another Newnhamite girlfriend, accepted my invitation to 'ordeal by sailing dinghy' for a few days in Bosham.

Trinity term and the year at Oxford culminated in Eights Week celebrations, the Bath and West show, plays, concerts, dances and a day in London to order kit from the tropical outfitters, Griffiths McAlister. The essential items were a Hounsfield safari camp bed with mosquito net and frame, a Tilley lamp and a water filter, plus some airtight metal trunks to protect one's clothes and books. Finally, in July, a frantic series of visits was squeezed into three weeks, beginning with home in Dartington, as the last time for at least 18 months, and ending with embarkation in Liverpool.

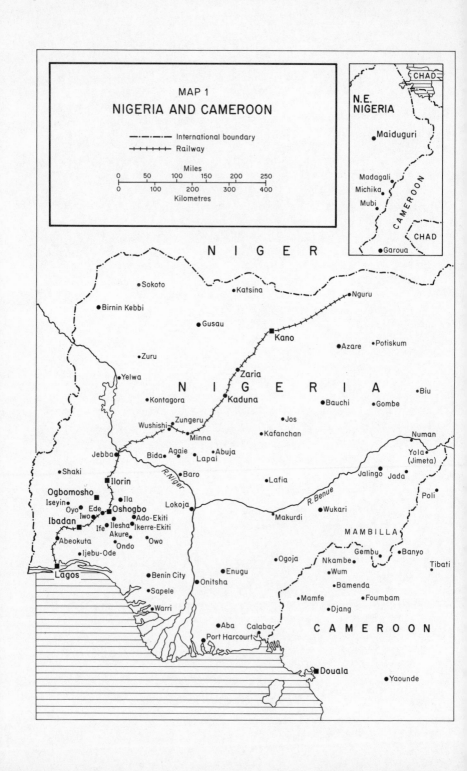

MAP 1
NIGERIA AND CAMEROON

—·—·—·— International boundary
+++++ Railway

Miles
0   50   100   150   200   250
0   100   200   300   400
Kilometres

N.E. NIGERIA

CHAD

•Maiduguri

Madagali•
Michika•
Mubi•

CAMEROON

CHAD

•Garoua

N I G E R

•Sokoto   •Katsina   Nguru•

•Birnin Kebbi

•Gusau   ■ Kano

•Zuru   •Azare •Potiskum

•Yelwa   N   I   G   E   R   I   A   •Biu

        •Kontagora   Zaria   •Bauchi •Gombe
                    •Kaduna

Wushishi•   Zungeru•   •Jos   Numan•
          •Minna   •Kafanchan   Yola•
Jebba■ Bida• Aggie• •Abuja   (Jimeta)
              •Lapai   Jalingo• •Jada
•Shaki   Baro•   •Poli
                                •Lafia
•Iseyin ■Ilorin   Wukari•
Ogbomosho• •Ila   Lokoja•
  Oyo• Ede• ■Oshogbo   Makurdi•   MAMBILLA•
Ibadan■ Iwo• •Ado-Ekiti
      Ife• Ilesha•Ikerre-Ekiti   Gembu• •Banyo
Abeokuta• Akure•   •Ogoja Nkambe•   •Tibati
    •Ijebu-Ode •Ondo •Owo   •Wum
Lagos■   •Bamenda
        •Benin City   •Mamfe •Foumbam
        •Sapele   Onitsha• •Enugu   •Djang
      •Warri
              •Aba Calabar•   C A M E R O O N
            Port Harcourt•

                              ■Douala   •Yaounde

R. Niger

R. Benue

4

Nigeria and Cameroon Policy in Practice

To revert briefly to the selection process that preceded the training in Oxford, given that the ASB in 1950 had rightly rejected me, what did the Colonial Office selectors think of me in 1956? Not so wet behind the ears, perhaps, but hardly with the appearance of a typical district officer (DO). Yet my interviewers did witness evidence of a sense of humour and a reasonably balanced personality when, in a time-honoured way, the 'trick cyclist' (psychologist) member of the board attempted to get a rise out of me by making derogatory remarks about my punt-building project. (The presumed theory was that anyone who took offence in the cool of a London office was likely to be a liability in the heat of the tropics.) My response was, 'If you had seen it on the water you would not be making a face like that,' whereupon the other members all laughed at him. Scoring a point at his expense was surely the key to my acceptability.

Elder Dempster Line, Lagos and upcountry
MV *Accra* sailed on 25 July 1957 — another key date — and called first at Las Palmas in the Canaries. A brief run ashore revealed some curious architecture in the cathedral and some camels sighted inland. My fellow passengers included not only the other four of my group of 'cadets' — Graham Donald, Robin

41

Jagoe, Clement Salaman and Bill Sharp — but also Robin Horton, an anthropologist returning to the field study of the Ijaws of the Niger delta. Also on board were the parents of Antony Shilling-ford, a prep school contemporary; his father was returning to Lagos as federal education adviser, and his mother was kind and hospitable when we disembarked.

It is at this point that my basically factual diaries begin to be supplemented by a substantial series of letters home, the first of which was posted from the next port of call, Freetown, Sierra Leone. Thanks to Murray Sanderson's advice to 'buy and learn to use a portable typewriter', carbon copies of my letters survive and can provide evidence of long-forgotten states of mind. My rela-tively frugal habits caused a somewhat censorious reaction to what seemed quite lavish and luxurious catering and other facilities; yet only 12 years later, returning from Malawi via Cape Town by Union Castle Line to Southampton, superior enjoyment would prove readily acceptable.

A glimpse from my cabin of the dockside in Freetown showed a crane inscribed with STODDART AND PITT, ENGINEERS, BATH, and an afternoon ashore provided the first experience of tropical heat and dust, street smells and market stalls. Takoradi, Ghana, was the next port and provided more first impressions — of ships plying the timber trade, of neat houses, of smart policemen and of a very large fishing fleet. Curiosity was reversed, however, when five fresh-faced 'cadets' landed in Lagos to be greeted politely but with some incredulity by our official hosts.

Back in Oxford in May, a letter from R. J. Purdy, Resident of Adamawa Province, had told me that my posting would be to Adamawa Division, and had given me essential advice about the camping equipment and stores ('beer, kerosene, soap') required for bush work, including the remark that 'a collapsible latrine seat is always useful'. My response had included the information that my baggage contained a portable seat 'which survives from my parents' honeymoon' — they had camped on Dartmoor — although subsequent experience was that resthouses normally provided thunder boxes. On arrival in Lagos on 7 August a further letter of welcome from Jack Griffith, senior DO in charge of Adamawa, awaited me, including his wife Cecily's *Guide to*

Buying Stores in Lagos Without Tears. This was invaluable for a young bachelor having difficulty in estimating what his consumption of basic necessities would be for an initial three-month period. John Purdy had written 'I hope you enjoy Adamawa. It is a splendid country even if a bit hot sometimes, and there is a very worthwhile job to be done here.' To this Jack Griffith now added, 'You are lucky to get to the province because it is interesting geographically and still relatively unspoiled. You will also be welcome when you come because we are very short-handed just now.'

The government coastal agent dealt with our baggage ('loads' from now on) and we were duly entertained by the Governor-General, Sir James Robertson, who was the senior of many 'retreads' from the defunct Sudan political service, and therefore knew my father's first cousin Ted Nightingale. We were billeted among various federal officials, mine being His Excellency's private secretary (Brown?) in the grounds of Government House. Two full days of familiarization, meeting people and opening accounts in Paterson Zochonis (PZ's) and Kingsway stores for subsequent mail ordering, were followed by the upcountry journey by train in which my letter home of 11 August was typed. This reported having sat at lunch next to Sir Ralph Grey, 'the Chief Secretary of the Federation, a very small sharp man who made very gentle but pointed conversation, and who is generally reckoned to be the brains behind everything here'.

What was the state of Nigeria at this time? The conference on the constitution in 1954 had pointed the way for federal independence to be preceded by internal self-government for each of the three regions. Whatever the timetable, it was extremely short. In a nutshell, the Hausa–Fulani Muslim north was regarded as backward but was bigger in every sense than the Yoruba west and the Ibo east combined, both being regarded as relatively advanced on account of their Christian mission-based education. Each region had within it significant, and sometimes vociferous, minorities of which more later. British administrators in the southern rainforests led a very different life from those in the savannah grasslands of the north where Lugard's doctrines of indirect rule exerted long-term influence. The common factor throughout

43

Nigeria, however, was that the time to train our local successors to take over could be seen to be running out with breathtaking speed. Even if it had been foreseen that the wicked imperialists would be replaced by corrupt politicians and military usurpers there was no way of prevention. We had to limit our concern to ensuring a smooth and peaceful handover within a timetable set by outside (and largely ignorant) world opinion and pressures. Sadly, only nine years ahead lay civil war, and later the excitement of oil revenue; then the disruption of budgets by the collapse of oil prices, accompanied by military coups and the current civilian despair.

The train northwards stopped frequently, passed Ibadan, rocked through the night, reached Ilorin in the early hours, crossed the Niger at Jebba, reached Minna in the afternoon and finally deposited us in the regional capital Kaduna by evening. For a second time we submitted to the scrutiny of official hosts and followed a familiarization programme. The first element in acclimatization was remaining hungry during two hours of work until breakfast at about 9.30, then another four hours until lunch at about 3.00 p.m. We were received by the Governor, Sir Brian Sharwood-Smith, taken to see the textile factory and soft drink production line, and given indoctrination talks in several of the regional ministries. A day trip to Zaria, further north towards Kano (and later to become familiar), included visits to the government publisher and two technical colleges. Dispersal to our posts was then the order.

One night in the train to Jos brought me within range of Adamawa at last, but with a two-day road journey yet to be covered. The acting Resident, Hector Wrench (later to come to Yola) kindly put me up, and a letter of welcome from Peter Crane, assistant DO in charge of the Yola provincial office, introduced me to the driver, Karfe Lamurde, with the warning 'The Bedford pick-up truck is new; please be sure to prevent Karfe exceeding 50 miles an hour.'

This was difficult because it ran so well, and my Hausa was still elementary, but rapport between us was adequate and, after a pause in Bauchi to pay my respects to the Resident ('Oh, hello, you're Jagoe, are you? — very sorry, no, I'm Nightingale and am *en route*; could there be some mistake?'), we reached the halfway point of Gombe for the night. The network of catering resthouses in the principal administrative centres provided hotel-type accommodation at this time. Next day we off-loaded my household in Numan, where the DO Neil Morrison was to be my mentor during the period of initiation, and pressed on to Yola — or rather, strictly speaking — Jimeta (the government 'station') and another welcome from Peter Crane and Jack Griffith. Almost four weeks had elapsed since embarking in Liverpool.

Learning the ropes: Numan, Jimeta, Mubi and Jada
The German Kamerun Kolony was dismembered after the First World War and a League of Nations mandate put a roughly north–south boundary separating French Cameroun from British Cameroon. After the Second World War this area became a United Nations trust territory. The British Northern Cameroon trust territory was administered as part of Northern Nigeria (and incorporated with Adamawa Division, plus small sections in Bornu and Benue — an unwise arrangement, as will be seen) while Southern Cameroon became a unit in the federation. Later both were unsettled after UN-sponsored plebiscites; the south joined the French part to form the Republic of Cameroon and most of the north became a new and separate Sardauna Province of Nigeria. Many awkward boundaries were involved; improve one, make another worse.

On the ground, at the grass roots, on foot, horseback or in a canoe, in close contact with farmers and herdsmen, such geopolitical complexities seemed irrelevant at first; but in due course the novice bush-whacker came to appreciate how the resolution of such problems impinged on daily life in remote places. Central government had little reality, but local government meant the close presence of a village head to collect tax (and perhaps provide a few basic services in health, schooling and justice) with the district head as the next level in the hierarchy, and above him the Native Authority (NA) within the division, at which point local and central government met. In the Northern Region the NA was ubiquitous, but was not always a Muslim emir; authority could be vested in a chief appointed as *primus inter pares* in an NA council.

As a trainee ADO it was my prime duty to learn as quickly as possible how to exert influence — one had little or no power — on the beneficial working of all levels of local councils and their staff.

Peter Crane is kindness itself and has become a lifelong (if often distant) friend. Always well beyond the call of duty, he helped me in Jimeta to get set up with Musa, who proved to be a wonderfully reliable cook, and with Paul as 'small boy' who was his steward Surhiel's younger brother and who became an excellent steward himself. Later he sold me his exceptionally fine horse, and was always generous in innumerable ways.

Neil Morrison in Numan, a mere 38 miles downstream from Jimeta on the south bank of the Benue river, not far from where it flows westwards from what was then French Cameroun into Nigeria, set me to tackle a variety of desk jobs in his combined NA/divisional office. One was to prepare new warrants for the nine native courts, another to bring the project list of the local development plan up to date, and later to sort out the items supplied by the Crown Agents for the Numan town piped water scheme. My letter of 31 August mentions checking 'some hundreds of pipes and fittings waiting in piles for the attention of the Public Works Department' and 'a very acrimonious dispute between two tribes over fishing rights'. Also the NA council had to be induced to sack its treasurer because the accounts for March and April had not yet been squared. Neil also introduced me to the techniques of using a bush resthouse. We went to Kiri for two nights, setting up 'camp' in a typical concentric-style grass-roofed mud hut. Woken in the night by a curious crunching sound, it seemed my duty, in spite of mild trepidation, to investigate. My torch lit up a dog munching its way through our egg supply.

Jack Griffith took over my further initiation back in Jimeta after my month in Numan. This comprised exposure to the machinations of the much larger Adamawa NA in Yola, together with fresh work from a desk in the provincial office. Regular exercise also began, either riding in the vicinity or tennis on the club court. Some time in the early evening also had to be devoted to Hausa conversation, and it was the government messenger, Malam Abubakar Azare, who challenged me during one such session to

46

explain the gradation of human skin colour by reference to the variation in exposure to the sun on the surface of the globe from the Arctic to the equator, and on to the Antarctic. Did he understand? An earlier letter home had recorded 'my vocabulary is not keeping up with requirements'.

The next hurdle was to acquire a car. Only the well-off could aspire to a landrover, and in any case the sort of terrain which required an especially tough vehicle was better tackled on horse-back, so the most popular car for junior officers at the time was the Standard Vanguard kitcar — the open pick-up style being very suitable for 'full touring loads', as defined for mileage allowance purposes. The agents in Lagos had only one immediately available and that was black — a cancelled order from an undertaker! Regardless of the ill omen my flight was booked Yola–Jos–Port Harcourt–Lagos, the kitcar was ready and prepared, a shopping list of 40-odd items from every friend in Adamawa took two days to gather, and then a very tortuous 1600-mile journey back to my base began.

The details of this ten-day slog, with many diversions caused by a prolonged rainy season, are of limited interest but my knowledge of the country was considerably extended. Many kindnesses *en route* included a night in Minna with the Stanbrook family, lunch with Michael Cardew at his Abuja pottery, a night in Jos with Francis and Enid Davies, and finally generous hospitality in Potiskum when the flooded Gongola river (a tributary of the Benue) forced a 400-mile detour and approach to Jimeta from the northern side. Tarmac was rare, and the laterite surfaces of the 'all season' main roads were easily rendered impassable, so that they were often barred by works department officials until the sun had dried them out.

The rest of 1957 was filled with more touring, miscellaneous provincial duties, December examinations in language and a variety of official regulations, and my first tropical Christmas. My newly acquired wheels took me to see Gerry Rees, the TONA (northern area touring officer), in Mubi and my letter home of 22 November describes the inspections performed in Hong and Song on the way back: 'nice names — I have recently discovered both Bong and Dong to exist too'. A continuation of the letter on the

47

29th goes into detail of two more introductions to the art of bush-whacking; first with Peter Crane as touring officer from Jada (60-odd miles south of Jimeta) and an entourage of 5 mounted and 25 foot followers, designed to hold meetings in half a dozen villages during overnight stops and to chase up the payment of *jangali* (cattle tax) by surprise dawn roundups (Peter took impish delight in these cowboy antics); second, a downstream trip with Jack Griffith, beginning by large dugout canoe to three overnight village stops and continuing by horse and on foot to three more — a week in all. Back in Jimeta my letter of 18 December says 'Being unable to escape the net of the station carol singers, a mixture of evangelicals and hard drinkers, I have taken over direction of them, a fairly satisfactory solution!' This filling of a musical vacuum did not seem very significant at the time, but eventually became a well-worn path during my British Council years.

Early in 1958 my first tour was an extended inspection of community development and other projects in the north, mostly beyond Mubi up to Michika and Madagali. Inspired by the network of Outward Bound schools, the Man o'War Bay training institute had been established near Victoria, Southern Cameroon some years ago, and its methods of developing self-confidence, initiative and leadership in its students included expeditions to unfamiliar parts of the country for involvement in community projects. Jack Griffith assigned to me the business of advance guard for this year's group of young men in the charge of John Wright (described as a 'professional tough guy') who were to join with local 'volunteers' in Michika to rehabilitate their market area. On the way up the usual checks in NA district HQ offices included their project books, wells and well tops, market stalls and slaughter slabs, the prison and/or village lockup (if any), the school, the dispensary, the *alkali*'s courthouse and possibly a reading room. In Michika it was necessary to organize food and accommodation for the party, to carry out my own survey of the supposed needs of the market area, to obtain the district council's agreement and to gather materials and tools for the job, including the strenuous use of my kitcar to transport stone, sand, cement, ring culverts, timbers and roofing sheets, shovels and head pans. During the week, while drains were dug, the old courthouse demolished and new *rumfa*s (market shelters) erected, my visits to nearby villages continued. One such was to the Cameroons Baptist Mission at Lassa which many years later became notorious for the lethal disease known as Lassa fever. In Gulak my diary records 'Lockup — five men and one woman waiting for various reasons. Warrants a bit shaky and the warder not in proper uniform' and, on the way back to Jimeta, as recorded in my letter home dated 26 January,

> I had the immense satisfaction of releasing a falsely impris-
> oned driver from the district lockup in Uba. Unknown to
> him, a man ran out to mount his moving lorry from the
> side, fell off and later died. Thereupon the local *alkali* put
> the driver in prison on a charge of murder, without any evi-
> dence whatever, before an inquest had been held, to the
> great financial loss of the owner of the lorry in a busy
> season, and when not one single eyewitness of the incident
> was inclined to attach any blame to the driver.

My diary also records having typed my touring notes in sex-tuplicate (many years before the photocopier), but they do not seem to have survived. Even so, my awareness of having passed muster became stronger, and there was talk of the possibility of 'getting a ship of my own' (in a very small way) by being posted to the much coveted job of the southern area touring officer (TOSA), resident in the Mambilla highlands. This prompted a letter home asking unexpectedly for a consignment of some warm clothes from my boxes in the attic.

Touring officer in the Mambilla highlands
The early months of 1958 were extremely busy. The *lamido* (Fulani for emir) of Adamawa and his NA councillors, with their various portfolios in the Yola offices, became a steadily greater concern, particularly my part in getting their five-year develop-ment plan agreed; and in the Jimeta provincial office there were tenders boards, boards of enquiry, loans boards and boards of survey. A proud moment was my cook Musa being overjoyed to receive the Burma campaign medal to which he had been entitled

but had hitherto lacked the right contacts to obtain. My letter home of 2 March speaks of buying Peter Crane's horse for £22; of the Chief Justice coming with his itinerant High Court to hear homicide cases; of the visit of the Minorities Commission (enquiring into 'oppression', real or imagined) and my taking one of the members of it out riding, namely Philip Mason, an ex-Indian civil servant and author of *The Men Who Ruled India* under his *nom de plume* of Woodruffe, and subsequently race relations expert; of the visit of the new governor, Sir Gawain Bell (another retread from the Sudan); and of a party to entertain Monsieur le Chef du Subdivision de Poli from across the border.

Meanwhile, tempers were rising with the late dry-season heat and increased humidity; my horse suffered from sluggishness on evening rides and loss of appetite was not uncommon among my colleagues. Peter Prince, who within less than five years would become my boss in Clarks Shoes in Somerset (see Chapter 6), arrived to take over Adamawa Division from Jack Griffith, who went on leave and transfer to Kano (very convenient for me the next year), and my preparations for Mambilla were enhanced by a week of local leave in the coolness of Jos. The first rain offered general relief in early April; Tim Healey came up from the south for handover discussions; an NA lorry took my household loads ahead; and my kitcar was duly chocked up in Mayo Selbe at the foot of the 3000-foot escarpment a few days later.

Although this degree of detail is made possible by diaries and letters, it cannot be sustained within the purpose of illustrating day-to-day work in the British Council. Yet it serves to bring home the later difficulty of finding work even remotely as rewarding as was district administration in the dependent territories of the Commonwealth. The balance of physical and intellectual challenge, the immediacy of results for effort applied and the validity (indeed, nobility) of the ethos made the roles to be played uniquely worthwhile.

What were my instructions when settling into my new role in Gembu, the district headquarters of Mambilla, with responsibility also for Gashaka and parts of Toungo districts? Nothing explicit, on the reasonable assumption that by a process of osmosis my initiation period accompanying experienced colleagues would have given me a fair grasp of policy in practice. Plenty of activity, yes, but was there any policy? Little that was evident in the front line, certainly no clear direction. Yet it was the scope for personal initiative that made the job so all-consuming of energy and commitment.

My two principal collaborators as touring officer were Mallam Usmanu Mukaddas, the district head and Alhaji Ahmed Tijjani Malumfashi, the livestock superintendent (see photograph) who subsequently became a distinguished animal health expert in Kaduna. Mukaddas and Tijjani had to be consulted almost daily since the keys to peaceful and constructive development in the southern area lay with the district council and its cattle control committee. When out of range on tour, my correspondence with Mukaddas was in Hausa (although he would have preferred Fulani) and covered the full range of our concerns. With Tijjani my official medium was English, although we conversed in Hausa as a means of improving my capacity. Tijjani had been in Britain for training and was a regional government, not an NA, employee.

A memorably inauspicious incident occurred within a day or so of my 'cavalcade' being met at the top of the escarpment in Maisamare by Tijjani and in Nguroje by Mukaddas. My horse slipped while beginning the descent of a stony path and sat down on all fours. My decision to dismount was disrupted by the animal's rising; one foot got stuck in a stirrup, and the stirrup leather failed to detach from the saddle. The horse dragged me, bumping over stony ground, but Tijjani caught him, saving me from serious injury or worse and limiting it to a sprained ankle. Fortunately, this dangerous and undignified episode did not accurately presage the future, but it did teach me the valuable lesson *always* to check the leathers, just as one would the ropes in a dinghy.

Gembu was four days' walk and 230 miles by road from the NA and provincial headquarters in Yola–Jimeta. Several alternative centres of power lay much closer; Benue to the west, Bamenda to the south and Banyo to the east. The year 1923 was a bad one for British decision-making; not only were the people of our chunk of ex-German territory condemned to what became maladministration at the hands of a Fulani aristocracy (which enjoyed ruling

without bothering to govern), but similarly unfortunate consequences followed from the granting of self-government to the
settlers of Southern Rhodesia. The first error was put right after
the UN plebiscite of 1959; the second not until 1980. But that is
to anticipate the evidence.

What were the salient features of Mambilla in 1958? Briefly
stated, the human population of 46,000 was a mixture of settled
small-farm cultivators in villages and nomadic Fulani cattle-
owning graziers without permanent dwellings — the same potentially explosive mixture as that in the Middle East to this day. The
dense cattle population of 161,000 thus outnumbered the human
by four to one, and the area of this high-altitude paradise was less
than 1500 square miles. The peace could only be kept by regu-
lating the movement of herds, by ensuring that the farmers could
obtain redress when crops were damaged, and by forestalling the
inevitable overgrazing and degradation of grassland if the natural
increase were allowed. To satisfy this last requirement we applied
a discriminatory rate of *jangali* (cattle tax) of 8/– rather than the
standard 5/– in the rest of the Northern Region. To find the cash
the Fulani had to sell enough cattle to the meat markets of the
Eastern Region. Trouble arose when some herd owners made
long-distance appeals to powerful but ignorantly sympathetic NA
councillors in Yola. Another concern was the risk of epizootic
diseases, rinderpest being potentially the most catastrophic, but
Tijjani and the veterinary authorities had contingency plans for
that. Finally, any number of specialist colleagues in education,
health, agriculture and works wanted to improve access by dis-
cerning a feasible route for a road up the northern escarpment, but
none had been found. 'Trekking' remained the only way up and
in. Yet a landrover track had been devised from the south, linking
with the Bamenda Ring Road, but that was less politically
desirable. Top people in Kaduna were keen on a site for an airstrip, and since all my predecessors had failed to find one my view
of the prospects was not very sanguine. One other factor in the
local scene was the tendency of the villagers to be animist
'pagans', exposed to the possibility of Christian mission prosely-
tizing, whereas the cattle Fulani were essentially Muslim in their
allegiances. Lord Lugard's settlement with the northern emirs had

precluded mission activity, but did this, or should this, apply to Cameroon trust territory?

As for flora and fauna, my initial experiences in the low-altitude orchard savannah had made baobab trees, guinea corn, cassava, yams, mangoes, lizards, fruit bats and screech owls very familiar; the mountain contrast was almost complete, with vegetable gardens able to boast temperate products, and more avocados from three trees in Gembu than anyone could consume. Eucalyptus trees were planted in and around all the settlements, both for fuel and for construction.

Towards the end of April, in a triple-length airletter home, I described the *salla* day celebrations, consequent on sighting the new moon and ending the fasting month for all good Muslims, and the return from leave of Frank Nelson, the agricultural superintendent, whose job was to develop the growing of arabica coffee as a cash crop. (Elsewhere in the region it was cotton and groundnuts.) Apart from Frank and Tijjani, no one in Gembu spoke English, but a short trek to the south across the Donga river brought me to Warwar, where Ken and June Goodman from Los Angeles had established their branch of the Cameroons Baptist Mission. For political reasons our contacts had to be very circumspect, but they became good friends despite my lack of sympathy with their particular religious outlook, and we kept in touch for many years.

Nothing very humorous survives from these days; life was earnest, and work was life (but see next paragraph). How can it be summarized? Familiarization with my parish dictated tours to the northeast and southwest (to take stock of the derelict road), then to the northwest and southeast (to dip my toe into the French side) by which time three months had elapsed and included three district council meetings and much paperwork. My portable typewriter produced full monthly reports to the senior district officer (SDO) in Jimeta. Very little feedback came. My knowledge of any news there might be came from *Rejiyo Kaduna* in Hausa, the excellent journalism in the fortnightly *West Africa* magazine (London, so slow in coming) and daily at 12 noon news in English announced as '*Ici Brazzaville, radiodiffusion television française*' heard loud and clear from French Equatorial Africa; also, of course, what was then the airmail *Weekly Times*.

In the absence of anyone with whom to share the humour of an absurd personal predicament one can only laugh at oneself. One day behind a resthouse my squat over the specially prepared hole for a natural function was maintained for a moment too long. 'Ants in my pants' — panic thoughts — they've got up my legs — can anyone see? No option but to remove all clothing and shake out thoroughly. Look round in mirth — pity — no one to share laughter!

The full year from April 1958 to taking leave in 1959 was packed with incessant action. Inspecting, touring, discussing and writing. News came of my being expected to attend a two-week course for ADOs in the Zaria Institute of Public Administration in August, but by the time the third set of dates reached me a late arrival was unavoidable — others were late too. Little of the course was relevant to my situation, but the social opportunities were valuable — as is normal. After visits to friends in Kano and official calls in Kaduna, the return to Adamawa was prolonged by the rains and such diversions as had been necessary a year ago coming back from Lagos with the car. By then Peter Prince had been replaced by Chris Rounthwaite as my boss, and within a few months it was Richard Barlow-Poole. My second journey to Gembu was in my kitcar followed by one of Alhaji Bakari's new diesel lorries containing my carriers and loads, all the way round the French side, enjoying generous Gallic hospitality in Garoua, Ngaundere, Tibati and Banyo before leaving the vehicles and walking up from Mayo Darle.

After ten days of routine in Gembu we were off again, down to the kitcar and on via Foumbam and Djang to Bamenda where contacts confirmed my conviction that officials there had knowledge and experience of closer relevance to Mambilla's problems. Then up the ring road to Nkambe and talk to opposite numbers there and back up to Gembu with the kitcar left on the south side. Meanwhile, my amateur road and bridge building had made progress; a reply from the Kenya Police Air Wing had produced evidence that a short takeoff and landing aircraft (STOL) could manage the minimal strip we had planned near Gembu. The rains over, December brought a flock of VIPs to satisfy their curiosity and a second summons for me to descend to provincial HQ.

Early in 1959 disillusion set in; my superiors seemed to under-value the work in the south, and the major task of registration for the federal election began to distort our priorities. My third journey into the mountains was prolonged by the need for 'registration propaganda' meetings *en route*. Back in Gembu briefly, my determination to complete the circumnavigation of my parish took hold, so a very long kitcar journey ensued, via Bamenda, Mamfe and Gboko to the Makurdi boatyard for ordering punts, and finally via Wukari, Serti and Jada back to Jimeta. March was entirely devoted to electoral registration, followed by a fourth and final session in Gembu for a visit by the Minister for Northern Cameroon affairs. An emotional leave-taking from Mambilla in mid-April and writing of handover/winding-up notes down in Jimeta became entangled with the question of whether my work would be wasted for lack of a successor.

Home leave, North America and romantic attachment
Vigorous argument for the necessity of a touring officer if peaceful coexistence of farmers and pastoralists was to be preserved had preceded my departure and, although a young Nigerian ADO was designated, an eight-month gap ensued, and it was not long before Tim Healy was drafted back to the task, by which time good order had deteriorated so far that he had to be given a police escort. Such a sad story gave me little satisfaction but illustrates the thesis that the better you do a job the less it is thought necessary to have it done.

Battle weariness after 21 months made my leave especially timely and, after a series of calls on colleagues in Jos, Kaduna, Zaria and Kano, my trans-Saharan flight in a BOAC Boeing Stratocruiser landed me back in the bosom of my family in Bosham and Dartington. The generous entitlement of a week's leave for every month served meant that a prospect of five months' pay without work lay ahead.

Leave offered time to reflect on the conflicts of recent months, since my reports and other writings had become increasingly bitter in the light of what seemed to me betrayals of trust. Explaining the implications of *mulkin kai* (self-government) in village meetings gave rise to a mixture of fears (and eager expectations) of a free-for-all under no government at all, in the absence of the *di'o* as umpire. We British were abdicating power according to plan, but we had already lost more influence than we needed to honour our UN trusteeship before it had expired. The capacity to correct mal-administration and to enforce good government had ebbed away before its time. One example of this was my being reprimanded for releasing a political prisoner in Gembu while lacking the tech-nically legal competence to do so. When my response was to ask rather heatedly, 'What the hell are we here for then?' my superiors were dumb. They thought, no doubt, that an arbitrary act, how-ever beneficial, set a bad example, even if it was employed to negate an equally arbitrary but malevolent act. My immaturity revealed, perhaps, but what price justice in bush conditions? No time was lost by the Premier's Office in Kaduna; a letter dated 13 May told me of a posting to Ilorin for my second tour.

Coming home after nearly two years was exciting. My constant concern to keep in touch by letter bore fruit; it was easy to pick up the threads. Few people could comprehend the way of life, yet in the late 1950s there was still a vaguely romantic view of the DO in the remoteness of Empire. Any 'Old West Coasters' knew the difference from the white settler areas of the East, and my family and friends seemed to find me relatively untainted — or at least unscathed — by imagined hazards.

Glyndebourne opera was affordable in those days and Rosemary Garton (who had my cello on long loan) came with me to *Rosen-kavalier* and later Mary Elspeth Milford came to *Così fan tutte*. (A third opera visit two months later would prove to have long-term significance.) Visits to Clifton, Oxford, London and Cambridge quickly renewed many friendships, and my plans for a trans-Atlantic expedition were becoming clearer.

Bill Gosling of Trinity had read economics with me and had taken a job in Canada. From Nigeria my enquiries to him had pro-duced the advice that one would need a minimum of $10 a day, and since the foreign currency limit was £100 which then equalled $280, my limit would be 28 days. My Kano–London–Kano leave ticket was soon extended at reasonable cost to take me, between 17 June and 16 July, on a round trip of amazing fascination and great pleasure. Montreal, Ottawa, Toronto, Vancouver, San Francisco, Los Angeles, Washington, Philadelphia and New York were the air stops, with intermediate points by road. 'You can't *fly* over the Rockies; it's sacrilege,' said everyone, but my view was based on the experience of all those long drives in Europe. Time actually on the move should be minimized.

One of my purposes was to find out, if Africa had to be forsaken, what attractions lay over the ocean; another was to see how the friends who had gone there were faring. Janet Roseveare had gone from Newnham to spend a year as a supervisor with the Bell Telephone Company. Not only did her friends in Montreal look after me; they also put me onto the St Andrew's University network, which proved so generous that, in the end, of 28 nights on the whole tour only two were spent in hotels. Job opportunities existed, in particular my interest was in the Department of Northern Affairs, which provided similar development services to those needed in Nigeria — if in a contrasted climate. Work was also available for graduates in law, banking and investment. But how well did British immigrants integrate with Canadian society? Neither Bill and Jennifer Gosling nor Roderick and Heather Fisher seemed likely to stay long, but those like George Marshall who had married Canadians were clearly settling in happily.

One of Janet's friends in the Canadian Broadcasting Corporation encouraged me to record a talk about Nigerian administration, but it was not used — not sufficiently light-hearted or anecdotal. The Botterell family in Toronto insisted on handing me on to the Turvey family in Vancouver with whom many students from the University of British Columbia were fraternizing. And so it continued in San Francisco with Peter and Foxy King, and in Los Angeles with yet another St Andrew's connection. There, however, my commission from the Milford family to try to persuade Sally to heed their pleas to come home had to be taken seriously. She was close to her late mother's younger sister, Gyp Napier, and to Tom Boyd, but my efforts were partially effective. Then a very warm welcome awaited me in 170 South Virgil, the Baptist Church base from which Ken and June Goodman operated in Mambilla.

The flight to Washington DC was memorable as my first in a Boeing 707 jet airliner, only just recently put into service, and doing 584 miles an hour at 29,000 feet. An American official, Taylor Rhodes, pumped me for information on Lagos where he would be helping to open a US embassy the next year. The quiet weekend near Philadelphia was with Donald and Louise Brian, friends of Lance Sieveking, my father's old flying comrade and BBC drama man. Finally, in New York my ingenuity was tested to the limit in the UN Secretariat building. Only by subterfuge could sight of the internal directory be obtained, but eventually this enabled me to declare my interest to the staff of the trusteeship division. Several had just returned from the visiting mission to Papua New Guinea, and some would shortly be observers of the plebiscite in the Cameroons.

What was my verdict on Canada and the USA? It was, at that time, that to live and work in Canada still offered a keen challenge, but that the opulence in the USA was overwhelming. The hospitality in both countries had been unimaginable, but home called and, within a week of getting back, trips to Dartington and Bosham to collect camping gear prepared me for the most crucial turning point in my life so far. My musical friends in the Cambridge–Oxford–London network had got me an invitation to the Music Camp they had all been attending for many years in Bothampstead near Newbury (later moved to Piggott's near High Wycombe). The level of competence of the singers and players was high amateur, or near professional, and among the sopranos was Diana Herdman; by the end of the week we were in love, and our closest well-wishers in the camp were John and Pat Shirley-Quirk.

Before parting, Diana accepted my invitation to come to Bosham in mid-August to meet my family and to see *Figaro* at Glyndebourne with them, but thereafter we were each committed in different directions, so some intense letter writing ensued. She went camping in France and on a singing tour in Austria, while my promise to go dinghy-sailing near Falmouth with my old director of music, Douglas Fox, had to be honoured, and a two-week Colonial Office conference in Cambridge attended.

Not until mid-September could our lightning romance make any further progress, but during a weekend working party at Music Camp Diana agreed to think about my proposal of marriage, which she accepted ten days later. This would involve giving up her training at the Guildhall School of Music and Drama. There followed a frantic series of visits, first to Epsom for me to seek her parents' approval, then to Dartington again, followed by the Gardiner family at Springhead, and finally up to Wilmslow to see Diana's grandfather, George Clarke and 'Auntie' Nora, his second wife. In mid-October my moment of departure drew near and our plans for a wedding were unresolved.

Ilorin NA, Ibadan wedding and Iseyin honeymoon

My re-entry problem after leave was compounded by recent emotions and the contrasted posting: from the eastern borders to the Yoruba-speaking southwestern corner of the Northern Region. But on flying back to Kano, Jack and Cecily Griffith gave me their usual sympathetic hospitality, as did Peter and Ann Crane in Kaduna. A three-day drive south with another night stop in Bida completed my journey to the provincial office in Ilorin.

Morale rose immediately on my discovery that Musa and Paul had loyally made the journey from Adamawa and had already arrived. The Resident, John Bell, and SDO Alec Smith, together with Nigel Stockwell in charge of the office made me welcome, and when discussing the implications of my engagement to marry, one of them said of me, 'He seems to have committed only one indiscretion in his short career.'

During our separation, letters between Diana and me flew thick and fast. By mid-November we had weighed up the pros and cons of being married at home or abroad, complicated as they were by severe political uncertainty concerning the future of the administrative service, the timing of my confirmation and eligibility for compensation if resigning, and the cost of passages. We decided that it was not feasible for me to fly home for a wedding, but that Diana (being admirably brave and determined) would come by sea to Lagos in the interests of her acclimatization, and that preparations for a local wedding would be my responsibility.

Meanwhile, what work had to be done? My official job was designated as ADO Central, to be the link at the most junior level between Ilorin NA, Ilorin town council and the DO in charge of Ilorin Division. My predecessor, Martin Bax, had left some hand-over notes, but there was precious little common ground between my new duties and the life in southern Adamawa. One thread did continue, however, from the process of electoral registration earlier in the year. The federal election dominated the last two months of the year, and my duty as polling officer for the central constituency involved the siting and staffing of 69 polling stations each of which had to be supplied on the day with an appropriate proportion of the 33,000 ballot papers made up into 660 books of 50. This first secret ballot election was to cost £1.5 million in 1959/60 and seemed unlikely ever to be repeated. It involved the mobilization of every single employee of the central and regional governments who was literate, regardless of normal occupation. My diary records that the paperwork required my signature 359 times, for one constituency.

There remained, of course, the usual functions of touring villages (by car, not mounted) in the districts of the division for a variety of checks and discussions (mostly as day trips), together with monitoring the portfolio-holders in the NA; and attention was diverted from the election for a few days when a ceremony was held for the installation of a new Emir of Ilorin by His Excellency the Governor from Kaduna, Sir Gawain Bell.

At the end of November casual leave of one day was granted and a 20-hour trip to Ibadan (capital of the then Western Region) enabled me to make some progress with organizing a wedding. The list of requirements was formidable — a licence, a church, a clergyman, a best man, someone to give away the bride, a place for a reception, a photographer, a cake and lots of friends. Arrangements had begun to fall into place by the time of my second visit at the end of January. David Wakefield-Harrey who worked for British Petroleum would be best man, Canon Anderson of the combined Anglican/Methodist theological college would officiate, the headmistress of St Anne's School, Kudeti, agreed to the use of her chapel, and Professor John Ferguson would be the bride's deputy father and give Diana away. John was the only person with whom the Herdman family had any connection at all — through a close friend of Diana's grandfather. He and Elnora were powers in the life of the University College, Ibadan (at that time connected to London), John being professor of classics, dean of the faculty of arts, a cricketer, a Shakespearean actor and a conductor of the chapel choir. A chance meeting with Michael Griggs of Clare (a friend of Geoffrey Hardyman, my Clifton contemporary) provided us with a pianist for the service. Another happy connection was with Stanley Fingland who had been guided by me round the offices in Ilorin when on a familiarization tour from Lagos. His job there, as a Commonwealth Relations Office official, was to prepare the ground for the opening of a British High Commission in time for independence in October, and to give advice on the creation of a Nigerian diplomatic service. He and his wife looked after Diana when she reached Lagos.

MV *Accra* was due in Lagos on 17 February, so the date of Saturday 20th was fixed as the most important in our lives. Ten days' matrimonial leave was granted until the 26th, and through the 'good offices' of several friendly colleagues it had been possible to reserve the VIP resthouse known as the Manor House in Iseyin for a short honeymoon. Meanwhile, my bungalow in Ilorin had been completely renovated and made fit for a bride, but we were in it for a mere long weekend before setting off for Minna. My general dissatisfaction with the nature of my work had been registered in Kaduna whence came news of a posting to Niger Province.

My swansong in Ilorin, however, was to be elected (or forcibly 'volunteered') as club treasurer. The election work had made me known to most members as an easy-going sort of chap, but they had not reckoned on a steely core. Collecting a vast sum in arrears of subscriptions did not contribute to my popularity in my final weeks! Happily this did not prevent many accepting our wedding invitation and making the journey to Ibadan.

Musa and Paul came with me in the kitcar via Ibadan to Lagos, and, after our nerve-wracking dockside reunion, they were able to help with all the shopping required. Diana's voyage had been just right; both of us had been teased — 'Oh, he/she will have changed his/her mind by the time you meet again' — but all was set fair. The Finglands took care of her for one night, then the Camerons in Ibadan for two. Our wedding was a joyous occasion. The choir of Nigerian girls from the school joined in, and an impressive number of NA officials attended. One who was unable to get away sent a telegram — 'WISHING YOU HAPPILY COUPLED' and my

parents' telegram said 'FELICITATIONS FROM THE WATCH PARTICU-
LARLY FROM THE OLD COCK AND HEN'.

At the reception in the Wakefield-Harrey's house and garden,
John Ferguson drew himself up to his full height and boomed,
'Socrates said, Ladies and Gentlemen — if I may advertise my
profession for a moment — that no man may marry a beautiful
wife and remain a philosopher,' thus implying that my chances
were minimal.

A heavy thunderstorm on the way north to Oyo was hardly an
auspicious beginning; it was frightening for Diana as her first
experience of a tropical downpour, Musa and Paul were soaked,
and on arrival in Iseyin the staff of the Manor House had almost
given us up, but it proved an ideally quiet and peaceful spot for a
honeymoon.

Criminal justice reforms in Niger Province

A combined house-warming and farewell party in Ilorin made it
possible to thank our well-wishers before tackling the tasks ahead.
The journey via Jebba, Bida and Zungeru to Minna was a bad one
— 12 hours to cover only 230 miles on badly corrugated laterite
roads — but Denis and Keturah Glason in the Residency received
us, covered from head to foot in red dust, like long-lost friends
despite being complete strangers. This augured well and my job as
DO Native Courts proved to be just the tonic required.

The introduction of a new penal code and criminal procedure
code for the Northern Region was a major challenge. The need
arose because the federal government had decided that at the
moment of independence on 1 October 1960 they wished to be
able to subscribe to the UN Declaration of Human Rights which,
among many things, required that no person be held or punished
for an offence other than against a written law. In the largely
Muslim north, however, the local *alkali*s (judges) applied the
Koran-based *maliki* code, and their law books were obscure and
in Arabic. In other parts some native courts applied 'customary
law' which was even vaguer. Precision in prosecuting and con-
victing was therefore impossible. But the northern emirs and their
legal advisers had first to be satisfied, by a visit from the Chief
Khadi of Sudan, that none of the proposed reforms was contrary

to Islam. Such reforms had already been carried out not only in Sudan but also in Pakistan.

So, after a week of settling in, working out the local implications with Denis Glason and meeting new colleagues, we were off again via Kaduna to Zaria for a ten-day course in the Institute of Public Administration — rather different from the mid-1958 one. While my daytime preoccupation was with a newly assembled bunch of native court 'specialists', trying to master the provisions of the new penal code and its translation into intelligible Hausa, Diana was able to enjoy a well-deserved extension of our honeymoon in the comfort of the catering resthouse and army swimming pool.

In Niger Province there were nine NAs, each one having a variety of judicial staff — *alkalis*, court presidents, assessors, court scribes and messengers. So back in Minna the rest of March was spent preparing a syllabus and hand-outs for a series of four-day courses designed to expound the new code. Into April we fitted a first course in Minna, a second in Bida and another for Lapai and Agaie combined. Diana, Musa and Paul came with me to the various resthouses, and each weekend we returned thankfully to The Cottage, an ideal if relatively primitive dwelling on a hillside overlooking the town and railway (single track main artery to the north) in the valley below. We completed the plan throughout the next two months with weeks in Abuja, Kontagora, Zuru and Kagara. Abuja included the pleasure of a visit to Michael Cardew's pottery training centre, but in Zuru a rather severe illness struck Diana down. It remained undiagnosed and lasted many depressing weeks before her strength and general happiness were restored. Eventually the doctor in Minna saw the refrigerator in the Kontagora resthouse and blamed it for harbouring bugs.

How was this work received? Contrary to some expectations, far from there being any opposition, the *alkalis* were delighted to have a modern text in Hausa that nearly everyone could understand and that could be quoted with authority. No longer would there be any need to refer to dilapidated volumes of doubtful authenticity. So we were batting on a better wicket than we feared and, in July, we started all over again with a series of courses on the new criminal procedure code, in some ways the more important of the two. This was preceded by a consultation visit to

63

Kaduna to meet the commissioner for native courts, Sammy Richardson (another retread from Sudan), who had oversight of the judicial reform programme. By this time various questions of interpretation and practice gave rise to correspondence not only with Kaduna but also with colleagues in neighbouring provinces. (At the end of July we frequently saw Globemaster transport aircraft passing over in the direction of the Congo.)

Throughout this period we were regularly in the company of Dennis Mann, DO Minna, who was a neighbour on the hill and who shared with us his worries about future employment. He was later posted to Kaduna, and eventually worked in the BBC Secretariat for many years. His successor in Minna was Musa Bello, whose wife was a daughter of Mukaddas (photographs show the likeness); he later transferred to the federal service. My view of the future, in spite of various schemes of special lists designed to retain expatriate staff, assumed that only senior and experienced men were really wanted and that we juniors should look for other work — hence my feelers in North America. But feelers in Britain were more relevant now, with a wife and the prospects of a family. No applications could be pursued far without being available for interview, but the ground was prepared in several directions, including the British Council and Clarks Shoes (see next chapter).

Another course in Abuja gave us the chance to witness the excitement of unpacking the wood-fired kilns at the pottery, and to arrange for the purchase of a *kakaki* (eight-foot trumpet) as a present for my father. The emir of Abuja, Alhaji Suleimanu Barau, was very distinguished and his brother had sent his son to Dauntsey's School where my father had been director of music. At the next course in Bida it was necessary to negotiate some extra evening sessions with the *etsu* Nupe and his court on the subject of homicide cases — as we had earlier with the emir of Kontagora. Grade A emir's courts had had powers of capital punishment, but Kaduna had persuaded them to surrender that part of their jurisdiction. By mid-September the two programmes were complete, but we still had to convert the old Railway Institute into a suitably dignified provincial court, furnish it, and provide it with staff and reference books.

On Independence Day, 1 October, my assignment in the role of the most junior ADO in the province was to the ninth and smallest NA at Wushishi. There Diana watched me, wearing for the only time ever the rather odd administrative service uniform, haul down the Union flag and hoist the green and white flag of Nigeria in front of a small parade of NA policemen, some school children, and the emir. In Lagos on that day Princess Alexandra had performed the royal ceremony of handing over constitutional instruments before undertaking a country-wide tour. So our next task was a week in Bida to prepare for Her Royal Highness's visit. My part was to organize and control a motorcade of 12 bright green Chevrolet saloons. Our VIP arrived on 11 October in a bright red De Haviland Heron of the Queen's Flight, drove into town to call on the *etsu*, and departed. Diana took masses of photographs at long range.

With my confirmation and resignation registered in Kaduna and a passage booked with Elder Dempster, the countdown to our final departure gathered pace in November. First, however, Denis Glason required from me the draft of a speech for him to deliver at the official opening of the provincial court; and then it seemed to me wise to do a quick tour of the southeastern parts to see how much of the instructions to court staff had sunk in. This little plan also satisfied my ulterior motives of wanting a night in the Katcha resthouse because of its wonderful view of the Niger valley, and to see the railhead on the Niger at Baro. Selling the kitcar was a sign that we were really on our way, and the counting of 1094 ballot boxes another indication. Concern mounted over the future for Musa and Paul; we paid them off with heavy hearts, sad to be breaking such strong ties. Happily, however, contact continued as late as 1967 when we were in Malawi and letters came from Musa in Yola and Paul in Sokoto. Did they both survive the civil war unscathed? We shall probably never know.

Our baggage 'not wanted on the voyage' was consigned to the government coastal agent, we took the train to Ibadan for a night with the Fergusons and to Lagos for a night with Peter and Lucy Gent (Oxford and musical friends) then in the British Council, and embarked on TSS *Calabar* on 1 December. A turbine steamship, formerly of the British India Line, she took only 100 passengers and plied to London not Liverpool. Compared with the MV mailboats of Elder Dempster she was vibration-free and stately. Also on board were Chris and Elizabeth Reynolds, he having just retired from service in the north which began in 1936. We shared a table, took runs ashore together in Takoradi and Freetown, and duly celebrated Diana's twenty-fifth birthday on 7 December. After calling at Madeira we had a rough passage between Finistere and Ushant, with much damage to ladders and guard rails above and to furnishings and crockery below. Into the Thames and up to Tilbury on the 16th, and Diana's parents met us for the road to Epsom.

5

London: The United Africa Company Ltd

After spending a family Christmas in Dartington it was agreed that we should go to Bosham and occupy the Old Schools, which had been converted by my parents, for a few months while we got ourselves and our possessions sorted out and made decisions about future employment. What had been learnt from the vivid experiences of the last three years?

Guidelines for job hunting
The objective set in Cambridge, of finding out about the apparent failures of British colonial policy by going and checking it on the ground, had been achieved. As implied in the last chapter, if there was a policy it was hardly manifest to those operating at the grass roots, although not until much later could it be said to have failed in any way similar to the upsets in Kenya and Cyprus. The symptoms were there, nonetheless; wishful thinking that all was well, then too weak a response too late. It is a sadly familiar pattern of behaviour that if a responsible official reports incipient unrest his superiors either lay the blame on him or do not believe him, so he is reluctant to admit the possibility. This applies to governors reporting to Whitehall no less than to a touring officer asking a provincial office for support. What had also been gained was understanding of, and admiration for, the basic work of 'bush

betterment' and the essentials of good government in pastoral societies; but the context of public service rules and 'red tape' had made me curious to try out contrasting methods in the private commercial sector. Once your horizons have been widened, however, can they be narrowed again?

Much of my thinking had been expressed in letters home and to friends, many of whom were similarly searching for the right path to follow, especially Mark Lowe, since our correspondence had continued all through school, national service and Cambridge. He too was a music scholar but had done his army service in Kenya, and later wrote to me in Nigeria from Germany and from Italy. He wondered about the reaction of selection boards to renegade musicians, and my letter in the autumn of 1957 was able to reassure him. Eighteen months later he questioned me closely and my five-page reply in January 1959 bears selective quotation:

> I convinced myself that I was being of real service to the people [of Mambilla] who suffer constantly from remoteness and official ignorance of their needs and circumstances ... [but] ... After 18 months of helping to run somebody else's country I begin to think that perhaps it's a mug's game. This is no time for a young man to allow himself to be condemned to abortive enthusiasms, and I think that frustration is inevitable unless one's exertions go into a society of which one is a properly integrated member. ... All we can expect [in Nigeria] in the foreseeable future is one-party government, with all hopes pinned to the wisdom of our philosopher-king, the *sardauna* of Sokoto [Northern Premier]. ... Specialist departmental officers are heavily reliant upon, and ever critical of, their administrative colleagues, but an occupation that requires indefinite qualities rather than definite qualifications is the first to arouse resentment because every man thinks he could do it better. ... The common man knows the DO to be a valuable friend, but he also knows that the [expatriate] DO must be the first to go if his country is to claim before the world that it is a nation managing its own affairs. ... What we encourage by imposed [non-sustainable] development is an epi-

demic materialism, whereas well-informed *amateur* advice is more effective because of the reduced gap between the outlook of the parties. Why put a professor in a primary school? ... Government paid my passage to a romantic and vitally interesting occupation; now I begin to see the sort of job I must look for, one for a lifetime.

Not much appreciation then that lifetime jobs would soon be phased out, but it was still possible to seek and be offered a 'progressive career' in most sizeable organizations. My basic criterion arose from the naïvety of having assumed that recruitment by the Secretary of State for the Colonies implied continuity of employment. On the contrary, working for whichever government to which one might be assigned meant being subject to the power of alien politicians. Hence my belief that one could no longer risk working abroad other than within a firmly British-based network. A secondary consideration was our desire to be in London for an initial period.

In February 1961 we celebrated the first anniversary of our wedding with a party for that large number of friends who had had no chance of being with us in Ibadan on the day. We were fortunate in being able to hold it in Bernard Robinson's 'studio' at 366 Goldhawk Road, and he arranged the performance of one of Bach's wedding cantatas. Meanwhile, a visit to Clarks Shoes in Street had been interesting but unfruitful at that time, and an interview with the British Council had revealed that they would have insisted on posting us abroad immediately, so that avenue was ruled out for a second time; we could have joined then if a home posting had been possible. Although some Foreign Office interviews were still pending we decided to accept what the United Africa Company (UAC) offered. UAC was the biggest single subsidiary of the Unilever concern (about one fifth of the whole), it was a household name on the West Coast, and the job for me in the recruitment section of Staff Department would use my graduate background and Nigerian experience directly. It also answered my need for private-sector work, and in a business that complemented the development ideals of government through profit-making commercial enterprise.

West African students in British universities

UAC had recognized the need to plan a programme of localizing its managerial and technical staff throughout its many subsidiary companies in Sierra Leone, Ghana and Nigeria. In the early 1960s there were still some 1200 expatriate managers 'on the coast', but the wind of change was blowing their way no less than in government circles. My task was to help John Lloyd, under David Cornock-Taylor, with the interviewing of staff for appointments overseas, but primarily to develop contacts in the centres where graduating students could be caught before they went home. My first day was 20 March.

Meanwhile, our search for a flat had resulted in a quarterly lease of a one-bedroomed, second floor 'apartment' at 37 Westbourne Terrace, quite near Paddington station. We were green enough not to have realized the importance of avoiding anything near a road junction, so we spent many warm nights that summer suffering from the acceleration of traffic when the lights changed either way. This lasted only six months because quite soon it became evident that Diana was expecting our first child, and it would have been a very poor environment in which to care for a baby. Luckily the Fergusons in Ibadan offered to let to us their house in Ashley Road, Thames Ditton, on the south bank of the Thames, not far from Hampton Court, and a good commute in to Waterloo. We moved there in October.

The work in UAC made good progress, beginning with enquiries of the various West African students officers in their high commissions about numbers and locations of their charges. Then a circular letter to all 24 area offices of the British Council in the 'home' network revealed that there were about 3000 West African students outside London. Some of these would be tied by sponsorship, but a high proportion were privately funded and therefore open to recruitment for service 'on the coast'. Nearly all the British Council offices responded helpfully, as did the university appointments advisers, so my first visits were to Oxford and Hull. Rooms for meetings and refreshment facilities were readily granted, and the news of my coming attracted anything between a handful and 20 interested candidates. My tour in June covered Liverpool, Glasgow, Manchester and Birmingham, and a later one in December took in Edinburgh, Newcastle, Nottingham and Shef-field. By this time, however, the limitations inherent in the whole enterprise had emerged and, although Bristol, Cardiff and Dublin were included in the following year, attention had to be given to internal discussion of the ethos of the company and its practical application to the methods of picking up Africans with managerial qualities.

Our musical lives gathered pace throughout the summer of 1961 and included taking part in Chelsea Opera Group performances of Berlioz's *Romeo and Juliet* in Oxford and in Cambridge; the wedding of Stephen Sandford and Pippa Norrington in Oxford (see Chapter 14); two visits to Glyndebourne (still affordable in those days); a week at Music Camp; Purcell's *Dido and Aeneas* done round the lake at Springhead in Dorset; a Whit weekend split between *The Barber of Baghdad* in the Shawford Mill Theatre and singing on the river near the Harnham Gate of Salisbury; a singing weekend at Claydon House in Buckinghamshire, seat of the Ver-ney family; and finally a Hoffnung concert in the Royal Festival Hall.

In midyear, six months after leaving Nigeria, the feeling per-sisted that my future direction was not clear, so a small investment in the Vocational Guidance Association seemed wise, only to be told that their analysis showed that either farming or diplomacy was the right road for me to take. The first option was recog-nizable as a genetic inheritance but not practicable at so late a stage; the second option, although not seen as *cultural*, was duly followed four years later.

On 18 January 1962 our first daughter, Sarah, was born in the Middlesex Hospital, and my role as proud father included helping the staff in a busy maternity ward and being allowed by the duty midwife to witness the delivery. This was such an awe-inspiring experience that my closer friends were bored by my telephonic accounts of it for many days to come. Within a week Diana had established the feeding routine and came home on the tenth day to the house in Thames Ditton, which proved the ideal environment for the baby.

In the same month my work in UAC came to the boil with a series of minutes, reviews and meetings. My efforts to attract the attention of qualified Africans as potential recruits were seen as successful and were favourably regarded by my immediate superiors, but we began to be aware of plans to reorganize the 'main trunk' of the business, particularly in Nigeria, where the company was having to face up to changes in the operating environment, especially the post-independence drive by local politicians to ensure closer control over 'foreign' mercantile enterprises. In short, retrenchment was in the air for the main commercial parts, but not for the many technical and specialized subsidiaries. We had been able to make 28 firm appointments in such fields as engineering, accountancy, technical sales and instruction, pharmacy, hire purchase and wharf management. The possibility for me to move into the commercial side in London shrank to nil, but the central Unilever management suggested that a secondment for two or three years to Political and Economic Planning could buy time for UAC to recover its poise. This would be research into various aspects of the lives of overseas students in Britain, but implied a long-term commitment to Unilever and being a London commuter. In early May my letter gave notice of resignation to be effective at the end of July.

A second round of job hunting

There was risk in this move, but at least my combination of understanding the realities of the west coast and knowing the ropes of the academic world had been put to good use, and now was the time to break free of this background. By this time, also, we wished to break free of the suburban existence, and in mid-June a visit to Street to explore the opportunities in Clarks Shoes opened an attractive vista of grass-roots industrial work in a rural setting. This was following up an earlier introduction for me from Patrick Wilkinson in King's to Michael Feilden in Street, but we did not jump too precipitately; there was time for many other interviews while working out my notice in UAC.

Little more than a year in the private sector was scarcely enough to form a judgement, and the Overseas Services Resettlement Bureau continued to encourage my interest in various aspects of the Foreign Office and the British Council. Further approaches to both proved abortive at this time and one or two attractive alternatives included Wiggins Teape's staff training in Beaconsfield, administrative jobs at London University and publishing with Longmans. Had my attitudes changed in any fundamental way since achieving fatherhood? The Nigerian experience had provided an insight of pastoral realities in primitive conditions; the Unilever experience had shown me the *modus vivendi* of one of the biggest corporation's private bureaucracy; now the priority was longer-term continuity in work that would not be rendered abortive through no fault of my own.

By the end of June we had decided to accept the offer to join Clarks Shoes' graduate induction scheme, with a view to my becoming a staff training officer, and to move to Somerset. Before then, however, we had to learn how to introduce baby Sarah to musical life, and the first opportunity was a ten-day Easter holiday in Cornwall. We drove 287 miles through the night to reach the coastguard cottages of Prussia Cove near Penzance on the farm of Michael and Romi Tunstall-Behrens, the main purpose being to join a large gathering of old friends in a performance of Monteverdi's *Poppea* in Godolphin Manor under the direction of John Carewe. We also did a concert in Penzance church under Robert Anderson. Our neighbours in the cottages were Michael and Rachel Moriarty with their young family, and Heather Harper and her husband. Later in the spring we again joined the Chelsea Opera Group, this time for Berlioz's *The Damnation of Faust* in Oxford, Cambridge and Lincoln's Inn. The Whitsun holiday found us in Salisbury where Mrs Blacking, widow of the cathedral architect (and mother of John, a distinguished anthropologist), generously baby-sat while we sang in Edington Priory and, for a second time, in an old 32-foot naval cutter on the river by the Rose and Crown at the Harnham Gate, organized by Chris Zealley and David Calcutt.

Ben Essex, Clarks Shoes' estate manager, arranged for us to rent a small company-owned house in Street, but before we moved into 58 Grange Avenue on 20 August we managed a trip up north so that Sarah could be shown to her great-grandfather, George Clarke, and 'Auntie' Nora in their fine house in a desirable part of Wilmslow, near Manchester.

6

Somerset: C & J Clark Ltd, Shoemakers

In earlier discussions Michael Feilden had expounded the ethos of Clarks Shoes in terms of maintaining a rural quality of life for people who would otherwise be obliged to drift into the towns. The family directors and shareholders had strong Quaker traditions to uphold, and could claim affinity to others such as the Cadbury and Rowntree clans.

Paternal industry providing rural employment
Tom Woods, ex-army and ex-ICI, was in charge of staff recruitment and development and had asked on his standard form for an indication of my values. Some of my responses were as follows: 'I am aware of having benefited from institutions that are well endowed with inherited and invested wealth that was the product of profitable enterprises in the past; hence the profit-making management of industrial enterprises is essential.' ... 'I do not wish to submit any longer to the racket that passes for life in the London area, and I do want to live and bring up my family in the country where I was myself brought up.' ... 'One thing I have learnt in the last five years has been the value and importance of living and working in the same community and of knowing one's colleagues in their complete home setting.'

The first principle of the company was that no one could expect to control the mass production of footwear without a genuine feel for the basic nature and construction of a pair of shoes, so all except the most specialized recruits were set to making one or more pairs of 'bespoke' shoes for themselves on a personal pair of lasts under the eagle eye of Bill Whitcombe. Not everyone took kindly to the painstaking manual work needed to satisfy the 'handsewn' expert, but my output eventually included a pair of walking boots for Diana, as well as two pairs of decent shoes for myself. This part of the induction programme took several weeks, but at the beginning one week of general talk about the ramifications of the Clarks Shoes' network had been handled by my subsequent colleagues, Bob Goree, who had been personnel officer in one of the factories and later joined Esso, and Ed Robinson who later joined Bookers' agricultural enterprises, at first overseas doing personnel work in the new sugar plantation near Jebba, Nigeria. My boss was Peter Prince, for the second time; barely four years previously he had been in charge of Adamawa Division, Northern Nigeria (see Chapter 4).

In the early 1960s Clarks Shoes was a keenly optimistic and expanding business with 18 shoe factories spread over the West Country, from Warminster to Plymouth, and several more factories providing rubber, leather-board components, lasts and engineering services. Only four were on the original site in Street. In what was a highly fragmented industry, Clarks Shoes was the biggest single manufacturer with about 10 per cent of total production. As became apparent, however, the weakness lay on the retail side. The training department was exclusively concerned with production, but that was to change radically during my time. In round figures, 10 million pairs of shoes were produced each year with a sales value of £25 million from a total workforce of about 6000. Despite some mechanization with powered hand-tools, shoemaking continued to be labour intensive, so Clarks Shoes tended to be a dominant employer in most communities and was very conscientious about helping to develop local facilities.

Operatives and supervisors
After bespoke handsewn shoemaking came operative experience, and my assignment was in the Shepton Mallet factory. Five weeks

spent on a variety of tasks in the cutting and making rooms, with many opportunities for nattering with workmates and their bosses, called forth what my staff training colleagues wanted — a nine-page account of human behaviour and attitudes to supervision on the shop floor. One cutter had been in the navy for 'hostilities only', but had remained in it for seven years and now half wished he had stayed on to enjoy an outdoor life and a chief petty officer's pay. Another was a part-time member of the county fire brigade; yet another had been a wartime RAF flying instructor in South Africa, and rather wished he had gone into civilian flying, but now believed that versatility was the best insurance against shortage of work. The most interesting one to me was a man who displayed the status symbols of having done 'sea time', that is he had unshaven cheekbones. It was no surprise when he said he had done 22 years and had been a chief stoker. But had he (my report asked) in taking to shoes, forfeited his chances of being reincarnated as a seagull? Comparisons between styles of foremanship were less frivolous, but in conclusion,

> I did not expect to make any startling new discoveries about the fundamentals of human behaviour, but it may be a little clearer than before that the industrial worker shares *some* common characteristics with the naval rating, the university don and undergraduate, the Nigerian peasant, the city businessman and the self-made African student. To elucidate the differences would require deeper reflection rather than further observation.

Peter, Ed and Bob were keen to ensure that the content of the courses offered was firmly supported by academically respectable research, such as would be recognized by the London School of Economics and the Institute of Personnel Management. January 1963 found me drawing up schemes for mounting a survey of what first-line supervision actually entailed, so that courses could be designed accordingly. Meanwhile, my role included taking charge for the first time of the existing programmes of two-day supervisory aptitude tests, one-week basic supervision and two-week advanced supervision courses and giving lectures, running exercises, producing hand-out notes and writing reports on the participants. A further ordeal, necessary to establish the minimum degree of credibility, was to act the part of a supernumerary charge hand for two strenuous weeks on the latest type of conveyor-belt making line in the Mayflower factory in Plymouth. Commuting from my parents' house (by this time in Totnes rather than Dartington) was easy, but standing, watching, talking, intervening and discussing on my feet all day tested my stamina to new limits and was not readily forgotten.

Music and drama in the local community

Domestic consolidation took priority for the first few months in Street, and we had a substantial stream of visitors, both family and friends, curious about our new surroundings and wanting to see how well baby Sarah was waxing. The local amateur dramatic group, the Street Players, put on *A Taste of Honey* in November, and Diana subsequently took leading parts in several of its productions. Before the end of the year we had heard the Bath Cantata Group under Beresford King-Smith (and later Jim Pescek) and been encouraged to join its Sunday evening rehearsals. The Street Subscription Concert Society elected me to its committee, and Lady Becket in Keinton Mandeville arranged occasional *hausmusik* sessions. About this time we came to know John and Phyllis Olive and their series of opera productions in their minuscule opera house at Shawford Mill, Beckington. As an extension of their normal repertoire they mounted a dramatized presentation of Mendelssohn's *Elijah* in St Mary's Glastonbury, and followed it up a year later with a similarly dramatic version of Berlioz's *Childhood of Christ* — a work we put on 25 years later in Addis Ababa. In June we went to Prussia Cove for a second time, sharing a flat in Porthenalls with Roddy and Serena Armstrong who were captivated by Sarah's charms at 17 months old.

The little semidetached company house in Grange Avenue was very convenient, but we had begun to feel well enough established to want to raise a mortgage and become house owners for the first time. Mick Wilson taught at Millfield School and lived with his wife Helen on the south side of Street in a modest but attractive four-bedroomed house in Wraxhill Road. They had decided (after some agonizing) to return to his native Australia, so we were lucky to be able to nip in and buy with help from the Halifax Building Society, the down payment being derived from savings while in Nigeria. Mick's full name was John Dunster Sinclair-Wilson and he took delight in saying that his second name owed its origin to his being descended from a bastard child of the Luttrell family of Dunster Castle in Somerset. He was indeed a colourful character who had been a leading actor while at Cambridge (and a King's College friend of Patrick Wilkinson), knew his way round the Far East, and was going to take up the post of master of Robb College, part of a private university in Queensland. We moved at the end of July, just in time for the annual factory holiday of two weeks (everyone but a skeleton staff of desk workers had to go at the same time) and another significant move for the staff training unit, from the 'prefab' aptly-named broiler houses to fine new space in the Barn of the old Grange.

Ordeal by management consultant — twice

My own report on the role of the first-line supervisor was duly presented in August after completion of my survey of 26 chosen supervisors in 20 rooms in six different shoe factories, together with the results of a questionnaire addressed to factory superintendents. The total number of charge hands and foremen was about 250, in the three types of room (cutting, closing and making), so my work had covered a 10 per cent sample. There was no claim of original enlightenment beyond an elucidation of the minute-by-minute demands on the supervisor's time and skills, and how this could be applied to the revision of our courses.

This was small beer, however, in comparison with the major overhaul of the entire Clarks Shoes' empire entailed by the McKinsey consultancy, which had been commissioned by the directors and senior management. A second consultancy by McIver in the following year dealt solely with the management of sales, by which time my interest had moved into that area too. The upheaval began in November with the recommended splitting of the business into three divisions — women's, children's and men's — whereby marketing, sales and production units would be grouped under their specialized product. This meant the recruitment of many new staff, particularly travelling salesmen, all of whom needed induction courses. Our planned programme was thrown into disarray, and in the first half of 1964 we 'inducted' no fewer than seven batches of new travellers and other staff, totalling nearly 40, including three recruits to staff training — Tim Orr, Hugh Stafford and Richard Marsden. A useful by-product of meeting this challenge was our gradual shift towards sales training, in contrast to the previous concentration on production staff. Hand-outs based on McKinsey's presentations had to be written and included in all our courses.

A review of my personal position led in the same direction. To make progress with a business career it was clearly necessary to be in the mainstream of commercial decision-making and not to be confined to service departments, such as the recruitment and training functions which had so far become familiar to me. Day-to-day cost consciousness based on time study and piece rates was certainly an obsession in Clarks Shoes' factories. But how was this realized as profitable turnover and increased market shares? It was agreed that the part-time course in Bristol on management personnel should be abandoned as no longer appropriate and that Bob Kent, the women's division sales manager, should take me on to assist him with his heavy burden. Before this transfer to an entirely new existence at the end of August it seemed right to review the achievements and shortcomings of the preceding year of somewhat chaotic improvisation. My 14-page frank appraisal did not go down too well with my immediate superiors, but must have been valuable as handover guidance for Tim and Hugh.

Family expansion and vocal adventures

On 9 March 1964 our second daughter Louise was born in our own bedroom in Wraxhill Road. Home confinement was fashionable at the time, provided no problems were expected, and Dr Rex Last's house was through the hedge behind us. On the strength of my previous experience in the maternity ward of the Middlesex Hospital, our district nurse accepted my help as assistant midwife. And this time Diana had taken her antenatal exercises seriously, so all went smoothly. At about 7.00 a.m., half an hour after the birth, we phoned Dr Last to report the successful delivery, glad we had not had to disturb his sleep earlier. To our surprise, he expressed acute dismay because, he said, he had a medical trainee staying with him to whom he had intended to demonstrate the ideal home delivery. What a chance to have missed!

Only a few weeks earlier my maternal grandmother had died. Known to us all as 'Me-me' (not Mimi), all through the two post-war decades her house in Bosham had been a base for family holidays, mostly spent on the water. Her cooking was legendary and she put up with visits at short notice with amazing generosity; but sclerosis had become so acute in the last few years that a nursing home in Portsmouth had become necessary. It was a great sadness that there was no way for me to get to her funeral; it was just impossible to ask for leave when the course in hand would have had no one to keep it going.

During these years in Street our vocal proficiencies — Diana's mezzo-soprano and my tenor — flourished rather more than in the past, either in London or at Cambridge. The newly built theatre, Strode Hall, was inaugurated with 'a kaleidoscope of theatrical entertainment' in which we sang (and acted) the light-hearted duet from Monteverdi's *Poppea*. Philip Moore conducted the BBC's Bristol Singers and welcomed me to join them on several occasions. John Simpson was an ordinand in Wells Theological College and a keen harpsichordist, so we did two programmes with him, one in the chapterhouse and another in the vicars' hall. As well as conducting the Bath Cantata Group, Jim Peschek was director of music at Monkton Coombe School. On one memorable day in March 1965 my voice managed without undue strain to do the tenor solos for Jim's performance of Bach's *Magnificat* in the afternoon and also to cope with the solos for a *Messiah* in Downside Abbey in the evening. Oratorio appearances in schools and churches became quite frequent, and Tim Reynish, an ex-NYO horn player, got me to do the Britten *Serenade* in Bridgwater and Minehead. A final effort was to do Mozart's *Impresario* with the Olives in Shawford, part of a double bill with Holst's *Savitri* in which Susan Longfield made one of her last appearances.

Sales administration: the year of truth
Bob Kent was a delightful person to work for — absolutely

straight, energetic and humorous — but he knew from the start that my enthusiasm for the job had been tempered by doubts. Plunging into a strange world at the deep end, my new environment in the central offices was slick and glossy but riddled with problems, particularly with crises over the delivery of orders. Control of the flow of stock from factory to warehouse and out to retail customers was achieved by feeding punched cards into one of the earlier models of an IBM data processor, which occupied an immense amount of space and needed 73 people to run it. 'The machine' dominated our lives, so much so that to get a single pair of shoes processed manually for a special reason required the chasing of one elusive individual colleague for approval. Only the operators of this system knew how to work it, so ordinary mortals were at their mercy; many of us began to think of them as high priests standing between the oracle and long-suffering humanity. After a year of this it was my resolution at the time never again to submit to such a regime, but the rather more user-friendly and compact systems of today were then a mere dream.

The immediate tasks concerned the deployment of our field sales force of 15 travellers in women's shoes through two regional sales managers, providing them with sample ranges, running sales conferences and monitoring their weekly sales returns. Everything was geared to the seasonal cycle of trade shows, which in turn were determined by forecasts of fashion and style. This was where my commitment began to waiver. Vance Packard's book *The Waste Makers* had exposed the planned obsolescence in car manufacturing. The fashion shoes for teenagers being made in Plymouth were intended to wear out within three months. It was naïve of me at the beginning to have imagined that Clarks Shoes had a prime interest in making good shoes; the actual motive was making money by ensuring that shoes were the medium for profitable enterprise, and if this meant going to America for inspiration so much the worse for the customer.

The last straw was my realization that a clique of fashion designers in Paris and New York were deciding what the colour-matching scheme for the next season was going to be, which London had to follow and to which our leathers and all other materials for promoting our product would have to conform.

After only four years in the private commercial sector it seemed the moment had come to recognize some awkward truths about my suitability. We were enjoying a good quality of life and were very reluctant to give it up, but, as much on the production side as in the sales team, the company expected mobility: indeed movement seemed to be an essential condition of progress, if not within a company then between companies. Why not make a virtue of necessity and join an organization (like the British Council) that would decide a series of career postings for you on a globally mobile basis, but without any break in employment and within a unified service? More significantly, would it not be better to leave the making of money to those who really enjoyed it and return to an ethos of public service? The feeling of being a misfit grew steadily during the early months of 1965. Morale had been raised by a substantial pay rise at Christmas time, yet there was no escape from my pastoral rather than commercial instincts, which were perhaps a genetic inheritance from a mixture of farmers, clergymen, seafarers and doctors.

One other home truth about the business world emerged from my Clarks Shoes experience, namely that the owner-directors of a family firm are those who benefit from a company's increased capital value (earned by good profit margins), but that salaried managers do not share in this wealth. Paradoxically, Unilever did issue annual bonuses to all its staff in line with the fortunes of its publicly quoted share prices.

My four-page letter of 8 March was addressed to John Aris, the British Council's director of staff recruitment, with some anxiety for fear that an approach at this stage, and for a third time, would be rejected out of hand. In retrospect, this move was effectively nine years too late, but Robin Twite saw fit to give me a fair wind and by mid-July my resignation from Clarks Shoes had been accepted.

PART II
The Second Age, 1965–92: In a Good Cause

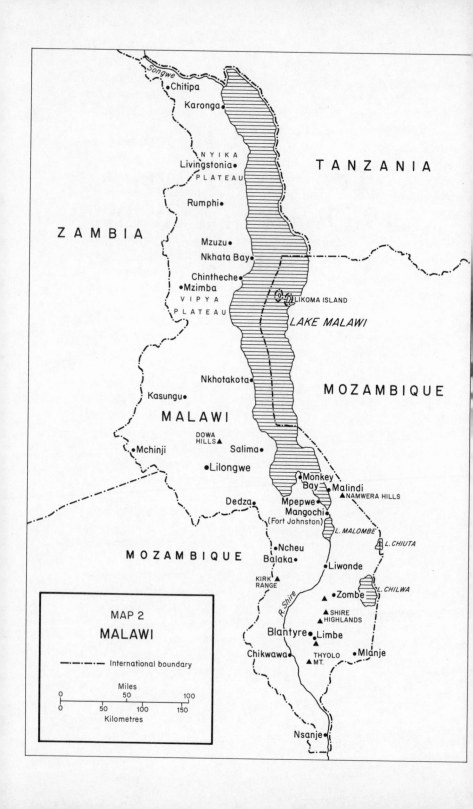

Songwe
•Chitipa
Karonga•

TANZANIA

ZAMBIA

N Y I K A
Livingstonia•
P L A T E A U

Rumphi•

Mzuzu•
Nkhata Bay•

•Chintheche
•Mzimba
V I P Y A
P L A T E A U

LIKOMA ISLAND

LAKE MALAWI

Nkhotakota•

MOZAMBIQUE

Kasungu•

MALAWI

•Mchinji

DOWA
HILLS▲
Salima•

•Lilongwe

•Monkey
Bay
Malindi•
▲NAMWERA HILLS

Dedza•

Mpepwe•
Mangochi•
(Fort Johnston)

L. MALOMBE

L. CHIUTA

•Ncheu

MOZAMBIQUE

Balaka•

Liwonde•

L. CHILWA

KIRK
RANGE▲

▲Zombe

R. Shire

▲
▲SHIRE
▲HIGHLANDS

Blantyre•
•Limbe

Chikwawa•

•Mlanje

THYOLO
▲MT.

Nsanje•

MAP 2
MALAWI

—··—··— International boundary

Miles
0   50   100
0   50   100   150
Kilometres

7

The British Council at Last: Malawi in its Early Years of Independence

The first six chapters of this book have been a necessary pre-liminary to the main purpose — to show that what C. G. Jung would have recognized as the individuation stage resulted, in my case, in the eventual and certain realization that personal fulfilment would be achieved through work within the British Council ethos and global network.

Lucky to get in so late
My letter to John Aris (mentioned at the end of the last chapter) apologized for abortive contacts in the past, but went into the detailed reasons for earlier decisions not to join the Council. It also pointed out that at no time had my candidature actually been rejected, especially by the selection boards that saw me in 1956 and in 1961. Diana and our new offspring seemed now well disposed, but 'in the short term I have no immediate desire to leave a very pleasant firm, many happy colleagues and friends, and local life enriched with plenty of music making and amateur dramatics of a good standard ... but in the long term I doubt my temperamental suitability to find it [moneymaking and wealth creation] of lifelong, absorbing interest'. Furthermore, 'My UAC

work extended my first-hand knowledge of the British Council from overseas places to area offices at home, and I continue to admire and be attracted by it. I have been aware for many years now that the Council is something to which I could devote my working life with pride in the service.'

The reply was characteristically generous, while warning me not to be disappointed if that year's selection board put me on a reserve list and/or offered me a contract appointment rather than general service entry. The question is often asked 'how did you get in? or 'what qualifications did you need?', so some account is required. The basic and formal necessity was an above average class of degree from a British university. My lower second was liberally interpreted on account of the commitment of time and energy involved in holding a choral scholarship at King's, but the recruitment department was clearly in search of certain ill-defined qualities such as are sought by many public and commercial concerns. Presumably my previous overseas experience, relative maturity and knowledge of personnel work counted in my favour, but those of a nervous disposition can crack up completely under cross-examination by an intimidating selection board. One very fast ball was bowled to me by a gentleman who leant back in his chair and said, 'Well now, Mr Nightingale, would you care to define the word culture for us?' As my mouth opened another member of the board leant forward and said, 'If I were the candidate I think I would require notice of that question' — a magnanimous intervention which afforded me those few precious extra seconds in which to offer a coherent response. My rescuer was subsequently identified as Morris Dodderidge, who has my eternal gratitude — and knows it. Other probings included such topics as my attitude to middle-class suburban Africans and state subsidy of the arts, and whether my music had been an asset or a handicap. My references to having recently read such authors as Matthew Arnold, T. S. Eliot and Raymond Williams seemed to be effective, and the result was much as Robin Twite had expected — an offer of a contract to be an assistant representative in Malawi. Vacancies in the established career service were unpredictable, but we had to take the risk of achieving that later, and it was happily justified (as will be seen) within a few years.

The British Council at Last — MALAWI

The never to be forgotten date of joining was 16 August 1965, but first we had to put our furniture into storage in Glastonbury (having made the unwise decision to sell our house in Street — although we could not be sure of tenants) and move the family to stay with Diana's parents in Epsom. Then followed three weeks of induction programmes and other preparations, and we embarked in mid-September aboard SS *Braemar Castle*.

The Union Castle east coast route to Beira

Two interconnected air-conditioned cabins on the port side were allocated to us, much to the disgust of the taxpaying sensibilities of my father-in-law who saw us off. Such apparent luxury became a basic need in the eastern Mediterranean and beyond, especially with Sarah aged three and a half and Louise only 18 months (bottom-shuffling rather than crawling) over an extended voyage of nearly five weeks. Not until the early 1970s were sea passages abandoned in favour of air travel; they were no longer justifiable in time or cost. Even so, the crafty individual could still work them occasionally and they were still available for our return trip four years later.

As during the three years in Nigeria, letters home form a valuable supplement to diaries and official papers in recalling incidents, states of mind and humorous anecdotes that merit space in this narrative. A quick run ashore in Gibraltar was followed by a more extensive family exploration of Genoa, but not during the passage of the Suez Canal, nor in Aden, from where my letter of 1 October was posted, describing my 24-hour trip from the ship in Port Said to the sights of Cairo and back to the ship in Suez, and the disturbed state of Aden itself.

> The journey would have been worthwhile if only for the hour spent among the literally fabulous treasures in the Egyptian Museum of Antiquities. I begin to understand the fascination of Egyptology. The significance of the Nile and its fertility, the hieroglyphics and symbols inscribed everywhere, the ingenuity and skill in execution of the craftsmen ... provided food for thought for several days. I also saw the Mohammed Ali mosque in the citadel ... sumptuously

decorated — all in abstract designs in accordance with Muslim precepts.

The next letter, from Mombasa, spoke of three families among our fellow passengers, especially Shirley Bloom and three children, whose husband Ronny was soon to play a leading role, not only in arranging a rescue party but also in being Higgins in a *Pygmalion* production in the Zomba club — but more of that later. They joined us for a self-drive hired car expedition to an Indian Ocean beach, 'so I was taking two wives and five children'. A letter from Dar es Salaam mentioned that we had made courtesy calls on the British Council libraries in both places. It also went into detail about my library of modern theology books, the concentrated reading of which was intended to help me face up to the problem of what my attitude to missionaries should be (never resolved from Nigerian days) and, just as significantly, what we should say to the children — Sarah having already asked 'what are churches for?' and been told 'for singing in'.

The last part of this letter, written after our delayed arrival in Blantyre–Limbe, described the sting in the tail of our voyage. The Trans-Zambezi Railway ran a single-coach 'diesel car' up from Beira (Mozambique) into the Shire Highlands of Malawi where the line connected on to Salima on the lake (until very recently Lake Nyasa). Mercifully, we had passed beyond the Portuguese border when it broke down, but a single-track railway has stringent rules which prevented the ready deployment of a locomotive to tow us. There was, however, a track-side telephone wire and Ronny Bloom, who had come down to meet his family, used the hooks on the end of a long pole (thoughtfully provided equipment for the driver) to shout an appeal to his colleagues in the British high commission to send two cars down the rough escarpment track to where we were stranded, 100 miles south of our destination. By the same method my first conversation with my new boss, Peter (R. P. K.) Harrison, the representative, was a shouted explanation. Even less auspicious was our first meeting because, after a very hot and sticky day, plus three hours of bumps with a sick child curled on top of me, the journey up resulted in my legs putting me straight from the car into the gutter, rather than advancing with dignity to shake hands. This was outside Limbe post office at 1.15 a.m., but fortunately was not an accurate omen of future relations, which quickly proved to be as cordial as anyone could hope.

First impressions and two immediate crises

Malawi had become independent in 1964, with Dr Kamuzu Banda as prime minister and Sir Glyn Jones, the former governor, retained as governor-general. What was it like a year later? For us there were many familiar features, in fact all the hallmarks of a former British Commonwealth protectorate — never a colony, please note. The machinery of government and the public services were still firmly in the hands of expatriate officials; the currency was still in pounds, shillings and pence; police uniforms were identical to the Nigerian ones; electrical sockets took 13 amp plugs with square pins; traffic kept (roughly) to the left; English was the medium of instruction other than at primary level; and, above all, the non-British foreign community was still embryonic. The USA, France and Germany were already represented and UN specialist agencies would soon follow. The British high commission itself was taking time to settle into its role, so the British Council was conscious of being an element in the continuity from pre- to post-independence — from the protectorate status of Nyasaland to the aid-recipient status of Malawi.

Contrasts between west and central Africa are, however, very marked, so although we felt quickly at home in many ways, the climate, altitude and extreme beauty of the environment underlined our need to learn the parts we had to play with fresh viewpoints, and urgently. Almost my first official duty was to help carry the coffin at the Catholic funeral of Peter Powell, a VSO cadet volunteer who had been on holiday from Zambia and had drowned while swimming with friends in Lake Malawi near Salima. Subsequently, my work inevitably included correspondence with his family in Britain and the commissioning of a headstone for his grave in the local cemetery. The second crisis, just three weeks later, was of an entirely different but no less disturbing order — the Unilateral Declaration of Independence by neighbouring Rhodesia. We could only guess at the possible consequences and, as the days of inaction turned into weeks and months of negotiation (and humiliation for some), it gradually became apparent that the diversion of industrial investment would be very much to Malawi's advantage.

The VSO (Voluntary Service Overseas) programme was launched in 1958 when compulsory military service was abolished. The idea caught on rapidly and widely — 18-year-old school leavers could offer enthusiasm and versatility, and graduate volunteers, with or without further qualifications, could make a valuable contribution in countries where skilled manpower was scarce. My post, as an extra assistant representative, had been created because there were already 26 volunteers in Malawi, with more to come, and the British Council's role as VSO's overseas arm was overloading the office. Expansion under Peter Harrison's benign direction (with Colin Perchard's exuberant support) was very much in the air and our work soon extended into aid-funded projects to advise on teaching English (Bryson McAdam and Graham Coe) and science (Stan Moss) and creating the Malawi National Library Service (Fred Johnson). The core of our work nevertheless continued to be running the main library in Blantyre, with small branches in Zomba and Lilongwe, organizing scholarships and technical assistance traineeships inward to Britain and bringing out expert advisers, both for short and for longer periods. With the higher education sector in the early stages of development, secondary school teachers and pupils took much of our attention, specially when we were touring in a landrover loaded with books, a film projector and a portable generator. It was also in the secondary sector that the volunteers were concentrated, although non-teaching volunteers were soon to increase rapidly.

New experiences crowded in on us. A happy family atmosphere pervaded the office team, and the Malawian library and clerical staff were invariably cheerful and diligent. As in Somerset and earlier in Nigeria, life and work were integrated. Soon we felt able to put our toes gently into the local musical scene. A letter in mid-November said 'Although I'm having to work rather long hours, as is inevitable when everything is new, it is most satisfactory to be working once more at rewarding tasks and in pursuit of a cause in which I really believe.'

An arm extended and a shoulder to weep on
We quickly got to know the volunteers in the immediate vicinity of Blantyre–Limbe by giving a couple of parties on Portuguese *vinho verde*, but extensive travelling was needed to visit the others. On the first such trip to the central region, Dedza secondary school had five volunteers, of whom two, Dick Bird and Robert Parsons, subsequently became close friends. The peripatetic life produces an ever-changing circle of acquaintances, but it is seldom easy to guess in advance whom among them will become long-lasting friends. It is inevitably a small proportion, and with those few one preserves carefully the means of contact. Dick joined the staff of VSO, did a stint as its earliest non-British Council field officer (in Papua New Guinea) and has remained a senior member of its team ever since. Robert had been the organ scholar of Peterhouse, Cambridge, and consequently suffered from our insistence on using his skills for musical events in Blantyre. He stayed on under contract to the Ministry of Education for several years, joined the Army Education Corps for a while, and then settled to teaching in Edinburgh.

Another opportunity to check on the welfare of upcountry volunteers and to look into the prospects for new projects came early in 1966 when John Isherwood from the VSO development section visited us for a comprehensive ten-day tour. Sharing a landrover for 1500 miles proved an excellent recipe for ensuring rapport between Blantyre and London on volunteer matters, and our friendship lasts to this day. He later left to ensure family continuity in his father's firm of solicitors and has given valuable service to Oxfam, among many other interests, including the current chairmanship of Wateraid. On this journey we saw two volunteers who later served in the British Council with distinction — Gillian Marsh at Lilongwe Girls' Secondary School and Peter Sandiford at the police training school. A potential disaster threatened when Brian Morris, in charge of the fisheries' training school at Mpwepwe (near the southern end of the lake) took us for a short trip in a boat with an outboard engine that promptly expired. After paddling ashore and walking back, it was a relief not to have to send a telegram to VSO in London saying 'REGRET ISHERWOOD TRAMPLED BY HIPPOPOTAMUS'.

91

Yet an actual disaster did occur one hot afternoon in mid-April when a pair of VSO women cadets from Livingstone in Zambia were hitching a ride south in a landrover, which exchanged a glancing blow with a passing lorry. Alice Ann Robinson had had her elbow on the right hand rear window ledge and it was so badly shattered that the only doctor in Ncheu District Hospital had taken the decision to amputate above the joint. Judy Rycroft, her friend, was mentally distressed by the realization that only moments before the accident she had changed places on the back seat. The driver was described as 'a typically quiet-spoken intellectual American' based in Botswana (Bechuanaland at the time). He was similarly shaken by the accident, which he could not explain. For us the consequences were a good example of how an incident of this sort could 'hit us for six'; this one monopolized our resources for the rest of the month. We did not know about it until two days after the event, when the doctor and his patient with the driver and his landrover came to Blantyre. Then followed complex discussions, messages and reports on the medical, legal and insurance aspects. We had to brief local solicitors and obtain their advice. As writs in the Malawi High Court seemed likely and as Alice Ann was a minor, my name had to be put down as 'next friend'. The driver's insurers, based in South Africa, began to wriggle in the hope of evading claims of general and special damages, but were finally induced to accept liability by a threat. The senior partner of the firm representing our side wrote to them: 'If you do not play the game I shall apply to have you struck off the list of insurers licensed to do business in Malawi.' Meanwhile, Alice Ann's wound was healing in hospital and Judy, who was staying in our house, was being given 'tender loving care' by Diana. My five-page letter giving full details of the entire episode to the director of VSO in London, Douglas Whiting, was significantly dated Sunday 24 April.

Happier events were two weddings, both in Zomba. In mid-July David Roberts, a VSO statistician assigned to the National Statistical Office married the daughter of his boss, Eric Bailey, an expatriate civil servant. Mrs Bailey was keen on amateur dramatics and gave a flamboyant demonstration of her 'deprived mother' feelings in the local Roman Catholic cathedral. The second wedding, at the end of the month, was of a pair of volunteers. Diana Leach was teaching at Malosa Secondary School and Robin Gray was an engineer with the Ministry of Works. Theirs was a relatively sober ceremony in St George's Anglican church.

The annual 'trooping season' stretched the overseas arm to its limits. In August of both 1966 and 1967 VSO chartered a Caledonian Airways Bristol Britannia (four turboprops) to deliver new and retrieve old volunteers in a combined operation for Zambia and Malawi. Approaching Blantyre for the first time, the aircraft made too tight a turn, came in fast, bounced once and then did an overshoot for a second attempt. We watched with our hearts in our mouths, knowing that nearly 100 volunteers on board were all our responsibility *in loco parentis*. Elaborate instructions in a circular letter made arrangements for the meeting and greeting of the newcomers, and issued dire warnings of the financial consequences of missing the outgoing flight for the leavers. It was an unpopular system but it was necessary for VSO, a charity, to minimize its travel budget. The aircraft went on to Lusaka and returned in the afternoon for an evening departure. In the first year some overnight accommodation had to be found, and we organized a pool-side barbecue for 90 people; the next year we avoided this with a slightly slicker turnround, but ran a buffet lunch for 150 instead. By 1968 the charter-flight system had been replaced by block bookings at special half-fare rates, resulting in our handling batches of 15 or 20 spread over two months — not much of an improvement.

While viewing this prospect with some anxiety, in July our boss Peter Harrison caught bronchial pneumonia. He and his wife Pat and son Andrew, all having meanwhile become firm family friends, were due for extremely well-earned home leave. Rather to my surprise it fell to me, within less than a year of first arrival, to be acting representative. Colin Perchard has since and very deservedly risen right to the apex of the British Council's organization, but at this time it must have seemed to Peter (with London's agreement) that his seniority in time served was outweighed by my relative maturity and 'outside' experience. This is only my conjecture without evidence, but in retrospect it seems a plausible explanation for what became a slightly delicate relationship — but only for a week or two; we were too busy and friendly to allow a sensitive issue to become destructive.

Never a dull moment: acting in charge of DIY
Viewed in the light of later knowledge of bigger British Council establishments in more sophisticated surroundings, it is hard to recall just how primitive was our working environment. Theorists will insist that long hours are the result of failure to delegate, yet no Malawian was available to whom office management and good housekeeping could be entrusted. Luckily we did at least have the stalwart support of two lady accountants — first Isobel Duncan who took enormous pride in keeping our figure work straight (and has kept in touch from Glasgow ever since), and then Daisy Kennedy who was equally good but had to leave to accompany her husband to New Zealand. Otherwise, our Malawian library staff, clerk–typists, driver–projectionists and messenger–cleaners needed the direct supervision of our British triumvirate — a team which was reduced to two at regular intervals.

We necessarily covered the entire gamut, from policy discussions with the British high commissioner (in our time an affable, sympathetic and supportive 'King' David Cole) through negotiations with landlords for premises and meetings with Malawi government officials, down to supplies of stencils for our Gestetner — there was no photocopying in those days. Still less were there telex or fax machines. International telephones worked badly, the airmail to London took most of a week and the only rapid method of reaching that far was by overnight telegram — which did not always make it in 12 hours. One of my earliest lessons was not to speak or write too clearly, nor out of turn. A particular minute sent to London was too forthright for the comfort of HQ, and Morris Dodderidge, who was in charge of the relevant overseas division, felt obliged to send me a mild reprimand. Many months later during my home leave, an interview was scheduled, but he forestalled it during my wait in his outer office by putting his head round the door and saying 'I trust you can read between the lines?' — followed quickly by — 'In that case we understand one another perfectly!' — a fine gesture by the very same rescuer of the nervous interviewee of two years before.

The lease on our house in Limbe had been due to expire soon after the Harrisons' departure. Efforts to line up an alternative one had been abortive over several months, so it became inevitable that we moved into their empty house in Blantyre. At the same time we began a long-running campaign to persuade London that capital was needed to buy a house because the market in rentals had fizzled out after the Rhodesian UDI. Owners wanted to sell. Despite the credit squeeze decreed by Harold Wilson's government, by Christmas our arguments had prevailed and we were authorized to buy a house being put up by a Portuguese contractor but which would not be completed before Peter's return. With characteristic generosity he insisted on lodging with a friend until we could move again. A letter of 25 September, reporting to Peter on my stewardship, dealt with all the goings-on and said of Diana — 'Our part-time unpaid assistant representative (social and cultural affairs) sends her love, as do all of us.'

Musical adventures and other recreations

The local amateur drama group was fortunate in having Trevor Whittock, a lecturer in English at the university's Chancellor College, as its producer for two plays, in the first of which Diana played Viola in *Twelfth Night* with great success, including the composing of her own version of the song, 'Come away death'. The very mixed audience in the small premises of Limbe Club included many Malawian students for whom the play was a set book. The action came to a surprise halt at the moment when Sebastian faces Olivia and says 'Oh, what *relish* is there in this dream!' Uproar followed because the word *relish* referred locally to the spicy food used to give flavour to the Malawian staple diet of maize porridge. An example of what? A cross-cultural curiosity perhaps. The second production, a change from Shakespeare, was *The Crucible* in which Diana played Mrs Proctor and had to weep on stage, so convincingly as to disturb me to the core. This time the venue was the hall of Chancellor College and the frequently tense and agonizing moments in the play evoked a strange response from the Malawian audience — and a disconcerting one for the cast — namely laughter. Perhaps that is explicable in terms of embarrassment.

'Have culture, will travel' is an oversimplified summary of the British Council's role, but it has been used as the title of a very good documentary film and it partially encapsulates my own attitude — but only partially because it ignores the strongly developmental motives inherent in my view. Even so, one need not be a cultural missionary to feel that it is unhealthy for musicians to limit their enthusiasm to their armchairs. Music should demand participation, but it requires someone to set a standard of value and taste. The musical activity around us in Blantyre–Limbe appeared to be limited to beat groups, church choirs and the odd comedy accompanied by a tinny piano, so after demonstrating our personal competence by taking part in the inevitable *Messiah* (with piano!) we tested the market. St Michael's CCAP (Church of Central Africa Presbyterian) had been built in 1891 by an amateur architect in the style of a basilica, using locally baked bricks — a truly amazing achievement which, as all fine churches do, challenged us to 'make a cheerful noise unto God'. We began with a recital of Bach, Brahms and Britten, accompanied on the organ by the aforementioned Robert Parsons, VSO from Dedza. This went down well, particularly with Tom Colvin, the incumbent CCAP missionary minister.

Small-scale efforts with a mere handful of executants would not, however, achieve the purpose of embracing as many people as possible. Larger-scale choral works had to be tackled and my belief — dating from my schooldays and Douglas Fox's influence — was that one should always aim to experience the masterpieces, inadequate though resources might be, and eschew second-class music at all costs. At the first attempt we mustered barely 20 singers, among whom our best bass was a Peace Corps volunteer. Conversely, there was an agricultural officer who droned and put the others off, but he was tamed by praise of the Eastern Orthodox Church's basso profundos and persuaded to sing down an octave whenever the part went above the stave. Audience reaction was unpredictable, but the sheer novelty of unaccompanied folk-song arrangements and part songs by Vaughan Williams and Britten held their attention.

Bach's *St John Passion* was acceptable to Tom Colvin, so we conceived a dramatized version (inspired by our Glastonbury ones) in which we replaced the singing evangelist with a Tasmanian schools' broadcasting expert reading from the pulpit, sobered the local comedian into playing Jesus and allocated the part of Pontius Pilate to a man who had played Malvolio brilliantly. The vigour of the trial scene and the beauty of the chorales wove a spell that broke only when the specially rigged spotlights caused the little pipe organ to expire. Yet our clarinet-playing friend provided a remarkably soulful substitute for the viola da gamba. Alas, she and Robert were stranded with a broken exhaust before the second performance, which was only rescued by the presence of my father who had arrived for a holiday — of which there is more later (see photograph of rehearsal).

So far so good, but the only instrumentalists available were the Malawi police bandsmen in Zomba, known to us because of their keenness to take the Associated Board of the Royal Schools of Music (ABRSM) examinations and because some of them had been to Kneller Hall for training. (On my next home leave, Avril Wood of our music department arranged for me to be given lunch there by four colonels.) The police bandsmen could read staff notation and liked an occasional outside opportunity. How would they take to Bach? His *Easter Oratorio* and *Ascension Cantata* attracted me as a double bill providing four choruses identically scored for three trumpets — but in D, not the normal B flat. Such instruments were specially ordered, and although our friend Matt Numero, the bandmaster, found the embouchure of the small mouthpiece none too comfortable for his African lips, he produced a spine-thrilling sound. Talent spotting and a bit of regular coaching produced some passable soloists from the ranks of the chorus, and the recitatives and arias were tackled with considerable panache. We enjoyed the help of seven bandsmen in addition to the trumpeters — on flutes, clarinets, euphoniums and timpani — and Robert on the organ filled in the string parts.

Something secular was needed next, so after the inaugural meeting of the formalized Music Society it was agreed that next time we should hire the full police band and choose an all-British programme, which would enable us to benefit from fuller support from London. The menu of Purcell, Stanford, Holst and Britten made a good St Cecilia's Day offering. Matt Numero conducted

Holst's *Second Suite for Military Band*, Roland Stamp (whom we had elected as the first chairman) sang the *Songs of the Sea* with appropriate gusto, the choir (now swollen to 40, including seven Malawians) tackled the *Choral Dances from Gloriana*, and we all took part under my baton in the 1692 ode, *Hail Bright Cecilia*. For this concert we had found, for the first time, one precious stringed instrument — a cello. Little by little unsuspected talent was emerging.

By this time, too, Jim Peto (an architect from Rhodesia) had appeared and was relieving me by doing some conducting; and John Maynard (a horn player and teacher of economics in the Malawi Polytechnic) organized some chamber concerts. Among the singers were two enthusiastic Malawian friends — Jake Muwamba, a government information officer, who was very keen to be taught how to read 'golf sticks', and Edson Lamya, an immigration officer on whom we confidently relied to welcome with a special smile our incoming volunteers and visitors at the airport. (Happily we found both of them still going strong 21 years later when we visited Malawi from Ethiopia in 1990 — see Chapter 14.)

Mozart's use of clarinets and trombones in his *Requiem* made me think of the police band again, but St Michael's CCAP was a bit cramped for large forces, so we enlisted the support of Peter Smith, a High Court judge (and a Catholic) to obtain his archbishop's permission to perform in Limbe Roman Catholic cathedral. Was this too ambitious a project? Would the ecumenical spirit unite the congregations? Would the Latin text be an obstacle? What were the electronic organ and the accoustics like? Above all, could we rely on a booking of the band if overriding political needs arose? And could we muster a string quartet to accompany the quieter passages? Grey Mtila was a trombone soloist with 'tuba mirum' well within his powers; instead of a first violin we got Helene Jones (a missionary from Nkotakota) on her flute; our second violin was a Seventh-Day Adventist who had to cut the final Saturday rehearsal and whose part was stolen from her car, necessitating eight hours of copying from the score; John Olive brought his viola from Somerset; and our cellist joined again with indispensable Robert on the organ. We rigged an enormous

1500-watt lamp on the end of a horizontal flagpole over the performing area, and the chorus had swollen to 55. The first performance on Palm Sunday 1969 was not satisfactory. Our 12 selected bandsmen had arrived breathless the previous day after an overnight journey from the central region in an open lorry, and the second euphonium had been observed on the cathedral steps emptying rainwater out of his instrument. Fly Limbalo, the timpanist, was cross-eyed. Was it fatigue, or ...? To a remedial rehearsal in Zomba the following day the bass trombonist turned up drunk, but the reward was in the second performance. About 700 people, babies and all, heard the *Requiem* live, Mozart did not turn in his grave, and we had made a bit of local history.

It should not be imagined that any of this was official duty for me. London's view was that the scope for cultural bridge building in such circumstances was strictly limited, had low priority and should on no account interfere with 'work'. Nevertheless, in later years it was acknowledged that the British Council people who are remembered in the countries where they have served tend to be those who have made such communal efforts in the visual and performing arts, in sport or in other ways, rather than limiting their efforts to the necessary desk work. On one occasion our rehearsal accompanist, Fred 'the Library' Johnson, had taunted me with 'your standards are so low', which was hard to forgive considering the importance of distinguishing between a high aim and a low achievement. In any case, the Music Society not only continued to flourish for the next 25 years but also grew branches in Zomba and in Lilongwe.

The Mlanje Mountain Club and the Ndirande Sailing Club were attractive for both us and our children. We all went up the mountain with another family once, but at other times Diana took turns with me. For a year or so we shared the ownership of Peter Harrison's Enterprise boat, but later joined in a project to build Mirror sailing dinghies. Leave delayed the completion of mine, but we did enjoy one season of racing on Sunday mornings and, after regularly coming in second, we eventually managed to win one race, just before having to sell the boat on departure.

Another extracurricular activity was newsreading for the Malawi Broadcasting Corporation (MBC). The MBC was instructed by Dr Banda not to tolerate poor pronunciation, so various Brits, such as our colleague, Bryson McAdam, and Paul Cole-King, the director of the new museum, were drafted in. My mistake was to use my own name rather than a disguise because it was not long before our high commission in Zomba told me to desist on the grounds that sooner or later there would be embarrassment over some news item or other. Although it was an interesting challenge, arriving half an hour before transmission but sweating to make decent sentences out of some of the material from the newsroom with one minute to go, it was a relief to stop, especially since demands to oblige tended to be at short notice.

More crises, a parental visit and mid-tour leave
Stuart Ginever, who taught English at St John's teacher training college in Lilongwe, suffered a dislocated knee while playing rugger on hard ground, and the efforts made to 'reduce' it caused a loss of circulation in his foot. A nurse in Lilongwe realized sooner than the doctors did that progress was not being made, but it was a week after the event before he was flown down to Blantyre as a wheelchair case; we were not informed until he was on his way. A Dutch surgeon with experience of dock workers' injuries struggled for seven hours to restore the circulation, but he failed and before long gangrene set in. We had to arrange Stuart's evacuation as a stretcher case on the BOAC VC-10 scheduled service to London, where amputation below the knee was deemed inescapable. Stuart was a delightful man; he was universally liked and was intending to specialize in physical education. The whole episode was distressing for all concerned, but at least we were happier with the news three weeks later that, with a prosthetic device, he was already up and playing. Director VSO was less understanding. He wrote that he 'hoped nothing of the sort would ever happen again' — seeming to blame us and underestimating the recurrent risks of being in Africa at all.

A more fortunate outcome, but a no less dangerous close shave, was the fate of Theodore Campbell-Barker, who landed up in hospital with a very high but undiagnosed fever. After he had survived the crisis point but was still a puzzle to the attendant physicians (few expatriates had much experience of tropical disease), a third opinion was offered by Dr Molesworth, who had worked in Singapore and was now with the local LEPRA (Leprosy Relief Association) team. He noticed a small puncture on the patient's arm and, when Theo Barker admitted that he had been climbing through undergrowth on Zomba mountain, diagnosed tick typhus fever. We took Theo into our family for a period of convalescence and he evidently enjoyed playing with Sarah and Louise when they came home from school. At one point he confessed that he had been expelled from his Jesuit school for radical views but that the fathers had nevertheless tried to recruit him for training, which he half expected to be going home to do at the end of his VSO stint with the Ministry of Information's visual aids unit. Imagine our amazement, therefore, when Theo wrote to thank us some months later and said, 'I was so impressed with the quality of your family life that I have decided to disappoint the Jesuit fathers, to marry my girlfriend and to come back to Malawi on contract to the government.' This he did and he stayed for several years.

Only a minority of our problems arose from accidents, injury or illness; most of them were concerned with local conditions and morale. Indeed, my role as an amateur psychiatrist almost merited a brass plate on the office door, or a distinctive numberplate on the landrover. We had to intervene between a VSO woman and her head of project after an unfounded accusation of improper conduct had got out of hand. Another woman became pregnant, but refused a termination and insisted on keeping the baby and being flown home. Word that yet another young woman was planning to marry her black American Peace Corps boyfriend reached her mother, who promptly appealed by letter to Dr Banda to stop it, thereby creating a diplomatic incident. It was in fact a storm in a teacup. The couple had already decided to postpone their marriage before all the fuss was made, but nonetheless we were still subjected to a considerable amount of abortive communication. One young volunteer cracked up within ten days of his arrival through little fault of his own. His capacity had been misleadingly described on paper, so there was a mismatch with the needs of the job. Another volunteer 'went native' and tried to avoid going back to what seemed to be an unhappy home. Much persuasion was needed to get him to face the impossibility (and illegality) of staying on. Also, a nurse had to be repatriated because she drove her companions to distraction by indulging in fantasy and delusion.

Sadly, of course, as the total numbers spread all over the country rose from around 30 to nearer 90, so the problems increased and prevented us from spending enough time with the happy majority of successful volunteers who made a significant contribution to all forms of development. In all this we collaborated with the Peace Corps, the Canadian University Service Overseas, small contingents from the French service civil (a substitute for military service) and a trickle of Germans.

My parents had acquired the epithets of Potty Granny and Dotty Grandpa, both with double meanings — pottery and mild madness plus music dots and mild madness. They did not really deserve such at all, but liked them anyway. Bringing up a family of five had involved steady and prolonged self-denial, so the last time they had taken a proper holiday together had been in 1938 in Scotland. Coming to stay with us in Malawi was a major adventure for them, and a very much overdue vacation. My father had to get Dartington Hall to agree to some 'sabbatical' extension of the Easter period, and my mother also needed leave of absence — again strongly deserved.

They arrived on the same VC-10 flight that took Stuart Ginever out, so the meeting and greeting at the airport was rather distracted. As already mentioned, my father was just in time to rescue our second *St John Passion* performance, of which the MBC made a tape and broadcasted it on Good Friday. The police band, having discovered my father's chief interest, insisted on his giving a lecture on the maintenance of wind instruments. The highlight of their visit was the arrangement we made to send them by train to Salima to embark on the lake vessel MV *Ilala*, for a voyage up to Nkata Bay, where my landrover tour of the north was craftily planned to coincide with their disembarkation. In this way they saw most of the country, including the Vipya forestry and Livingstonia mission, and several other remote VSO projects on my check list. In several suitable spots my mother employed her talent for watercolour sketching, and many Malawian scenes (and later

Romanian ones) now hang in our home. On most such tours we had our long-serving driver–projectionist Elias Sanudi at the wheel. He had an unblemished record and proudly insisted that the only damage ever sustained by a British Council vehicle had been the fault of a British colleague. At one notorious spot he never failed to announce, 'This is where Mr Fox [a one-time assistant representative] turned over the landrover.' Even so, one feature such drivers never, in my experience, understood was the working of back axle differentials and the reason for the lack of traction on one wheel if the other was allowed to spin in mud or sand. Much revving was wasted.

Before we could take what we felt was a well-earned leave there was one remaining hurdle — the making of a 50-minute documentary film by Rediffusion TV in aid of VSO recruitment. It was flattering that Malawi should have been chosen for this, but we viewed with consternation the filming team's plan to be round our necks at the height of the trooping season — not just incoming volunteers were arriving but about 80 students under a variety of schemes were also being prepared for going to Britain. Even worse was its refusal to take advice on the selection of volunteers and projects; instead of good examples it preferred to use atypical but photogenic subjects. A political clanger in the commentary on some shots of Dr Banda being greeted on his return from a trip was almost disastrous, for he was described as a 'near dictator'. Had this become known in Malawi it could have caused the expulsion of every VSO volunteer in the country and, by association, would have damaged the British Council too. It fell to us to send vigorous appeals to the high commission to press the Foreign and Commonwealth Office (FCO) to lean on the company to delete the remark before transmission, not just in Britain but also in Canada, Australia and the USA. It had to be, and was done, in only 24 hours — rather too close for comfort.

Diana and the children flew home a month ahead of me, which gave me the chance to make a series of semi-official visits by a circuitous route. A plan to stop over in Nigeria had to be given up when the worsening civil war closed Kano airport, but the alternative proved fruitful, my itinerary providing some instructive comparisons with British Council modes of working elsewhere.

103

The Victoria Falls Hotel provided an ideal unwinding spot for two nights, but first a flight to Salisbury and a visit to Ranche House College, 'an oasis of sanity', where discussions with the principal, Ken Mew (ex-ICI) and Sir Frederick Crawford (ex-Governor of Uganda) enabled me to make a case to VSO for an English teacher to be provided, despite the sanctions in force. Then, in Lusaka, an evening spent enthusing about musical projects with Hugh and Elizabeth Crooke, was followed by a weekend in Kitwe with Murray Sanderson (ex-Cambridge and Kenya) whose Medwich clothing business was a model of industrial relations. Gerry Coombes (ex-Northern Cameroons) was in charge of the British Council's regional office in Ndola and helped me sort out a muddled air booking to Nairobi. There a useful link was made with a Kenya Air Force flight lieutenant who ran the Duke of Edinburgh's award scheme (renamed the President's scheme) in which the Malawi Young Pioneers had expressed an interest. And finally, a meeting with Graham Hyslop, a semiretired 'guru' with long experience of integrating Western and African music, was an inspiration.

Home leave without a home base, however welcoming and hospitable one's family and friends, is not to be recommended. Having learnt this lesson we never allowed it to happen again, but in 1967 Sarah and Louise were still young enough to be 'in orbit' indefinitely without worrying, so long as we provided the vital feelings of love and security. We split our time between Diana's parents in Highcliffe and mine in Totnes, spending Christmas with the latter. We borrowed John Olive's caravan for an extended tour to Glasgow and Edinburgh; we looked up former colleagues and friends from Nigerian and Clarks Shoes days in huge numbers; we spent several weeks with the Shirley-Quirk family based at Flackwell Heath; and flew back to Blantyre on an ill-starred flight from Gatwick the day after Boxing Day, leaving seven hours late, missing our connection in Lusaka, and arriving two days later.

Second tour and changes of staff

Peter and Colin welcomed us as warmly as ever, but alas, this happy band would be dissolved before the year ended. Colin was posted to London in April and his replacement, Keith Fenwick, did not arrive until August. In the middle of the four-month gap a surprise summons arrived, for me to attend a VSO conference in London followed by a British Council staff conference in Cambridge, so Peter was left single-handed for two weeks. He handed over to Edge Semmens in November and left for a posting to Manchester. It was the end of a six-year period of continuous expansion in all fields of our concern, and we felt not only pride in having been part of the team but above all gratitude for the privilege of having enjoyed such excellent tutelage. Farewells for the Harrisons were reluctant and heartfelt, yet not without comic relief — as when the copper tray, to which the staff had contributed as a present, came back from the engravers with a crooked and misspelt inscription.

'Excuse me, Sir, but I have a warrant for your arrest.' A Malawian policeman stood apologetically in my office doorway, then showed me the paper issued by the magistrate in Limbe. Failure to pay a fine, it said, and the offence had been not stopping and 'dismounting' when being passed by (the then) President Banda's motorcade. After pleading a misunderstanding, my phone call to the aforementioned judicial friend, Peter Smith, revealed that strictly speaking, once issued, a warrant had to be executed, but that if my cheque went by return with the policeman the matter would probably be closed — and it was. Phew!

Our last year and a half in Malawi included another VSO staff tour, this time by Myra Green (who was to be my closest collaborator in London a mere five years later) and two more weddings. First, Sue Jenkins, a VSO teacher of English at Kapeni College, married Ken Patterson 'under British Council auspices', for Peter gave away the bride, Colin was best man and Diana sang. And second, our neighbour Penny Dean, the LEPRA nurse, married Ian Flemming in St Paul's Anglican church in Blantyre, with a choir to sing a Purcell anthem, Matt Numero on the trumpet and — guess who? — Robert Parsons on the organ.

We are often asked how much choice we got over postings. The system involved an annual opportunity to fill in a postings preference form, and it was now time for ours to be noticed. After a total of eight years in Commonwealth Africa it seemed sensible to suggest 'a genuinely foreign country in the Far East' as the best way to broaden my experience. So we had no cause to complain then when, in May 1969, our posting to Japan was confirmed. In due course, Andrew and Peggy Crease arrived as our successors and, after a week for handing over, we flew down to Cape Town on 1 November.

RUSSIA

CHINA

HOKKAIDO

• Sapporo

• Murorar

N. KOREA

• Hakodate

Aomori •
• Hachinohe

• Moriok

• Akita

S E A   O F   J A P A N

• Sendai

Yamagata •

H O N S H U

• Niigata

Nikko •   • Hitachi

S. KOREA

Takaoka •

• Nagano

Utsunomiya   • Mito

Kanazawa •

Kofu •

■ Tokyo

Gifu •

Yokohama •

MOUNT FUJI ▲

■ Yokosuke

Nagoya ■

Shizuoka •

Himeji •

Kyoto ■

• Nara

Okayama •

Kobe ■■

Hamamatsu

Shimoda

• Hiroshima

Osaka ■

• Wakayama

• Fukuoka

SHIKOKU

Sasebo •

• Kurume

• Omuta

KYUSHU

• Kumamoto

• Nagasaki

• Miyazaki

• Kagoshima

PACIFIC   OCEAN

MAP 3

JAPAN

—·—·— International boundary

Miles

0   50   100   150   200

0   100   200   300

Kilometres

8

Japan in Frenzied Expansion

F our nights in a family hotel in Cape Town, waiting to embark in RMS *Pendennis Castle*, gave us a wonderfully refreshing spring (southern hemisphere) holiday, and also a taste of the political problems of South Africa. This knowledge was very handy some five and a half years later when we had to weigh up the pros and cons of a posting there — resolved negatively in favour of going to Malaysia instead. Close friends in Malawi had been John and Veda Carver and family, and Veda's sister Sandra, married to Peter Hewitt, took us to their vineyard near Stellenbosch for an unforgettable Sunday. Their veranda had a view of Table Mountain from the north, with an ocean on each side — the Indian to the left and the Atlantic to the right.

Transfer leave and a surprise legacy
At this time there were five Union Castle mail ships operating a strictly scheduled cycle of sailings taking precisely ten days on each voyage, with a turnround at each end related to the fortnightly tides. Soon they would be driven out of business by jumbo jets, but for a few years yet the mail contract was worth more than the passengers. For us it was a luxurious experience and much of my time was devoted to getting halfway through the Linguaphone Japanese course. Diana and the children revelled in the deck games. An afternoon in our cabin making Pooh and Rabbit masks with scissors and paste secured us the first prize for fancy dress.

109

We docked in Southampton on a frosty November morning and were in Highcliffe by lunch time. Then followed family visits to Totnes and Bosham, and a few days in London to be debriefed on Malawi and briefed for Japan. But the top priority was to go house hunting with John Olive as our guide to the district around Bath. Underestimating the need to live within commuting distance for the inevitable London posting in the future, we decided to get our furniture out of store and establish a permanent home base in Somerset where so many friends lived. We saw 34 houses in a week and settled on a four-square stone house in Beckington. In the same period we began visiting possible schools for the girls. While engaged in negotiations for a mortgage and raising the required down payment, we went to Totnes for Christmas and were astounded by the news that Seton Lee's will had nominated me as the residuary beneficiary, with enough money for at least two houses of the type we had in mind. 'Aunt' Seton was my father's first cousin, being the daughter of one of his mother's sisters, both in turn daughters of Sir Andrew Clark, who had been a well-known doctor and president of the Royal College of Physicians. She had endured a lonely existence since her mother died in 1938. During the war and for many years my parents had welcomed her to stay in the family home whenever convenient, but my last contact with her had been during my year in Oxford and no inkling of her intention had been evident.

We attended her funeral in Dawlish and then set about long and complex correspondence with the solicitors in London. There was much speculation about a mysterious locked trunk in the basement of a bank in Maida Vale, where it had been kept for 32 years. After valuation for probate we received a fine set of monogrammed table silver and other precious items. There was also furniture in store in Bournemouth, but time was so short that most of it had to stay there for another two years. January 1970 was a month of intensive DIY, making our 'new' house, with many superficial blemishes, fit for letting against the deadline of our departure for the Far East.

Acute culture shock
'I'm sorry, ladies and gentlemen, but we cannot fly over the North

Pole with a defective gyrocompass.' That was our captain explaining our delayed takeoff on the long haul via Anchorage in Alaska and across the international dateline to Tokyo, the most disorienting experience of our lives. Both time and space became confused, and the domestic exertions of recent weeks combined with jet lag to cause fatigue from which we took a week to recover.

Meanwhile, Robin Duke, our new boss, had evidently got wind of our propensities in the extracurricular field and deflated us by remarking, 'We don't indulge in parish pump activities here. Our job is to support the professionals.' This was true enough in the light of the plethora of cultural events imported from Britain under British Council auspices, especially in this year of Expo 70 in Osaka, but he might have been wiser to have waited to judge the level of our proficiency as amateurs before worrying about overzealousness. As we shall see, two years later when our time was up, he changed his mind.

The contrast with our former life could hardly have been greater in every way. We had moved from a small town in Africa to a teeming capital the size of London; from a rural environment to a concrete jungle; from a tightknit group of colleagues able to see the effect of its work on the development of the country to a large team of specialized colleagues struggling to compete for a discernible impact on 100 million people; from a British Council operation almost totally independent of the high commission to one closely dependent on our embassy and officially regarded by the host government as its cultural section; and, most significantly, from an Anglophone community to alien linguistic surroundings where the use of Chinese ideographs prevented any normal approach to learning one's way about and presented a major intellectual challenge.

We had asked for it, it was hard going at first and it was salutary. In future no one would be able to question our adaptability and resilience. Japan in the early 1970s displayed rampant capitalism, with few planning restrictions, construction in concrete replacing wooden dwellings everywhere, severe pollution of air and water, and little concern for the social infrastructure. Even during our two years, however, the atmosphere began to change — buyers lost their hold over the labour market as the reserve of workers from the countryside dried up and some hitherto unheard-of strikes occurred. By the mid-1970s, too, building restrictions were being enforced and pollution control was given legal sanction at last. The American occupation of postwar Japan under General MacArthur had lasted from 1946 to 1952, so it was not always possible for a relatively ignorant Brit to disentangle the effects of American influence from what was genuinely Japanese. On the whole, we admired the reforms achieved and the education system had certainly been very deeply influenced.

When Uncle Bill, my father's younger brother who had been an Indian railways' engineer, heard of my switch from Clarks Shoes to the British Council, and knowing that cobbling was the lowest form of life on the subcontinent, he wrote saying 'I'm glad to hear that you have recovered caste!' — a remark which could also in some people's eyes have referred to our move from the developing to the sophisticated world. Robin Duke had made it clear that the subject of the war was taboo and that on no account should it be mentioned in conversation: but he had also implied that we should avoid referring to previous service in 'colonial' countries, since this might suggest to the Japanese that we were unworthy to work with them. Was that a serious view, or projected snobbery?

Whatever the truth, the core of my work consisted of interviewing candidates for postgraduate (and some postdoctoral) places in British universities. The British Council (pronounced Bu-ri-ti-shu Ka-un-shi-ru) was well known for this service, which encompassed not only its own scholarships offered annually but also a wide range of officially and privately sponsored students. As with VSO in Malawi so with students from Japan, this was a rapidly expanding business. As affluence increased, more Japanese people became interested in exploring what lay behind America, particularly Britain and other English-speaking countries in northern Europe. The process of finding places, via London and our area offices, was fraught with uncertainty, but the ministries of foreign affairs (*Gaimusho*) and of education (*Monbusho*) relied on us, as did the National Personnel Authority and many banks, investment firms and other businesses. As the third-ranking generalist in the office, pressure was put on me to act as a long stop in handling VIP visitors, giving lectures (without any preparation time) and

112

accompanying visiting performers, so anything could be demanded and the family suffered long hours of neglect.

The deputy was Paul Hardwick (later Martin Beatty), a gentle and easy-going man of wisdom but unhappy with much of what went on, and around us were the specialists — English language officers (Verner Bickley followed by Jean-Jacques Dunn), two television officers (Don Gillate and Mike Barrett, assigned to the NHK, the equivalent of the BBC) and a librarian (Derek Cornish, then Tom Maughan as book promotions officer). We also had a regional office and library in Kyoto (Peter Martin succeeded by Julian Harvey). Each of us had a 'Japanese mouthpiece' — a secretary with or without competent typing in English and/or translation skills. Before long a top management visitor from London abolished both television officer posts and the administration officer, Reg Curling. *English by Television* enjoyed audiences of over a quarter of a million early on Saturday mornings, and the didactic sketches were dramatized with parts played by local British amateurs, including Diana (and on one occasion the whole family to sing a Christmas carol). Such programmes were replaced by a cheaper alternative — off-the-peg material from the BBC.

Expo 70 World Fair in Osaka

At the top of our tree Robin Duke was in his element, wheeling and dealing with high-powered impresarios and museum directors, negotiating the presentation of the best of British performing and visual arts, invariably with lead times of two or more years. Wearing two hats, as representative of the British Council and as cultural counsellor in the embassy, he played the sort of dual role that puzzled many but became familiar to us in several places later. Hitherto in Malawi our contact with the diplomatic service had been at arm's length; here in Tokyo we had to learn quickly how the hierarchy of a large embassy worked and how colleagues in it impinged on our own 'alternative' setup. Sir John Pilcher had been a language student of prewar vintage, and was an old-style ambassador. To our instant and lasting advantage, the head of chancery was Brian Hitch, a linguist and musician of the 'wizard' sort (language scholar and organist of Magdalene College, Cambridge) whose musical and general hospitality rescued us in a way that forged a long-term friendship, including that of his wife Margot who is a potter and sculptor.

The fruits of cultural diplomacy were evident in Osaka when the Scots Guards band and the Cardiff Polyphonic Choir appeared in the British Pavilion on our national day in April. A Barbara Hepworth exhibition in the Hakoné open-air museum opened in June, and an English landscapes one in October. We also danced attendance on the New Philharmonia Orchestra (NPO) in August, and on the English Chamber Orchestra (ECO) in September. In the same period we helped look after visitors such as Lord Montague, Prince Charles, Michael Stewart (the then Foreign Secretary) and Lord Fulton, our chairman who resigned almost immediately on his return to London. Especially rewarding for us were the opportunities to entertain — Edward Downes and Janet Baker when the NPO was in town and (for a good laugh) Raymond Leppard and Robert Tear with the ECO.

The Japanese were deeply and intensely interested in Western music. They also experimented with using their traditional instruments, the *koto* and *shakuhachi*, to perform Vivaldi, for example. A group called the Nipponia Ensemble devoted itself to this. Reciprocally we felt the need to attempt to understand the *Noh* drama and the *Kabuki* theatre, but the language barrier was rather daunting. One *Noh* play, *Sumidagawa*, was of special interest as the inspiration for *Curlew River*, the first of Britten's trilogy of church parables, and sadly it was only towards the end of our time that Colin Graham came to explore the chances of presenting those works in Japan.

Before the world fair closed and the autumn school term began, we took Sarah and Louise to Osaka and visited 14 national pavilions in a day. We found the smaller countries' ones less crowded and more enlightening, especially the presentations of Singapore as a 'garden city' of lush greenery, and of New Zealand as the land of a well-balanced diet — that last appealed to the children's appetite.

The Imperial Household Agency and the Bank of Japan

Two aspects of the 'sharp end' of cultural relations were a surprise to me. The first was the assumption that part of my duties in

Tokyo would be to visit His Imperial Highness the Crown Prince (now Emperor) Akihito several times a week so that he could practise English conversation. The second was a similar requirement to help Mr Tadashi Sasaki, the Governor of the Bank of Japan, improve his understanding of what he read in English. My acquisition of two distinguished pupils in this way was anomalous in the light of my lack of qualification, but since no formal teaching was involved — just general discussion and scrutiny of texts — my inexperience was ignored.

After initial meetings with the chamberlains of the imperial household (presumably there had been vetting on paper too) my first session with His Imperial Highness the Crown Prince was in May 1970; a year later we had met 39 times. He had been well taught and already had a good command of conversational English, but suffered from a speech impediment which sometimes halted progress. We talked of a wide range of topics and sometimes an article in the *Listener* (BBC's weekly, now ceased) or the *Weekly Guardian* offered a basis for discussion. We discovered a mutual liking for the pictures of John Piper, and he asked to read some of the Duke of Edinburgh's speeches. He took pride in his profession of marine biologist, particularly ichthyology, and made a special study of goby fish. This was nearly my undoing, for he expected the English of his scientific papers to be corrected, which was a severe trial for a non-scientist. More my line was checking the expressions used in a letter to the King of Thailand or to Princess Beatrix of The Netherlands. We always drank green tea and ate some delicacy, which itself provided a talking point.

By the autumn a routine of Wednesday mornings at 8.30 had been agreed, which had the advantage of my being collected from my house by official car and delivered to the office afterwards. Early in 1971 the idea of reading poetry, both aloud and for study, came up. This was embarrassing for me, being very ill read in that field, but Browning and Wordsworth were in favour and gave me the opening to say that Diana was a much better reader than me. This suggestion was registered in the appropriate quarters and when Diana came with me in March for our thirty-fifth session we found Princess Michiko (now Empress) there too and keen to read Wordsworth, which we enjoyed four more times.

Soon, however, Mike Barrett was introduced to the agency and in due course took over from us. Later Mrs Opal Dunn became tutor to the whole family.

We had to decline to resume attendance because Diana was expecting our third child, but we were honoured and delighted, just before leaving Japan the following spring and after Jessica had been born, to be invited to dine with the Prince and Princess. Sadly, he had a heavy cold that evening and we felt the need to say farewell rather early. By happy coincidence, however, we have been privileged to meet again twice. Their state visit to Romania occurred while we were posted in Bucharest and we obtained an invitation to a reception in the Japanese embassy. Again, not many years later, they came to Finland during our time in Helsinki and we were able to secure a 20-minute audience, during which it was pleasing to observe that not a trace of the Crown Prince's impediment remained.

Mr Sasaki also settled for Wednesdays and on those afternoons his car would whisk me through the security gates in the basement of the bank and we would discuss an article he had read in *The Economist* or an item of hot news. We began in November 1970 and our last session (the thirty-second) was in February 1972. Sometimes he would cancel to travel to an international meeting or because of a dollar crisis, but he read widely on such subjects as the Bayeux tapestry and the canal age. Quite frequently a text would be sent round with a request for me to scrutinize its style. When he had to make a speech to the Bank for International Settlements in Basle he sent round a pocket recorder for me to make a tape for him to listen to *en route* in the aircraft. A bit of homework was needed when he cross-examined me on the British attitude to the Irish, the significance of the Orangemen and the background to the troubles. Often we simply spoke of his visits to Rome, London and Washington. When we left we were given two very fine *kakemono* (wall-hanging silk-mounted scroll paintings), which are displayed only on special occasions.

The art of getting about locally and escaping permanently
The domestic scene was rather bleak. A metropolis the size of Tokyo can be thoroughly enjoyed by young couples without chil-

dren or by middle-aged couples with teenagers or older offspring, but having children of primary school age implied both the need for baby-sitters if we had to go out (many evening functions were obligatory) and inescapably sending them to an American-style international school with several shortcomings, combined with suffering them to breathe very polluted air and to drink dubious water. As parents we wanted to get them out to find some fresh air whenever possible. However fascinating the country, the cultural surroundings and rich opportunities for adventurous work, we knew that one tour of two years ought not to be extended.

Speaking elementary Japanese was helpful for finding out where to go and how to get there, but it was far more useful to be able to read the labels, notices and instructions all around. The snag was that this required familiarity with all three systems, which are combined in writing the language — the *kanji* Chinese-style ideographs and the two *kana* syllabaries, the cursive *hiragana* for normal words and the angular *katakana* for transliterated foreign words and names. My chance discovery of a very clever little American book called simply *Read Japanese Today* launched me on an addictive interest in *kanji*, and a programmed textbook on the syllabic systems enabled me to grasp those by studying in the bus for half an hour on the way to the office each day. A persistent illusion, fostered in ignorant circles, was the idea that *romaji*, the romanized form of writing Japanese, had much future. It was possible to buy a map of Tokyo with everything labelled in this way, but it bore no relation to what you saw about you. Conversely, a map for walking in the country beyond Tokyo, covered in *kanji*, was only made useful to us by Brian Hitch who kindly and painstakingly annotated it with legible notes.

To get out at all at weekends it was necessary to keep the diary clear of commitments once a month, to make an early start on a chain of several suburban trains and to avoid (by not using the car) any risk of traffic tailback getting in again. For longer family holidays, in our first summer we had a wet week by the Chuzenji lake, but by Christmas time (and for the following Easter) we had discovered the ideal log cabins to rent in the frugal atmosphere of a kind of secular missionary establishment known as Kiyosato Experimental Educational Project (KEEP) on the north side of

117

Fuji. Even a little reading ability was an aid to navigation; we eventually recognized with confidence many place names and the difference between an entrance and exit to or from an expressway. Another game with reading was to surprise a new acquaintance who presented his or her *meishi* (name card) by looking at the *kanji* and pronouncing it. Mistakes invariably caused amused concern rather than offence, and there was a fair chance of accuracy because of the limited variety of surnames.

Parish pump or no, little by little we got involved in music, frequently through Brian's chamber music contacts. When an embassy colleague, Melville Guest, married the daughter of the Argentinian ambassador in Tokyo's magnificent Roman Catholic cathedral, we sang the duet from Bach's Cantata No. 155 in the organ loft. Then my secretary, Hirasawa-san, was married in a colourful ceremony that not only combined Western and traditional customs but also obliged me to make a speech in Japanese and Diana to play something on the piano. Although we were not involved, one of Robin Duke's sons had married a Japanese woman and his daughter a Japanese man. Whenever the subject came up Robin's favourite remark was, 'I do think that is taking cultural relations rather far.'

Julian and Guinevere Harvey in Kyoto provided another lifeline for the jaded Nightingales. On one of our trips to the Kansai — always a welcome break — we joined a Japanese lutenist in a recital of lute songs. A more memorable occasion arose from another Hitch/Cambridge connection. This was with Hiro Ishibashi who had a Ph.D. in English literature and was principal of Ueno Gakuen ladies' music college. An enthusiastic teacher of the viola da gamba ran an early music group somewhat ahead of the field. Diana was seven months pregnant but in good voice, so we were persuaded to do some songs with their consort of viols in a concert in the Tokyo Bunka Kaikan Small Hall — the equivalent of London's Queen Elizabeth Hall — both of us in formal dress and me conducting in front of an invited audience of the diplomatic circle. This was very much to Robin Duke's taste and, in muttering congratulations afterwards, he said 'We must have more of this' — rather too late, within a few months of our departure, to reappraise our competence.

118

There were no hard feelings though, and when Jessica was born Robin was delighted to be the first to get the news by my phone call to his office. Promptly the next day, no fewer than five of the Japanese secretaries and librarians said that they were third daughters in their families, so a society should be formed. In Jessica's honour they elected me as president of the Third Daughters' Association, British Council Tokyo Branch, and my duties were to take them all out to lunch once a month. When our new baby was six weeks old we observed their custom of a coming-out party which was held in our book display room. Incidentally, our offices and library were then on the eighth floor of a ten-storey block called the Iwanami Jimbo-cho building, over a subway station and conveniently surrounded by the book-selling area. It had a habit of swaying during the frequent earth tremors, and my standing instruction to our charming staff was, if frightened, to hug the nearest British colleague.

Towards the end of our second year we felt we had learned to turn most problems to our advantage. For a non-academic with no previous teaching experience other than training industrial and commercial staff, the burden of lecturing to first-year British area studies classes at Tokyo University had been heavy, but reformation of the British Council Scholars' Association had been rewarding. Meetings of the Cambridge and Oxford [sic] Society yielded new friends and even Japan–British Society functions could be useful. After freezing for two winters and boiling for one summer we had moved out of an uninsulated house into a centrally heated and cooled apartment (with a view of the Crown Prince's polo ground from the rooftop), and for seven weeks of our second summer the family enjoyed the coolness of the old mission station overlooking Nojiri lake in Nagano prefecture. The London Symphony Orchestra and the Royal Shakespeare Company had been and gone, and the number of applicants handled by my placing service had trebled. Sarah had begun flute lessons with Marie Lorenz Okabe, a Dane married to a Japanese architect, and we had bought a Muramatsu silver-headed open-holed flute to take back as an eightieth birthday present for Dotty Grandpa.

Early in 1972 we anxiously awaited news of a posting, which when it came we greeted with modified rapture. Although it was to London and on promotion, to be sent to one of the most unpopular departments in HQ could have been a fate worse than death. Happily that proved a false assessment, as will be seen. Robin Duke, making what he knew to be a hopeless attempt to hang on to us, said to me 'You know, it is rather difficult nowadays to find chaps who are neither drunkards nor womanizers.'

In April the family flew to Hong Kong before my successor, Richard Gravil, could arrive, but within a few days Martin Beatty saw me off to join them for a relaxing long weekend and, thanks to the good offices of Derek Beard in New Delhi, we enjoyed the facilities of the empty flat of a colleague on leave. Taking advantage of a VSO project-vetting day trip with Audrey Lambert to Agra enabled us to see Fatepur Sikri and the Taj Mahal, while baby Jessica was entertained with Stephen and Helen Mawson's child of a similar age.

Heathrow and home begins another chapter.

9

London:
Four Jobs in Three Years

On arrival at Heathrow with a four-month-old baby in the family we were stunned into incredulity by the suggestion that Jessica would have to be put into quarantine because we had stopped over in India where smallpox was endemic. Our explanation that medical advice had been against vaccinating a child of under six months cut no ice and a vigorously healthy baby lay in the carrycot; only after a telephone discussion between the Airport Health Authority and the medical officer of health for the Bath district were we allowed to go, directly to Beckington and on condition we reported next morning. The delay caused the friends who had come to meet us to give us up as not being on the flight, but at least our self-drive hired car had not disappeared.

Being posted to the centre of the network after experience abroad is to turn from poacher to gamekeeper, and each of the four gamekeeping jobs employed in various ways my understanding of the poacher's point of view. It is odd but true that each of my posts prepared me for the one after the next — Malawi had a close bearing on Malaysia and later Ethiopia; and Japan provided important insights which helped in Romania and later Finland. On the art of working, if not in fact necessarily living, in London, we had had a dummy run while with UAC, and this first stint in the British Council's headquarters offered essential lessons for the second one almost ten years later. The common factor in the four otherwise unconnected tasks undertaken during these three years in London was the overriding need to introduce coherence, or at least a vision, which had previously been absent.

Conditions of service for staff and teachers

Many junior colleagues at 3 Hanover Street, where Service Conditions was accommodated, thought that their role was to apply the rules, whereas the proper purpose was the positive one of providing sensible logistical support for a total of over 1000 career staff and contract teachers spread all over the globe. Viewed in this way the work could be much more rewarding than simply handing out unpopular answers when questions of interpretation arose. To interpret the rules in an imaginative way, based on knowledge of the circumstances of daily life and work overseas, was not easy for home-based staff, so it was an important aspect of my work to bring common sense to bear on the decisions made. The welfare and morale of our 'clients' abroad could be critically improved by ensuring that our service was seen by them as a support rather than a hindrance, and that as much regard was paid to the spirit as to the letter of the rule book.

How should Bloggs travel to his new post? Would his family accompany him? Would they find reasonable accommodation? How should his baggage be sent? What car could he have shipped, or bought locally? What schooling was available at primary level? When could holiday visits be arranged for any older children at boarding school in Britain? What medical attention was available if or when needed? When and where could leave be taken? And, interdependently, would he get the right pay and appropriate allowances? All these questions would arise again as soon as there was any talk of a transfer, whether mid-tour or combined with leave. The tone of the exchanges between the gamekeeper and the poacher on all these topics reflected the quality of our service very accurately. Experienced poachers could become quite indignant if not handled with care, and rightly so, since the issues involved were often of vital importance in personal matters.

Surprising though it may seem, it was possible to derive considerable creative satisfaction from applying the required liberal attitude, encouraged by the benevolence of Oliver Elliott, director at the time, and supported by my two section heads, David Rogers and Ivy Murfett. We had to be sceptical of standard Whitehall dogmatic administrative 'theology' in its inapplicability to situations abroad, and we found close allies in the FCO's Personnel Services Department whenever HM Treasury or the Civil Service Department had to be convinced that a change was needed to prevent an awkward section in the rule book creating any more hard cases. Whenever discretion was exercised, or a specific issue referred upwards for a ruling, 'case law' was created and had to be recorded; but there was constant awareness of 'the unperceived laminations of reality' — a phrase engraved on my mind during a public poetry reading. Whether too vague or too restrictive, no rule can envisage all circumstances, so when an inequitable result is implied the good administrator sets about redrafting whatever wording has led to a lack of common sense. Achieving piecemeal reforms in this way was unspectacular but offered unexpected job satisfaction.

While my official enlightenment proceeded well, the weakness in our earlier decision to find a house in Somerset became apparent. We were too far from London for a daily commute, so my routine had to be weekly. This incurred the expense of digs for four nights, with a late arrival on Monday mornings and a late departure on Friday evenings. My luck in finding a room in the houses of three congenial families held up, but the strain on Diana and our family life was severe at times. Weekly commuting is definitely not to be recommended to anyone. Even so, during our first year at home we both took part with John and Phyllis Olive in performing Walton's *Façade* in Shawford Mill, and later Diana had leading parts in their opera double bill of Vaughan Williams's *Riders to the Sea* and Lennox Berkeley's *Dinner Engagement*. Sarah, aged ten, had to begin boarding school without delay to minimize the re-entry difficulties after her American-style interlude (fortunately her initial schooling in Malawi had been British style). She was bright enough to respond to the good teaching at St Christopher's, Burnham-on-Sea, and in due course, with hard work, achieve the necessary common entrance standard. Louise, aged eight, went to the Church of England village primary school for a year before joining Sarah, and Jessica was christened in Beckington church.

It was evident when my parents came to spend Christmas with us that Dotty Grandpa was not well. Back at work in Totnes in January 1973 he suffered a severe stroke (cerebral haemorrhage). His right side was paralysed, but after a prolonged rehabilitation process he was able to balance and walk a little; most distressing, however, was his total loss of the power of speech while continuing to understand all that was said around him. For another two and a half years he suffered frustration, and Potty Granny, in spite of being 17 years younger, was almost worn out caring for him. All members of the family helped when they could, and my way was to split my weekends between Totnes and Beckington every two or three weeks, thus depriving Diana still more.

Meanwhile, certain members of VSO staff who had known me from Malawi days began to invite me to take part in the occasional selection board in their offices in Bishop's Bridge Road, the old Great Western Railway's parcels office at Paddington station. The commitment was restricted by agreement with the British Council and limited to one every few months, until suddenly, late on a Friday at the end of March, came a summons to Personnel in Davies Street. Michael Ward had been asked to provide someone on secondment from the British Council to fill an unexpected gap in the VSO hierarchy and my name had been suggested. A turmoil of thoughts over the weekend ensued. Would it be a wise move? It was tempting to accept what had emerged as a popular request, but what was behind it? What timing was envisaged, and would it not be better to stay put and follow through my pet initiatives? And whose job was it anyway? My feelers went out to many for advice, but a month later secondment for one year initially was agreed, and two months later the process of extricating myself began. At my little farewell party in the basement of 3 Hanover Street my friends gave me a long-playing set of records of Haydn's *Six Last Masses*, which is still treasured. Colleagues become friends more readily in a department with a strong *esprit de corps*, probably born of an assumption of unpopularity. Being aware that my year with them had been somewhat unorthodox and radical, my thanks included the remark — 'Never again would the

British Council appoint anyone to this post who had an Irish great-grandmother — one of mine came from Cork.'

Voluntary Service Overseas in transition
This was not a career move for an ambitious climber, but it did become an intensely absorbing 11 months of strenuous activity with enormous scope — and even worse neglect of the family in Somerset. John Shaw had been head of teaching volunteers but had been successful in the supplementary competition for entry to the civil service, and he left VSO to join the DHSS. The obvious person to replace him was Dick Bird (see the Malawi chapter) but he was in Papua New Guinea being the first non-British Council support officer. Hence the gap for me to fill. Douglas Whiting, the long-serving and much admired director, had just retired and been replaced by David Collett who was experienced in voluntary social work but of the sort that lacked any overseas dimension. Hugh Carey, the deputy, knew me, as did Myra Green, Margaret de Bunsen (now Wilson) and several others on the staff.

Whereas the British Council was (and is) a second level public body depending on the FCO and the ODA (Overseas Development Administration) as sponsoring departments for its government grant, VSO was very much a 'third rank' public sector NGO relying on voluntary fundraising for basic support, the ODA for financial underpinning, the British Council as its overseas arm, and the good opinion of recipient countries — not forgetting also the favourable view of British officials resident in them.

This was a time of very low staff morale, of widespread mis-understanding of the 'imperial legacy', of suspicion of the British-ness of the British Council and of the lifestyle of some of its staff abroad: and pervading everything was a loss of confidence in the validity of what VSO was about. My British Council background proved advantageous in improving staff relationships, in counter-ing an atmosphere of dispirited disarray, in reforming the manner in which volunteers were administered, and in improving the tone of correspondence with the overseas arm. The top priority was to give a lead in moving from a policy of 'calculated vagueness' to one that was explicit and defensible. My responsibility for over 800 teachers was two-thirds of all volunteers in the field, the balance being a growing number of 'development' volunteers who came under the deputy director. Within a month my six-page 'Notes Towards an Operational Philosophy' had been chewed over and generally accepted as a reasonable stopgap until such time as the new director could take stock of his options and deliver his own line.

The work was subject to an inexorable annual cycle of recruitment, selection, posting, training, supporting while abroad, repatriating and finally debriefing. The whole process was coordinated by ten regional executives (earlier known rather inadequately as secretaries) who had geographical groups of countries to look after all the year round and, according to season, had to play a succession of roles — giving talks in universities to attract applicants, running selection boards, matching the curricula vitae of selected volunteers to the project-vetting reports on requests from overseas, designing and running briefing courses and monitoring arrangements made by the overseas arm for in-service/in-country training, liaison with project heads and so forth. In practice, this was done for all volunteers, not just those in education, so my side had a broader charge than appeared on paper and my next effort, a six-page 'Constructive Critique of Headquarters Organization' sought to recognize this openly. Many of my recommendations fell foul of certain personalities, but within a year of my departure the essential changes were made. Meanwhile, the briefing season was on us and it fell to me to do the opening and closing of courses in Reading, Isleworth and Tottenham, which required the preparation of suitable speeches.

For our summer holiday we borrowed John Olive's caravan and took the whole family to Music Camp. Jessica aged 18 months had begun to toddle, but camp has never been too good for toddlers and we had to work a shift system to keep her happy. The other two were able to join in the singing and most activities, but the experiment was not an unqualified success.

On returning to VSO in early September, I received news of a fatal accident in Kano. A VSO nurse, Mary-Jane Garnons-Williams, had been knocked off her motorcycle in a head-on collision with a bus on the airport road. As Nigeria had only recently switched from driving on the left to driving on the right, and it was also dark, it was assumed that one or other of the parties had forgotten which side to drive on. Her father was a major in the military vehicle establishment in Virginia Water and in due course my job included taking a few of her personal effects to him. (Motorcycles were a constant worry: a similar fatality occurred in Malaysia a few years later.)

With recruitment publicity and the selection board season in full swing the next month, my self assignments took me in quick succession to Aberystwyth, Cardiff, Bangor, Bath and Oxford. During this time we also issued the first revision since 1969 of the 'Notes for Guidance of the Overseas Arm' — a task requiring much homework, but essential for reducing the cumulative discrepancies between theory and current practice. Most exciting for me, however, was the need for a troubleshooting tour of Southeast Asia. A staff tour of this area had been postponed twice, but even my availability for it was limited by London commitments and it had to be set up at very short notice. Volunteer dissatisfaction had been surfacing for some time, especially in West Malaysia, Brunei, Singapore and Laos, so a programme appraisal on the ground was becoming urgent. With seldom more than two nights in each place the tour was squeezed into less than three weeks of November, but the follow-up extended to Christmas.

In retrospect, there was an absurd amount of detail in my 60-page report, but it did contain a 'mine of information' on the background, personalities and state of play in each of the six centres visited. Robert and Bina Arbuthnott's generous hospitality in Kuala Lumpur set the scene for my conclusion that his relatively new broom (as British Council representative) would in due course take the sting out of the current discontent: what neither of us anticipated at the time was the opportunity it had given me to 'case the joint' before my posting as his deputy less than two years later. Similarly, in Sabah, Ken Lambert (British Council regional director) and his wife put me up in their house in Kota Kinabalu and arranged meetings which produced many positive openings in education, fisheries and medical services. This was traditional volunteer country where satisfactory projects would abound.

Going on to Brunei, my host in Bandar Seri Bagawan (which means city of the sultan's father) was the Acting High Commissioner, John Moffatt, who met me at the airport in a car with no numberplate — in its place there was a crown! Was that the peak of anyone's career? (Brunei was then a constitutional curiosity, not part of Malaysia but an oil-rich mini-state allied to Singapore; the resident Brit had the dual role of representing Britain in Brunei as well as representing Brunei to the rest of the world.) Its affluence made it unsuitable for volunteers and the result of my tactfully expressed determination to prevent any further abuse of VSO's services was that, the following year, the Crown Agents filled all requirements by recruiting teachers on contract at the market rate. Peter Sandiford (British Council assistant representative) looked after me in Singapore, but even he, a former VSO volunteer in Malawi during our time, could not deny that similar arguments should prevail there.

The Royal Laotian Airlines' flight into Vientiane was of the sort one would prefer not to repeat. Dr John Hay, first secretary (Aid) in the British embassy there, was the overseas arm. To operate in an atmosphere of political instability, superpower influences and civil war was an unenviable task; and the volunteers found the Francophone environment discouraging. Pathet Lao troops in Chinese-style uniform were 'in town', which made me want to get out as soon as possible. The programme had either to be reformed to make it an effective complement to the American International Voluntary Service (IVS) programme, or it should be abandoned.

In Bangkok, the British Council assistant representative, Walter Curry, made my visits in Thailand a memorable pleasure. As elsewhere, we had a struggle to make much impression in comparison with other (more liberally-funded) volunteer agencies, but the individuals were reasonably happy.

Immediate tasks back in London included the chairing of regional selection boards in Leeds and Manchester, a briefing course in Tottenham and plans for 'more time with the family' during Christmas leave. A pleasant change from recent concerns was an Epiphany concert in Beckington church, where we performed Parts 5 and 6 of Bach's *Christmas Oratorio*.

In January 1974 the implications of my troubleshooting activities began to sink in, and David Collett discussed the details with great care. There was a growing sense, however, that my concern

128

to improve British Council/VSO relations, both at home and abroad, was becoming superfluous because VSO planned to cut the ties as soon as possible, and that he and Hugh Carey were on a collision course. My secondment needed to be reversed as soon as convenient and before the explosion became imminent. Meanwhile, regional boards took me to Swansea, Cardiff, Belfast and Bristol plus recruitment talks in Cheltenham and Birmingham, but on the home front all was not well. Diana was suffering from nervous exhaustion brought on by too many visitors combined with a very demanding Jessica, and relief was available during the week only from kindly neighbours. Equally dismal was an office subject to energy saving in cold weather, followed by the general election in which Edward Heath lost to Harold Wilson. Much homework was needed to complete the first radical redraft of the 'Guide for Volunteers' since 1968. By the end of March the search for a new assignment within the British Council became active, and by early May a graceful exit from VSO was accomplished. Dick Bird had returned from his stint in Papua New Guinea and with my recommended reorganization now possible, he took charge of overseas operations while Myra Green headed the home operations.

For a part of the Easter holiday, Diana's parents came from Highcliffe to look after the children and we went to farmhouses in Wales for a bit of walking on the Pembrokeshire coast. We also celebrated Grandpa Herdman's seventieth birthday.

Didactic displays and circulating exhibitions

It was time now to be a little less earnest. There had not been much scope for frivolity in the last year, but one advantage of London is being able to keep one's ear close to the ground; thus a rumour reached me that Geoffrey Tribe, the controller of Arts Division, was planning to appoint an assistant. He was a little surprised by my call and asked 'What sort of interest do you have in the arts?' to which my response was 'Well, er, I am an amateur musician with a long background, and while in Japan I deepened my interest in the visual arts, and — er — in any case, I like the idea of working with you.'

This was the way to find a job without the help of the Personnel Department. Nevertheless, it was clear that the British Council still put education before the arts in its order of priorities, so the first half of May saw me in Manchester on a course designed to display the workings of a big local education authority. There was time to visit the Whitworth Gallery and the Royal Northern College of Music (statue of Chopin) and, one afternoon in the cathedral, a rehearsal with full orchestra and organ blazing away. It was Chetham's School, but what was the music? Accosting a man who looked as if he might know, the reply came to me 'It's a Gothic monstrosity!' — in short, it was Saint-Saëns's organ concerto they were rehearsing.

Before joining Arts proper, my initial assignment was to give urgent help in Aids and Displays, a cosy little unit in Euston Road, sharing premises with Fine Arts, and later known as General Exhibitions. Unhappily its director Pamela Grimmett was very ill, soon recognized as being terminally ill, having to be in and out of hospital and unable to work more than spasmodically. If ever there was a challenge to bring order out of chaos this was it — to work off a serious backlog, to sort out the muddles and to restore the morale of a distraught little team of devoted staff. Derek Dooley, the deputy, was preoccupied with the only designer on a massive and overwhelming project to deliver a complex travelling exhibition to a site in Brussels, and the accountant was about to leave, so the rest of the team — a handful of researchers — was being held together precariously by the only secretary/typist, Elsie Garstang, who was a wiry, mince-no-words, middle-aged woman. Within a few days of my appearance in her domain, apparently in despair of summing me up, she asked bluntly, 'When's your birthday then, Bruce?' (just a trifle ahead of her time in not using surnames) — and on being told, she said, with a sigh of relief, 'That's or'right, then. We don't want no more Virgos 'ere!' From that moment on she evidently felt able to relax, secure in what she thought to be my placid Piscean characteristics.

As with Service Conditions and VSO, Aids and Displays had a global responsibility (despite its diminutive size) to provide multiple sets of visual material, photographic displays and circulating exhibitions, both of a didactic nature and of prints or posters with their own inherent merit. Clear and unambiguous terminology was needed. Also, a systematic method of collating requirements and commissions from our 80-odd offices abroad, together with a watertight manner of planning the itineraries of the product, were basic essentials. Files of letters and minutes that could not easily be found quickly were useless, so my invention of a set of visual control panels was effective in showing the whereabouts and future plans for any item at any moment. Inevitably these became known as 'Bruce boards' and were still in use many years later.

We took our summer leave in two parts. A week at the end of June coincided with speech day and an exeat for Sarah and Louise from St Christopher's (Burnham-on-Sea) and with two Bath Festival concerts. We then spent another week at the end of July on the Shirley-Quirk's narrowboat *Amelia di Liverpool*, cruising from Worcester up the Severn to Stourport and then on the Staffordshire–Worcestershire canal. This was an ideal family exercise; the two elder girls would take turns either to help Diana with the lock gates or to guard little Jessica from straying overboard, while the skipper handled the vessel. Some time was also devoted to house hunting, for we realized with much regret that Beckington was noisier than many places much nearer London and the strain of weekly commuting was not to be prolonged. We looked both in the Basingstoke area and in southwest London, but when the offer we had received was withdrawn, the whole venture was delayed for another year. During these two months also, three visits were paid to Wexham Park Hospital near Slough to see our dying colleague; she never returned to work and died in September. Before all this it had been arranged that Miss P. Lighthill would be posted substantively to take over my acting job, so releasing me to begin my intended Arts Division role in mid-August.

Coordinating the departments of Arts Division

It may appear that much of this work in headquarters can hardly be described as the sharp end of cultural relations, but the nuts and bolts of bridge building in the arts were closer to *our* daily work than to that of many others in London. Of the six departments, three were big-spending 'senior' ones, namely Fine Arts, Drama and Music, and three were relatively modest, namely Literature, Films, and Aids and Displays. Geoffrey Tribe had taken over the division determined to implement reforms that

131

would answer certain long-standing criticisms once and for all. The directors of the big three were specialists in their fields, with a professional reputation among the experts in Britain, whereas the 'junior' three directors were normally without specialist qualifications and were often staff posted home from overseas (see Chapter 12). The performing and visual arts constituency in London tended to expect us to promote their offerings abroad and the advisory committees exerted their influence in support; but our overseas offices needed to procure the best available and most appropriate British offerings in support of their overall purposes, not as ends in themselves. To reconcile these conflicting viewpoints was the core of the problem, and it needed tackling from several angles.

First, it took Geoffrey several years of chipping away to reach the stage where, however specialized the staff of a department needed to be, the director would be a generalist with experience of being in charge of a British Council representation or directorate overseas. The second approach was the dissemination of much more information for the advisory committees on the nature of our priorities in the countries in which they were interested, in the hope that a better perspective would result. This in turn required a third innovation, which is where my job began.

Geoffrey had worked in Tanzania and Eastern Nigeria, in staff training and development, and in Education Division. His purpose in enlisting me was to introduce the same rigour in the distillation and application of policy in the arts as we had learnt to apply in our educational work. So the drafting of country arts policy papers — involving description, analysis, diagnosis and prescription — dominated my time for the first two months until diversion onto the forward plan became necessary. A draft of each paper went to the office in the country concerned for comment and amendment. Our basic motive was no longer to accept the notion that activity in the arts was an optional extra and not really 'work', and to restore arts work to a proper place in the overall strategy. Too many colleagues thought that if it were enjoyable it could not be work, so cutting at the root of our belief in mutual enjoyment as an essential element in bridge building.

Are these administrative details too boring? Is there a danger of relapsing into theory? No, because what is recorded here is the framework for effective working practices and, before long, the next overseas posting would take us back to the sharp end. Meanwhile, on the domestic front, although we had failed to move closer to London it remained easier to split weekends with Totnes, where my father's condition had stabilized without, alas, any prospect of recovering the ability to speak. Sarah aged 12 plus had entered Sherborne School for Girls where, the following year, she was awarded a music scholarship. The rich offerings of theatre and music in London were exploited by me within the limits of a shallow pocket, but a catalogue would be pointless. One evening a week saw me in Morley College at a woodcarving class under the tutelage of Mark Harvey. My parents came to stay with us — fetched by me in their own car — for ten days of Christmas leave, providing a brief respite for my mother from her burden of caring.

The year 1975 was the British Council's fiftieth anniversary and the celebrations included a visit to the Spring Gardens offices by the Queen, the publication of a book (Frances Donaldson's *The British Council: The First Fifty Years*) and a concert in the Royal Festival Hall. Personally, however, while the coordination of arts work continued to be absorbing and constructive, our overriding concern was where we would be posted next. Somehow it came to light that my name was on a list of those suitable for 'sensitive posts', one of which was the regional director in Cape Town. This was, we knew, physically attractive but politically repulsive; yet for several months we thought that would be it, and even a degree of enthusiasm was engendered in conversations with Dennis Frean, recently retired from Pretoria. Even so, there was a vocal minority of colleagues in London who took the radical view that we should not be working in South Africa at all. Top management eventually issued a paper justifying all that was being done, which has since been proved entirely valid. Unfortunately, the domestic implications were very off-putting, since the travelling throughout the Cape Province would have left Diana isolated while Jessica attended a local school. This would have replicated the weekly commuting pattern and the more we thought about it the less we liked it.

A surprising deliverance was at hand. Geoffrey Tribe told me to aim higher and backed his judgement on paper. So, one day in June, a visit to Personnel elicited the following: 'We have just decided to move William Brown from Kuala Lumpur to Cologne. How would you like the deputy post in Kuala Lumpur?' It took me barely a second to say 'yes, thanks very much', knowing for certain that it would suit us, having seen the setup during my VSO staff tour of 18 months earlier. It is not given to many to have any first-hand knowledge of a post before getting there, so the switch from Arts Division via South Africa to Malaysia was made, with a few hurdles yet to take. Once again the ear to the ground and luck of the draw syndrome had been illustrated. No matter how well qualified, availability was the key to a good job.

The biggest outstanding task was to prepare for the annual Cambridge staff conference, which that year was to be on the subject of our informational role — by which was meant our activities in the arts, books, science, education and English teaching, as opposed to our role in technical assistance and development aid. The FCO's Cultural Relations Department could be assumed to have a critical interest in this, since it represented the 'diplomatic wing' as opposed to the ODA's 'aid wing'. In the event, the background material ran to 12 pages, but my attempts to proselytize in support of the need for cultural profiles were choked off. My thesis was that cultural bridges could not be built without comprehensive understanding of the nature of the abutments at each end. More significant, fortunately, was the opportunity that Geoffrey got to expound 'Tribe's theory of tingling', namely his insistence that the test of an effective arts event was 'does it make you tingle at the nape of the neck?'

No better principle could be applied to our subsequent work in Malaysia, but several storms had to be weathered before we could fly there in October. At last we managed to move from our reluctantly sold, elegant stone house in Somerset to a very uninspiring brick, four-square box in Bourne End, quite close to the Thames between Marlow and Cookham — but a reasonable commute into Paddington. We fitted in a second canal holiday, this time on the Shropshire Union canal from Penkridge, and Diana took Sarah to Music Camp while her mother came to keep Louise, Jessica and me company; but Grandpa Herdman collapsed while out walking and was taken into intensive care for a few days. The next disaster was my broken front tooth, which would have been a relatively minor problem had it not happened just before we were due to sing as a solo quartet with Neville and Jane Coulson for the wedding in Essex of William Wilson and Margaret de Bunsen. The next week was spent on an ODA course at the Institute of Development Studies at Sussex University, and on the following Tuesday my mother phoned with the news of Dotty Grandpa's death, quietly during the previous night. Cremation was at the weekend. On our return home we had packers in the house and had to make arrangements with agents for letting. A visit from my mother, loose ends in the office, a final briefing — and we were off.

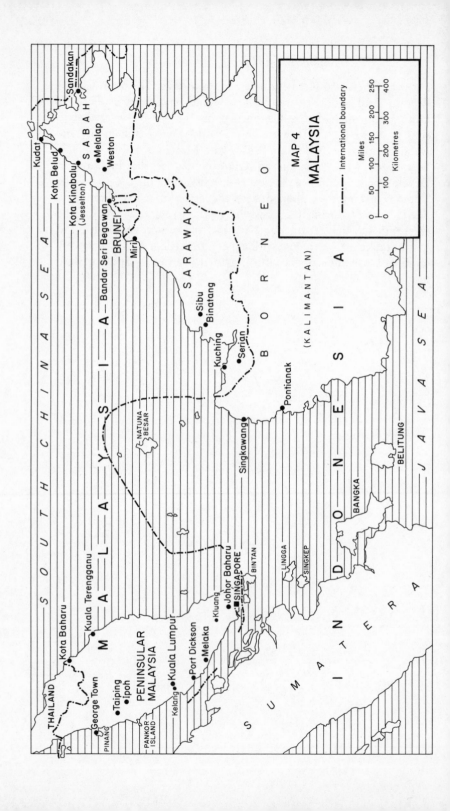

MAP 4
MALAYSIA

------- International boundary

10

Malaysia in Economic Takeoff

O n stepping out of an aircraft in Kuala Lumpur one is enveloped in a warm damp blanket — you are at sea level and near the equator. My previous visit on the VSO troubleshooting tour had prepared me for this, and also for the red earth and smells of vegetation on the road in from the airport. It was all new for Diana and Jessica, now aged nearly four. The contrast between the tropical Africa we knew (Nigeria and Malawi) and the Southeast Asian tropics lay in the effects of human activity. In Africa one had to assume an environment of dirt and potential disease; here the Chinese influence produced meticulous cleanliness.

Mid-1970s Malaysia: what was it like?
Malaya [*sic*] had become independent in 1957, three years before the end of the 12 years of jungle war emergency — 1948 to 1960 — during which Chinese-inspired communist guerrillas had been contained and eventually defeated by British-led security forces. Then, in the mid-1960s, there had been a period of confrontation with the Indonesians who disputed the inclusion of Sabah and Sarawak in the Malaysian Federation, preferring to think of those parts of Borneo as being integrated with what they called Kalimantan. Now, however, the preoccupation of Malaysian politicians was the delicate constitutional balancing act in keeping their multiracial society in flourishing condition. That

they have succeeded for so long is a tribute to their skill. The population is a rich mixture of Malays, Chinese and Indians, each community having a distinct occupational bias in the economy and different religious affiliations. The indigenous Malay peasants are Muslims, and their traditional rulers are sultans, forming the top and bottom levels of society. Following Portuguese and Dutch activity, British hegemony was established in the nineteenth century and development depended on three features — the import of Indians to run the infrastructure of railways, postal services and the police; the import of Chinese to work in the tin mines; and the encouragement of Malay farmers to work on the rubber estates. The Indians are mostly Tamils and if not Hindu tend to be Protestant, whereas the Chinese tend to be Wesleyan Methodist or Catholic.

This inherently unstable society was held together for many years by British administration and the English language, but communal violence had erupted in Kuala Lumpur as recently as the early 1970s when rioting Malays burnt down Chinese shops. We saw the area, which had deliberately not been rebuilt as a reminder to everyone of the importance of learning to live together peacefully. Government policy was aimed at eliminating the Malay population's economic disadvantage through special education and training programmes, but this in itself made the other communities feel insecure and fear discrimination. An especially contentious issue was the role of English, which was progressively being replaced in the schools by Bahasa Malaysia, the Malay language (also the basis of Bahasa Indonesia) which had crept up as far as the universities in our time. The serious disadvantages of such a policy, which ignored the example of India's experience, was suddenly noticed by the senior members of the Malaysian establishment in the late 1970s, and it was just as we were leaving that the British Council was called upon to devise a major remedial programme to try to reverse the damaging decline in the country's capacity to communicate with the rest of the world and to do business internally.

Here was a challenging background for what proved to be a very full and pleasant life. The economy was booming in a newly industrializing context. British interests, which were partly concerned with politico-commercial matters and partly with capital aid and technical assistance, were balanced equally between the FCO and ODA. Robert Arbuthnott headed the British Council, which was physically at arm's length but operationally closer to the high commission than we had experienced in Malawi. He plunged us into our first truly multicultural Christmas. The Philharmonic Society of Selangor (the state in which Kuala Lumpur lay until the capital territory was created) had a long tradition of musical and theatrical activity and its chamber choir formed the nucleus of its annual carol concerts, which (in our time anyway) were staged in the British Council's 300-seat auditorium above the library. When Keith Hunter had been in charge of Penang he had run a choir there and when he was transferred to Kuala Lumpur he brought the choral library with him. Robert conducted the assembled forces until it became my turn the following year.

Robert had also arranged that a main proportion of my official duties as his deputy (at least for my first tour) would be the monthly planning and execution of the centre programme of cultural activities, both local and imported. In spite of a steady increase in American (Lincoln Centre), German (Goethe Institute) and French (Alliance Française) activity in this field, the local clientele tended to presume a degree of British leadership, an expectation encouraged by the coincidence of more British Council staff than usual having appropriate interests and skills. Two heads of local music schools, Harold Ashcroft and Albert Reverger, were also active in exploiting our platform. The normal pattern was at least one chamber concert, recital or poetry and music event each month, with twice-weekly film shows, plus other meetings, lectures and exhibitions. The detailed work of support in running the programme was in the hands of Haji Osman, a versatile and resourceful colleague of long standing, known as the 'centre secretary'. My job was to think four or five months ahead and to slot in whatever could be made available and whoever could be encouraged to collaborate. More of DIY later.

Candidates for the Regional Rhodes Scholarship award
One of my less frequent chores as the deputy was to act as secretary to the selection committee that exercised patronage in

making an award tenable in Oxford once every two or three years for Malaysia, Singapore and Brunei combined. Early in 1976 the Trustees indicated that our turn had come again, so we placed advertisements and fixed a closing date and a day for interviews. The requirements were so stringent — candidates had to be under 25, have an honours degree, be unmarried and be keen sportsmen — that we had only four qualified applicants.

The committee duly assembled under the chairmanship of a distinguished Malaysian diplomat with the four interviews carefully timetabled, whereupon a note came to me from Robert saying that a late candidate had arrived unannounced from Singapore, and that he was expecting to be interviewed. The committee instructed me to respond that they were sorry, there was no case for admitting him to the competition. Then Robert sent in another note. He had been telephoned by 'our man in Singapore' who put him in an awkward quandary by claiming that the extra candidate was the personal nominee of the Singaporean minister of education and that if the committee did not admit him then relations with the British Council would be seriously impaired. This case was explained by me, but the committee saw no reason to change its view. At this point Robert could see that my role as secretary was to provide a service to the Trustees, but as his deputy my duty lay to the British Council and its reputation. An issue of principle had arisen. How should the rules of the game be interpreted?

His third and last note said, 'If you do not see this man, heads will roll.' The only course open to me then was to halt the proceedings and show the note to the chairman. No sooner had he explained the nature of this attempt to influence them than the two Singaporean members, who were senior government employees, said most emphatically 'This is irregular. We do not allow politicians to push us around in this way! All is not lost. This man can try again in two years' time.' Immediately my bacon was saved and the imperturbability of our experienced chairman was vindicated. No news of dire consequences ever reached us, our chosen candidate (also incidentally from Singapore) was unanimously regarded as outstanding and happily went off to Oxford. Mr Ong Teck Chin studied for a doctorate at Wadham College.

The Watford Palace Theatre Company on tour

Drama and Dance Department in London is engaged in a constant search for theatre companies able and willing to tour abroad, but no responsible colleague can afford to endorse a proposal unless and until the actual production has been seen. Because negotiations for a contract actually to send a drama group may be squeezed into a few months, possibly only weeks, the lead time tends to be uncomfortably short. (This is in strong contrast with the world of music where engagements are based on reputation and are made a year and a half or more ahead.)

The Watford group was not so much a company as an *ad hoc* assembly of television actors held together for the purpose of the tour and offering us *The Merchant of Venice* and *Pygmalion*. Once the contract had been signed in London we went ahead with negotiating for the local arrangements to be handled by the only available local impresario, Rajalingham. He had worked with us before and seemed confident of being able to tackle the requirements of booking venues, organizing publicity and ticket sales, and reserving accommodation and internal transport. When Val West visited us from London on an advance tour, she vetted the venues and helped scrounge the rather formidable list of stage furniture needed for the *Pygmalion* set. Other nuts-and-bolts details, such as the rate of subsistence to be approved by Equity, had to be sorted out, but Rajalingham lost his nerve. First he went quiet, then he hid away and, when found, said he was withdrawing from the enterprise. So much for supposedly contractual obligations — and there were only three weeks to go before the company was due to arrive.

To rescue the tour entailed mobilizing every member of our generalist team. Some 12,000 tickets had RAJALINGHAM PRODUCTIONS printed on them. This had to be blacked out by hand and each ticket, whether sold or unsold, had to be checked and reconciled with the seating plan — done in my house, mostly after midnight. We organized ourselves into separate task forces to deal with the logistics of customs clearance and transport, immigration and hotels, technical needs, publicity, programmes and invitations. Five British and four Malaysian staff had to drop other commitments for two weeks and, on the days of performances, all our accounts staff, secretaries and drivers were on front of house duty.

141

The company flew in from Calcutta, but its costumes and props failed to appear. Acid remarks circulated among the 'reception committee' on the steps of our library and Diana burst into tears. We had visions of playing *The Merchant of Venice* in hastily improvised batik outfits, but some desperate telegramming (no telex or fax in those days) persuaded the Indians to put the baggage on the next flight — which mercifully happened to be, but might well not have been, the next day.

Our choice of venue had been much criticized by the old hands among the amateurs of the drama fraternity, who said 'You cannot possibly be heard in the university examinations hall' (otherwise known as the Dewan Tunku Canselor). My response was defiant. We thought we took a fair risk because so far only amateurs had tried it. Sure enough, when Shylock delivered an entire soliloquy with his back to the audience every word was heard. We were vindicated — the professionals could do it. Each play was given twice in Kuala Lumpur and once each in Penang and Ipoh, with audiences totalling over 7000. (Later they took *The Merchant of Venice* to Sarawak for six performances, but that was outside my jurisdiction.) Two of the leading ladies gave poetry recitals, and a drama teachers' workshop was enthralled by a group of actors giving a demonstration of the discipline and eye contact essential in a stage fight with swords. The company enjoyed many pool-side parties. There was just one show of temperament and a single case of imprudent sleeping on the beach with consequent loss of money and documents. Eventually we could all relax and enjoy the common endeavour, but — phew! — not again just yet, please.

Bach, Shakespeare and Purcell

Such were the hazards of imported cultural events that we often thought it quite as rewarding to mobilize the available local talent. One colleague, Leslie Beckett, who was an experienced science teacher working in the Curriculum Development Centre, had the great courage required to get together not just one but two choirs and orchestras and to mount three performances of Bach's *St Matthew Passion* in the Wesleyan (Chinese) church during Holy Week, just when the Watford Palace group was in town. The double requirement stretched resources to breaking point and some movements did, it must be admitted, fall apart; but the multiracial collaboration was heartening and the achievement inspired my own future planning. The dates had to be the three days between the Watford group's last night in Kuala Lumpur and its opening in Penang because only then was it possible for me to sing the tenor soloist evangelist part. That was the (two) week(s) that was — TWTWTW — 12 days without any let-up, but we survived.

A nightmarish if minor fiasco surrounded David Stone and the Stradivarius violin on which he gave a recital in Penang under our auspices. We had arranged to hire a local Yamaha upright for his accompanist, but on arrival it was found to have been tuned almost a semitone sharp. The very thought of trying to tune up a valuable violin is too excruciating to contemplate, so my embarrassed appeal to the assembled audience was for superhuman forbearance while half an hour was spent tuning the piano down to the correct pitch. Only one old lady walked out and got her money back.

Another colleague, Malcolm Cooper, was a language expert running the University of Malaya English for Special Purposes (UMESP) project. He and his wife Jane were keen on both acting and singing, and between us we worked on a scheme (not, it must be said, entirely original) for reintegrating the very fine music in Purcell's *Fairy Queen* with Shakespeare's *Midsummer Night's Dream* as originally intended. To reduce both the text and the score to a manageable combination involved a weekend of hard bargaining in a holiday cottage; uncut the two together would have lasted nearly seven hours, but we contrived to reduce the play to under two hours and to embellish it with more than an hour of music. We used the OUR rectangular auditorium diagonally, with Malcolm's actors on stage along one side and my musicians off stage across the end, equipped with individual shaded lights, as if in a nonexistent 'pit'.

The onstage cast and the offstage singers and players were a memorably multiracial mixture. Oberon was played by a well-known but rarely persuaded to act Malay Malaysian, Puck was an 11-year-old Indian Malaysian boy, and Diana played Titania —

143

described as 'gorgeous and majestic'. Malcolm and Jane were one of the pairs of lovers, and John Gardner, our library adviser, played Wall. The other mechanical roles included the oldest inhabitant of the dramatic fraternity playing Bottom, and Gino the gay hairdresser playing Thisbe. The fairies' choreography was beautifully produced by Anna Kronenburg, our Cape Coloured dancing teacher. Our 'ready-mixed' chamber choir of 25 sang the choruses, a Belgian woman the soprano solos and Eddie Chin (Chinese Malaysian) the baritone ones — until he backed out in a fit of temperament. This misfortune, typical of the risks taken, was more than counterbalanced by the magnanimity of Robin Gritton who happened to be in town as the visiting examiner for the ABRSM. He confessed to being a cellist and willing to join us, so we enjoyed the little dreamed of bonus of a rock-firm continuo. Our principal trumpeter was Colin Stuart, a high commission colleague, and three Malays from the Royal Malaysia Police Band provided oboe, double bass and timpani — a small contingent, but auguring well for extended collaboration less than a year later.

The four performances attracted full houses and only one of them suffered any noticeable shortcomings. We were able to present a locally made pewter bowl to Robin Gritton, and we all had the satisfaction of knowing that such a reconstruction was not uncommon and was professionally acceptable.

Learning to fly — and other relaxations
Meanwhile, 'the work' was carried on. Apart from Robert and myself, the other generalists were Gerry Liston, Joyce Taylor and Jim O'Hara. Gerry had a first-class Oxford degree in physics, had done a stint as a VSO volunteer here in Malaysia and had later been posted by the British Council to Kumasi in Ghana. His special interest was in looking after scientific visitors and, in recent years, he has risen high in the London hierarchy as the overlord of innovations in the area of information technology. Joyce looked after the programme of technical cooperation traineeships and other awards, and Jim's main responsibility was for the small VSO programme. Our librarian colleague has already been mentioned; our English language expert was Bryson McAdam whom we had known previously in Malawi and who knew Malaysia well, having

144

been the Chief Education Officer in two of the states before independence; our educational technology colleague was George Grimmett; and our science education adviser was David Bates.

David was a keen pilot and was very soon to become a qualified flying instructor (QFI) based at the Selangor Flying Club at the old airport, a mere ten-minute drive from the office. This was too good to be true for one who had cherished a longing to fly ever since failing to join the Fleet Air Arm for national service. Such an opportunity could not be ignored — it could hardly be expected to recur — so my documentation as a student pilot was duly completed, ground school was attended and, throughout the early months of 1976, David took me up at least once a week. He was a born teacher, with just the right manner for inspiring self-confidence in a novice in charge of a lethal machine. He also had a professional interest in the use of club aircraft, for the time saved by not toiling overland on bad roads enabled him to visit two secondary schools in one day, landing on the nearest grass strip after a low pass to clear off the footballers or other live obstacles. After several sessions of 'circuits and bumps', stalling recovery exercises and practice forced landings, David introduced me to cross-country procedures. Diana came with us on a trip to Johore and back to Malacca with an overnight stop in Kluang, but tended to lose her normal composure when she was seated behind us and unsure of which of us was actually in control of the plane.

In due course David judged me ripe for a first solo circuit, but not until after my safe return did he confess how anxious he had been. An assistant flying instructor has to obtain a second opinion before sending a pupil solo for the first time, but as David had recently achieved the status of QFI he was sending me on his own authority. He was biting his nails very hard as he stood by the runway watching me take his advice to abort my first approach (if unhappy with it) and to follow the overshoot procedure. But once safely down after the second attempt, there was the obligatory round of champagne for all — and a greatly relieved Diana was summoned by telephone to join us. That was 5 July.

Sarah and Louise flew out from their boarding schools to join us for the summer holidays and, having already spent a few week-ends either on the coast at Port Dixon or in the coolness of

Fraser's Hill, we took a week of local leave in mid-August, spending half of it at the Seaview Hotel on Pangkor island (off the west coast) in company with Rex and Mavis Hunt and family (later of Falklands' fame but then Deputy High Commissioner) and the other half at the Lutheran bungalow in the Cameron Highlands. It was when doing one of the signposted walks up there that Sarah outpaced me for the first time — a memorable humiliation for Daddy! We saw the unsurprisingly derelict airstrip at that altitude and found the Boh tea estates interesting.

On the domestic front it was time for Louise to leave St Christopher's and join Sarah at Sherborne, so Diana planned to leave Jessica with me and fly home three weeks before term began to organize the transfer. In attempting this we endured an emotionally shocking experience at the airport, unwittingly falling foul of the immigration bureaucracy almost as badly as on our arrival at Heathrow from Japan and India. An observant official saw that Jessica's photograph and details were on Diana's passport as a dependent child — if one were travelling both must go; they could not be separated. We pleaded in vain. It was no excuse that Diana had a ticket to come back in three weeks and that Jessica would remain in her father's care. (Too late did we learn that a warning about the tightening of the rules had been circulated in the high commission. The authorities feared a trade in unaccompanied children.) Diana's suitcase was retrieved from the British Airways jumbo and we went home, shaken and disconsolate. Two days later, with a separate passport for five-year-old Jessica duly provided, Diana went as intended.

Acting in charge during an interregnum
There was a seven-week gap between Robert Arbuthnott's departure and John Lawrence's arrival. Our contribution to the series of farewell parties for Robert and Bina was a musical-menu dinner, into the spirit of which our children entered by making coloured cards as a guide to the entertainment. The inexorable cycle of local chamber concerts and imported recitals continued, while several friends, such as the Coopers and the Bates, went off for summer leave at home. Colin Perchard, our old friend from Malawi days, came with his family for a stopover holiday *en route* from being in

charge of the British Council in Korea. Because of Diana's absence they stayed with Joyce Taylor, but we all went to Port Dixon for a weekend.

John Singleton Pettit was a consultant dermatologist with a long history of presenting poetry readings as part of our centre programme, but in the process he tended to be very aggressive, not only to me but also towards Haji Osman and other Malaysian colleagues. He made the mistake of trying to exploit my vulnerability during my occupation of the hot seat, so precipitating a showdown which he lost.

A large number of public holidays is characteristic of mixed societies and in Malaysia we naturally observed all the Muslim feasts and Chinese New Year, as well as Dipavali and Christmas. It was customary to spend most of the day making a series of calls on all who had indicated they would be 'at home' with open house, beginning with local colleagues and progressing to VIP contacts. As acting boss it fell to me on one such Muslim holiday to call on Dr Mahathir Mohammed, then Minister of Education but now (for many years) Prime Minister. Knowing he was a keen family man with a preference for informality, we took Jessica with us and when they shook hands, in her happy little-girlish uninhibited manner, she swung Dr Mahathir all round his entrance hall.

An extra feature of life at this time was the acceptance of invitations that normally passed me by, such as the regular series of national days in the diplomatic circuit — a phenomenon which became much more familiar in later years. The Austrian one was significant for us because the Ambassador's wife, Helga Ziegler, was a keen singer who organized several of our chamber concerts. We also fielded more visitors from London, such as Peter Martin whom we had known in Kyoto, Japan, and who now needed a comprehensive programme of interviews with our contacts in education and science. Mr and Mrs Sutcliffe, the then headmaster of Atlantic College in Wales, descended on us with little warning, but enjoyed lunch with me at the flying club.

John Lawrence arrived in the middle of the Dipavali celebrations and we were able to welcome him with Robert and Martina Frost and family who were staying with us from Singapore. The usual enormous office party was held a week later.

Not long after this we were shaken by a fatal accident. Helen Swift was a VSO nurse working at Gombak Hospital a few miles of very dangerous road out of Kuala Lumpur. She used a motorcycle for getting to and fro: a timber lorry killed her. My least pleasant task of all time (so far) was to go with Gerry Liston to the mortuary to identify her body; at the funeral a week later in St Francis Xavier Roman Catholic church in Petaling Jaya, the large congregation created such a moving atmosphere that Diana, who had undertaken to sing a short piece, could hardly do so for the lump in her throat.

More immediately distressing, and barely a month later, was the heart attack suffered by one of our drivers, Joned, in full view of all the library staff. By chance we had visiting us from London a trained welfare officer, Jan Webster, who applied resuscitation manually, but he died in the ambulance and we all went to the Muslim cemetery in Ampang for his burial the next day.

The zenith of an amateur conductor's efforts

The Philharmonic Society's committee had hoped to put me in charge for our second Christmas with them, but fortunately my official duties had been accepted as adequate excuse to limit my role to conducting the carols contributed by the chamber choir. Sarah and Louise arrived for their fourth holiday in time to enjoy the concerts and other festivities, including Jessica's fifth birthday party and a few days up in Fraser's Hill.

Since 1977 would be the Queen's jubilee year, we planned a very special chamber concert of works by a galaxy of British composers. We also took part in a poetry and music programme devised by our friend Tim Gee, head of chancery in the high commission who would later become consul-general in Istanbul and finally head of the FCO's Cultural Relations Department. More significant, however, were my plans to put on performances of Bach's *Mass in B minor*, since the required talent seemed to be almost all available, albeit in some areas somewhat diluted. As with flying, the opportunity might never recur. It is surely rare to be able to muster the five soloists needed for this work in an amateur group: we had a reliable soprano in Daphne Squire (Canadian), Diana was our mezzo, Helga Ziegler (Austrian) was our contralto, Leow Siak Fah (Chinese) was an operatic tenor who set me a challenge to moderate his style for the *Benedictus*, and Eddie Chin was the baritone.

Bearing in mind the proven versatility of the Malawian police bandsmen, an interview was arranged for me with the Royal Malaysia Police Band's director of music. Some of his musicians had already helped us in the Purcell *Fairy Queen* orchestra, but since they were nearly all Malays (and therefore Muslims) we wondered whether it was at all feasible to expect them to take part in what was one of the greatest Christian-inspired works for performances in the Anglican church of St Mary's on the *padang*. On hearing my frank explanation, the director reassured me immediately, dismissed my concern and expressed his belief in broadening his men's musical experience — especially into Bach. So our minimal string orchestra, led by Winnie Cheah, a local teacher, was augmented with six police bandsmen playing trumpets, oboes, a string bass and timpani. As before, Colin Stuart took care of the top trumpet. There were also four flutes of diverse nationality, a clarinet and a trombone. Crucially, too, we had Jim Chopyak, a Peace Corps volunteer, to play the horn obligato for *Quoniam*. In the absence of bassoons, however, we had to persuade Lawrence Wragg (a merchant banker) to use the reed stops on the pipe organ, although his reluctance to practise enough almost led to disaster. The missing rapport was only achieved with an extra lunch-time session after the final full rehearsal.

Worse problems had threatened in the final week when Jo Speelman, our continuo cellist, went into hospital for a hernia operation. We operated a contingency plan, asking our pianist friend, Esther Chan, to simulate a continuo line for the solo items on a small electric keyboard. Then came the surprise and a serious quandary — a smiling Jo presented himself with cello for the first performance. We could not possibly turn him away, yet he had been unable to rehearse at all and knew nothing of our cuts and other special markings. There certainly was more raggedness in the first performance than we had hoped. Even so, the five soloists and 25-piece orchestra did well, and the 50-strong chorus made a brave attempt to overcome a degree of under-rehearsal. But the proper spirit prevailed in the second performance, the work was favourably received by many and we were able to donate some of the proceeds to the Malaysian Association for the Blind. John Shaw, who was Acting High Commissioner at the time, wrote me a nice note of appreciation. Contrary to what most outsiders assumed, none of this intense activity was comprised within my official duties.

We were personally proud of Sarah, whose very musical playing of the flute obligato for the *Benedictus* had turned a few heads, and it was good for the second sopranos to have Louise among them, while Jessica was in the audience in the care of Potty Granny.

My mother had been under severe strain before my father died some 18 months earlier and was understandably taking time to recover. She stayed with us for nearly three months and saw much of Malaysia, coming with us on several trips out of Kuala Lumpur as well as sharing our busy life. Malaysian visual and plastic arts were quite sophisticated — witness their batik painting and decoration and some of their elaborate pottery — and this was more her line, although our attention was not restricted in any way to the performing arts. There were frequent exhibitions by local artists, sometimes on our premises, as also of foreign artists imported by the various 'cultural agencies' such as ourselves. The Swiss Ambassador was a regular attender of vernissages. He was the brother of Erni, a well-known painter in Switzerland, and we had the agreeable surprise of meeting him even more regularly in Romania after our transfer there.

Most imported exhibitions were of prints, posters or photographs, for it is unreasonable to expect owners of original works to lend them for exhibiting in places where conditions may not be under control and the handling *en route* may be risky. Durable items could, however, be circulated and my earliest such exercise in Malaysia was to mount Dennis Mitchell's bronzes (one of which is now in the Tate of St Ives). Later we exhibited a set of prints by Howard Hodgkin.

True to her name, Potty Granny went on a day trip to the ceramics department of the Mara Institute of Technology in Shah Allam. She was disconcerted to find that the clay was being

150

imported rather that dug up locally, and even more so to be asked to do a demonstration of throwing. Despite a wheel that rotated in the opposite direction to her own she managed to pass this ordeal first time — never a relaxing task! We also celebrated her sixty-ninth birthday, took her to Port Dixon and Malacca, managed a business with pleasure weekend in Penang, travelling via Ipoh and Taiping, and finally a most memorable trip to Kuching. Unfortunately, our colleague in charge of Sarawak, Andrew Norris, was on leave, but we had no room to manœuvre on dates. Thanks to Mr Chua, the senior member of local staff, and James the driver, we included a longhouse visit; and thanks to Hashim, the son of Haji Osman, we were privileged to visit the Istana by sampan across the river and to see the Rajah Brooke memorabilia.

Mid-tour leave: Seychelles, Kenya, Algiers and home

It may be thought that the link between the nitty-gritty of making cultural connections and the planning of elaborate globetrotting journeys is rather tenuous, but in my view there are important gains to be made from taking every opportunity of seeing one's work in a few familiar countries in perspective with others' work in many unknown countries. My family teases me about never wanting to make a simple journey from A to B and there may be an element of self-indulgence in such a habit. Even so, my mid-tour leave journey from Malawi via Zambia and Kenya was very instructive; and our family end of tour journeys from Malawi via Cape Town and from Japan via Hong Kong and India all served a good purpose, at the very least in helping to fill in the gaps in our geographical knowledge.

This time we combined these motives with a legitimate desire for a short break on sunny beaches and wanting to see our cousins in Naivasha and our diplomat friends in Algiers. To get from Kuala Lumpur to the Seychelles we had to change flights in Colombo, which gave me an opportunity to speak by telephone with my Sri Lankan friend, Lal Jayawardena. He had read economics at King's and since become a top civil servant and banker; we were to see more of him in Finland ten years later when he became director of the UN's World Institute for Development Economics Research (WIDER). Another pleasure in Colombo was to take lemon tea and ginger cake on the ocean-facing veranda of the Galle Face Hotel, served by waiters in traditional dress.

As our British Airways VC-10 approached Seychelles airport, the captain addressed us by saying: 'There is news of some sort of armed revolution on the ground here. Those of you planning to disembark may wish to reconsider.' We preferred to accept the advice of some fellow passengers who said they knew of a route to the Coral Strand Hotel that avoided the centre of the town. Even so, it was true that there had been a *coup d'état* while the current strong man was out of the country attending a Commonwealth conference, and our taxi was held briefly at gunpoint. After a quiet night we found that an emergency curfew had been decreed by radio and that no staff had been able to reach the hotel. Breakfast was being cooked and served by volunteers among the guests. Diana and Jessica were disappointed by a denial of the beach as being potentially dangerous, but by the afternoon we were allowed to go walking. Then a surprise connection developed through a stranger who knew Roland Stamp, our friend from Malawi music days who had been employed by the Electricity Corporation. He was now doing the same here and got police permission to drive from his home and have tea with us. News then came that a British Airways jumbo would be coming in the evening to rescue stranded passengers, and we reached Nairobi only a day late.

Our Nightingale cousins live a two-hour drive northwards up the Rift Valley, at their Nunjoro farm on the edge of the Kinankop escarpment overlooking Naivasha and the lake beyond. My father's first cousin Ted has already been mentioned in connection with my need for career advice, and his wife Billy is a formidable lady who shares with him a deep love and wide experience of Africa. Their four children Peter, Daphne, Charles and Richard are my second cousins, but we meet only at long intervals. This visit of only three days included walks for sighting colobus (black and white) monkeys, the viewing of an immense variety of birds and other wildlife around Lake Naivasha and Lake Nakuru, and an introduction to their turkey-raising work. Some 15 years were to pass before we had the chance again for a week there, on our retirement journey home from Ethiopia.

The route from Nairobi to Algiers, which had to be by Swissair via Zurich, was done with characteristic efficiency and punctuality. Margot and Brian Hitch (then the commercial counsellor and number two in the embassy) lived in a fine, cool house with a distant view of the sea — very Mediterranean in style and very peaceful. We called at the British Council's establishment just to satisfy curiosity, but remember best our visit to the Bey's palace and a supper picnic in the foothills of the Atlas mountains.

The final leg of this 12-day journey was by British Caledonian BAC 1-11 to Gatwick, but we could not go straight into our Bourne End house because we had been obliged to compromise with our tenants over the date of their removal, balancing their family's convenience against ours. This meant hiring a dormobile for ten days and 'going into orbit', taking Sarah and Louise out from Sherborne with some of their friends for a picnic, going to a couple of Aldeburgh festival concerts and attending a college lunch in Cambridge, relying meanwhile on the infinite hospitality of Peter and Kay Orr to look after our baggage.

Once in our house we were able to renew friendships by receiving rather than visiting, and the move two years earlier into the London commuter belt made this much easier. My somewhat misguided enthusiasm had made me sign up for some courses run by Staff Training Department. They always seem an attractive prospect, but when the time comes to interrupt one's leave there is a tendency to regret the commitment. In favour of them, however, is the social benefit of meeting new colleagues and the opportunity for a rapid updating on aspects of life at home, such as is needed for representing abroad. This time we had no complaints about six days spent on the arts in Britain and three days on trends in tertiary education in Britain.

In early August 1977 we went as a family by overnight motorrail to Stirling and drove on to stay with the Russells in Forglen House, Turriff, north of Aberdeen for five nights. Tris and Joan had befriended us in Kuala Lumpur, his family firm being owners of tea estates and our children being of similar ages. We did not know how or why they had acquired such an enormous mansion and whole wings were closed off, but we enjoyed a bothy ballad competition, fruit picking, bonfires, hedge cutting and a trip to

153

Banff on the north coast. The return journey southwards included a call on Isobel Duncan (ex-Malawi) in Glasgow, two nights with Diana's Aunt Sallie in Whickham near Newcastle, and a visit to Emmanuel Church in the village of Holcome north of Manchester where my great-grandfather, the Revd George Nightingale, had been the incumbent for 25 years.

Our final escapade was to live for a long weekend aboard *Shawford Lily* (the Olives' narrowboat moored on the canal in Bath), which we used as a base from which to see their production of *Fidelio* in which John Shirley-Quirk was singing; and then, joined by Peter and Pat Harrison on a beautiful autumn day, to voyage down to Bristol docks in company with the Shirley-Quirk's boat *Amelia di Liverpool*. Meanwhile, John Lawrence in Kuala Lumpur was keen for me to return to my desk so that he could take some leave and, although Diana and Jessica stayed on for another week to see the other two back to school, by mid-September we were all at work again.

An overseas arm for the IUC

Supervising the programme of cultural events tended to drag me into too much personal involvement and, since the work was not all that well appreciated, it was a welcome relief for me to take on the very different role of (effectively) the overseas arm of the Inter-University Council for Higher Education Overseas (IUC). This body, a postwar creation charged with founding new universities in all those countries in the process of becoming independent, achieved some very distinguished establishments, including the universities of Ibadan and Makerere. All five universities in Malaysia relied heavily on its services, which were funded by the ODA, but its administration was soon to be merged into our Higher Education Division. Our 'specialist tourist' category of expert visitor or academic consultant overlapped with the IUC's own programme of academic staff exchanges and interdepartmental links. Similarly, the IUC's training awards overlapped many other sources. In brief, there was a plethora of funding agencies for all levels of academic liaison and it was my task to draw the threads together in so far as British contributions could be monitored coherently. Besides the universities, there were half a

154

dozen research institutes and more than 20 professional associations, all eager for expert advice.

Focusing on this work was helped by having to field a visit by the IUC's director, Richard Griffiths, during John's short leave, and by a repeat of Butterworth and Beavan's 1976 visit in January 1978, for which my comprehensive documentation provided the background. Another development during this time was the publication of the think-tank (Central Policy Review Staff) report on overseas representation. Our director-general then instructed us to lobby local heavyweights and to get them to write letters to the Foreign Secretary (then Dr David Owen) seeking to prevent our proposed abolition. Several powerful letters were obtained and duly transmitted.

Before the end of 1977, however, our most significant visitor was the Assistant Director-General, Tony Sherwood, who had Malaysia in his parish and came to carry out a policy inspection. Such 'visiting firemen' from London are a regular feature of life in posts abroad, but the way you handle them requires a subtle appraisal of their declared purposes, their self-esteem and your own view of their usefulness or potential for mischief. Since overseeing the Penang office was one of my more pleasurable duties, it fell to me to fly up with the ADG and to do my best to impress him with the quality of our contacts in the north.

Diana and Jessica joined us at the weekend and we were all accommodated together in the exclusive Penang Club at the generous insistence of Mr I. K. Cheah, a local Chinese Malaysian businessman. After a gruelling series of appointments we began dining quietly in the club, but our distinguished guest was informed politely by the waiter that it was customary to wear a tie in the evenings. The locally accepted alternative was to wear a batik shirt with a mandarin collar and it was my fault for failing to notice his open neck. My nervous observation of his surprised reluctance to conform was relieved when he accepted the tie proffered by the club's obliging servant. In slight defiance, how-ever (it was indeed hot and sticky), he promptly undid his shirt-sleeves and allowed them to flop around ostentatiously. Relatively relaxed conversation then continued and, at this point, Jessica aged six appeared to say goodnight. She quite spontaneously kissed Tony Sherwood, including him in the family round with Diana and me. Ever seen a man melt? He had a reputation for toughness, but was also known to be a proud father of four and he was away from home. Since that moment my firm belief has been that Jessica secured my next posting (on promotion) to Romania.

The news of it lay several months ahead and, although essentially welcome, it was greeted by the family as a very mixed blessing. At the end of the year Diana had enjoyed a great success in the role of Madame Dubonnet (in some dazzling costumes and with several appropriate poses) in a local production of *The Boyfriend*. Our third Christmas had been enlivened by a change of High Commissioner and invitations from Sir Donald and Lady Ruth Hawley to make music at Carcosa, the British high commissioner's very impressive and historic residence. Also, we had just managed to move house from Damansara Heights to Jalan Ampang on the other side of town to be nearer the British Army School in which Diana was teaching music part time in return for the admission of Jessica slightly below the normal age. The bungalow was owned by the Rubber Research Institute and was next door to our friends Peter and Waveney Jenkins. He has been chairman of the local chamber of commerce for many years and she is a sculptress of considerable repute. So the idea of moving before a full tour had been completed was not very popular, although there was time enough for plenty of excitements yet.

Despite the IUC visitation we managed to take a little local leave in January 1978, travelling with all five of us by car to Singapore and enjoying the hospitality of Robert and Martina Frost for a few days. Robert's father Richard Frost had been a long-serving British Council representative — oscillating between Nairobi and Oxford as it was once possible to do, more or less — and wrote an excellent account of postwar pre-independence Kenya entitled *Race Against Time*. So Robert is one of a small band of second-generation British Council colleagues. He and Martina, who comes from the very small Romansch-speaking Swiss minority, have a house in Marlow, not far from the one we had in Bourne End, and their daughter went to the same girls' prep school in High Wycombe as our Jessica. We took them to Fraser's Hill in

156

April and, some 16 years later, we were able to take a holiday in Cyprus, using their flat in Nicosia as a base and benefiting again from their lively hospitality.

Sailing rather than flying, and yet more music
To obtain a pilot's licence it would have been necessary to have invested in many more hours of practising solo cross-country flying and passing more exams. After David Bates's departure my enthusiasm waned. There seemed to be less time than ever and other uses for our money, but we continued to patronize the Selangor Flying Club for social purposes. It was a pleasantly airy place in which to entertain visitors to a light lunch and was only a few minutes' drive away from town. It became clear that trips to the coast at Port Dixon were more therapeutic for the family and, after several attempts at racing in 'lasers', we discovered that one GP14 sailing dinghy remained from the half dozen once provided by a British Army recreational fund. It was strictly the responsibility of the defence attaché in the high commission, but we had a free hand to use it. Cannibalizing the remains of some of the others made the vessel complete, but it leaked faster than we could bail out on the first short trial. After applying no fewer than five fibreglass patches the boat was seaworthy and fit to take anyone interested.

Our favourite place to stay nearby was the Malaysian railway cottage on the headland, which had a panoramic view of the Straits of Malacca, a sea lane so busy that we counted as many as 11 ships visible at once. Here we took John and Pat Shirley-Quirk during their rare escape from John's singing career. There was an unfortunate misunderstanding over his willingness to do a recital while on holiday, but we arranged a master class for local singers, and our multiracial chamber choir, which had an ever expanding repertoire, submitted to an 'observed rehearsal' of four contrasting pieces, with buffet supper and improved performance to round off the evening. We also took them for a weekend in Penang.

The membership of the chamber choir was very near the ideal in numbers and variety — nine women and six men offering divisible upper and lower parts according to need within reason. A pair of friends formed the loyal core of the upper voices — Ivy Daud and

157

Khaw Yen Yen. Ivy was a princess of the Negri-Sembilan royal house and Yen Yen was a doctor specializing in gynaecology; about this time she married an American diplomat and ten years later we visited them near Washington DC. Chew Hock Ping was our most stalwart tenor and Eddie Chin a firm bass. The European (or as the Japanese say 'Caucasian') expatriate membership was drawn from the shifting population, but Malcolm Cooper (who did some conducting too) and Richard Fisher (teaching in Seremban) together with Daphne and Gordon 'Buff' Squire (Canadians) and Francis Carnwath (merchant banker) formed the basis. Ling Ai Ee, a near-professional pianist obliged by her parents to be a doctor, also sang with us, as did Frank Doyle (a Catholic priest) and Mary-Ann and Peter Lawrence (who were local, although their names would suggest otherwise).

An invitation that stretched my programming ingenuity to the limit came through Ivy Daud from the Lake Club to entertain its St David's Society diners on 1 March. We learnt that the previous year they had had a cabaret, so we doubted our suitability to follow that sort of act. In the event we need not have worried, despite my greater nervousness about that than about any other undertaking. By finding some four-part arrangements of Welsh folk songs and, with an especially vigorous rendering of *Men of Harlech*, we made them 'tingle' all right and got plenty of encores. Two months later we put an expanded programme of folk-song settings, jazz Bach 'swingles' and some Gilbert and Sullivan excerpts into one of our regular chamber concert series, and repeated it by invitation the following night at Carcosa, the High Commissioner's residence.

A strongly contrasting exercise was my attempt at a multimedia presentation of Vaughan Williams's *Job: A Masque for Dancing*, which was inspired by William Blake's *Illustrations to the Book of Job*. The published orchestral score contains stage directions for the ballet (first produced in 1931 and revived in 1948) so my scheme entitled *New Life for a Neglected Ballet* required a combination of three systems — a recording of the music to be heard stereophonically, transparencies of Blake's 21 engravings for the overhead projector, and about 100 slides of the stage directions (to indicate the narrative) for projection on a second screen.

Seated between the two visual media with the score on a stand, with concentrated practice it was just possible for me to co-ordinate each of them as the music progressed. The audience was small and select but appreciative.

Coming within sight of the end of our time it was pleasing to find that one or two conductors less transient than ourselves were emerging. Dr Oliver Thevathasan had taken on the chorus of the Philharmonic Society of Selangor two years back, and Mervyn Peters put on three performances of Haydn's *Creation* as the last major effort in which we took part as soloists.

A final stint acting in charge

In mid-April John Lawrence went off for ten weeks' home leave, coming back just a couple of weeks before our own departure in mid-July. Confirmation of our posting to Romania came before he left, with an instruction to learn as much French as possible in the remaining three months and letting me know that six weeks of intensive Romanian language tuition would begin as soon as we got home. The Alliance Française accepted my enrolment the next day for two two-hour morning sessions each week.

The publication of the think-tank report (mentioned above) had stimulated some articles in the British Council's house journal (then called *Compass*) on the various options being canvassed for the future pattern of representational services overseas. My contri-bution sought to elucidate the functions of a British embassy or high commission compared with a British Council establishment in terms of PECDAIC (political, economic, commercial, defence, aid, information and consular) and ESC (education, science and culture). Entitled 'Shopkeepers with Music', the article drew on my Arts Division background to argue that there was no need for us to continue to be derided as 'a nation of shopkeepers in a land without music' provided we were prepared to accept a degree of integration of the staff devoted to PECDAIC and ESC. This was heresy, as seen from London, but in the middle of John's absence we were officially asked to discuss with our high commission colleagues the precise pros and cons, in the particular Malaysian context, of various types of integration with the diplomatic service and of the diplomatization of our staff. In due course reports on this subject from all over the world were collated in London and a vague consensus emerged, which has lasted a long time now, the general belief being that the public is largely indifferent to the status of individuals (whatever governments may think) but that the British Council needs separate premises (if nothing else) for effective working. Even so, much work went into analysing tangible and intangible benefits, drawbacks and possible physical arrangements before we could respond adequately.

Another inescapable task was the writing of a country brief and annual review of 1977/8 for Malaysia, in the prescribed format, plus a statistical profile, running to 12 pages in all. No comment was made on my unauthorized innovation of unconventionally classifying all our work as services to the public, to the government or to individuals.

This and the two earlier periods of cultivating a mentality of 'the buck stops here' were a good preparation for my subsequent postings in command of my own ship, however small. No longer 'reluctant to occupy the middle ground' (as had once been said), being temporarily in charge required of me several extra roles in relation to senior colleagues, such as welcoming John Dobson on his first arrival for Sabah and giving farewell parties for Malcolm and Jane Cooper and for Bryson and Alma McAdam. More significant perhaps was the experience of attending weekly 'prayer meetings' in the high commission, being sensitized to the politico-economic realities that preoccupy HM missions abroad and being privy to the funding problems of our sponsoring departments — the FCO and ODA. Before long similar issues would become familiar to me when working inside the embassy in Bucharest. Acquiring a sense of British interests, rather than just British Council interests, was a gradual process, exemplified in the concern felt in the high commission that we should maintain our presence in Sabah and Sarawak following the withdrawal of deputy high commissioners from Kota Kinabalu and Kuching.

Reverting to the human aspects, a delightful and moving incident should be recorded. Through a common interest in music we had come to know Professor Marian Soltys and his wife Audrey. He was a distinguished veterinary microbiologist working, as a retirement job, in the agricultural university, Universiti Pertanian

Malaysia. (They later went to Guelph in Ontario where we stayed with them in 1988.) One of our visitors to Malaysia was another academic of Polish origin, Professor Rotblatt, a specialist in medical physics and famous for organizing the series of Pugwash conferences. The Universiti Teknologi was celebrating its first con-vocation with a long invitation list. Soltys and Rotblatt, in ignorance of each other's presence and not having met since leav-ing Poland some 40 years earlier, each recognized his long-lost friend in a corridor and fell back in amazement before embracing ecstatically. It was a heart-warming scene to witness.

An account of my stewardship, or 'handing back notes' for John's return, mentioned the invaluable help of Jean Malcolm who had come earlier in the year, both to keep alive the science education contacts after David Bates's departure and to fill the gap before my successor, Julian Davey, could arrive. In writing my 'continuity notes' for her and for him, mention is made of a second device, similar to the 'Bruce boards' in Aids and Displays, enabling a visual check to be kept on the plethora of academic and professional visitors we were handling. Jean had worked in London for many years before getting a post in Tanzania, and she later went to Botswana before returning to London. Her many friends were very mournful at her sudden death, caused indirectly by a minor car accident.

A more immediate tragedy in Malaysia was the death of Richard Sherrington, a much respected colleague in the English teaching field, who unluckily had happened to be on board the Boeing 737 that was hijacked between Penang and Kuala Lumpur and, after trying to land in Singapore, had plunged into the muddy swamps near Johore Bahru. A ministerial armed bodyguard had been allowed onto the aircraft and had engaged in an argument with the pilot, but other than that little explanation of the incident has ever emerged. Security at the Penang end was notoriously lax. We spent a panicky morning in the office trying to answer demands from London that we obtain local confirmation of the names on the passenger list. In the meanwhile, Richard's distraught wife had been waiting at Heathrow to meet the connecting flight he had failed to take.

It was inevitable that we would be out every evening of our final two weeks, but the most memorable was the chamber choir's farewell dinner in the best Chinese restaurant, the Imperial Room. They presented us with a picture of a street scene with satay sellers' stalls and we sang informally till late. Jessica's school term reached a convenient end and, in mid-July, we took a Thai International flight to Bangkok with a fantastic breakfast *en route*.

Our night in the Hotel Oriental was at KLM's expense because our onward booking to Athens was with them. In spite of sleeping a great deal and enjoying room service, we managed to visit 'The House on the Klong' and to take a trip in one of those terrifyingly powerful outboard-engined boats up to the Grand Palace. We had hoped to see Julian and Guinevere Harvey in Athens, but the dates did not fit so they had booked us into a modest hotel. The city was hot and dusty, so we chose to take a one-day cruise to the islands of Aegina, Poros and Hydra. In the evening Iain Sutherland entertained us in his ambassadorial residence — we had delivered a present for his daughter from our Sarah: they were school friends. An Air France flight to Paris enabled us to spend a day in the suburb of Esbly visiting the family with whom Louise was staying for two weeks of 'French immersion'. Two days later Peter Harrison (ex-Malawi) met us at Heathrow and took us to our Bourne End house, which he and Pat had been borrowing. After an all too short weekend for settling in, my daily commute to London for Romanian language tuition began.

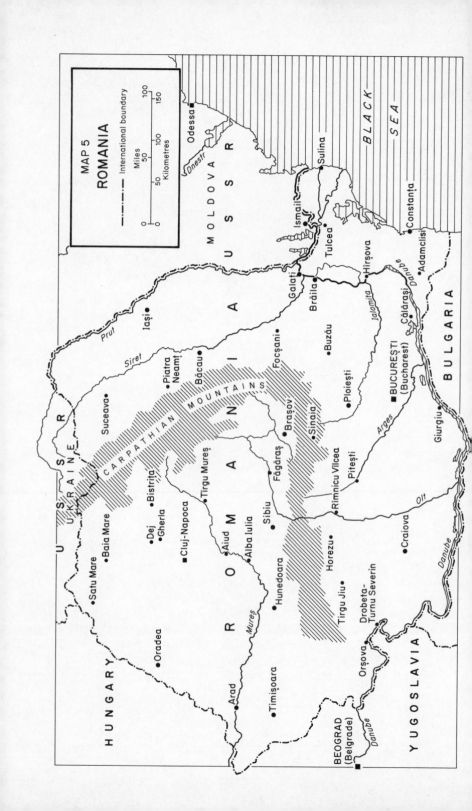

11

Romania in Decline: The Bear in the Balkans

The prospect of a one-to-one pupil–teacher relationship caused me some quiet worries for fear it might overstretch my rather limited language-learning capacity. Would the attempt drive both parties to distraction? Fortunately, my teacher Lucian Gafton, who was an Orthodox priest attached part time to the London University chaplaincy, had similar misgivings and at our first session we agreed to review the state of our nerves at the end of the first week. When that moment came we felt that reasonable progress had been made and that neither of us was feeling undue strain. Happily, my prep school Latin was proving a considerable asset, for Romanian is the fifth (and largely ignored) Romance language of Europe. It has survived in a form very similar to Italian and derives from the language of the Emperor Trajan's legions and their creation of the province of Dacia Felix. The Slav and Turkish elements constitute a mere 15 per cent, so the bulk of the vocabulary is recognizably Roman and, as is often said, the language remains a fiercely defended island in a Slav-speaking sea.

Language tuition and an overland journey
Lucian Gafton also did some work for the Romanian section of the BBC World Service in Bush House. He was in voluntary exile

taking refuge from the harassment of the communist regime. (We did once manage to call on his father who was the Bishop of Rimnicu Vilcea.) Staff Training Department had arranged for me to be given the maximum allowance of 180 hours of instruction, so we settled down to a routine of two sessions of an hour and a half each morning and afternoon — 6 hours a day for five days making 30 a week for six weeks. At the end of this time it was just possible for me to maintain a halting conversation with a sympathetic listener, thus providing a solid foundation for subsequent lessons with Costache Popa. We contrived to vary the teaching/learning process and enjoyed compatible values, but it could otherwise have been a very trying experience for both parties.

Meanwhile, the family enjoyed a summer holiday based around our Bourne End house. Our heavy baggage had been consigned directly from Malaysia by sea to the port of Bremen with the intention that it would be sent from there by road into Romania, but it was actually put into a rail wagon and effectively lost for several months — see below. Our car had also been shipped, but to Avonmouth docks from where Diana retrieved it, but events were to prove that we would have been wiser to have sold it in Kuala Lumpur and begun again with a new car for Bucharest — see further below. The consequences of both these errors took some time to emerge. We got used to living for many months with what could be packed into a few suitcases and a trunk or two, within the limits allowed for air freight, and an ordinary car could not take much more. After many journeys to and from posts by sea and air, the prospect of driving to a post in our own car some 1800 miles right across Europe was a novel challenge requiring plans and preparations of a very different sort; more like the type of expedition done in my student days in the mid-1950s to Italy, Turkey and Austria.

Being on the list of people 'suitable for sensitive posts' had nearly landed us in Cape Town and was now at least partially responsible for assigning us to an eastern bloc country in which the British Council had to operate from within an embassy. Though not the case in Poland or Yugoslavia, in the Soviet Union itself and in East Germany, Czechoslovakia, Hungary, Romania and Bulgaria our staff needed the protection of a diplomatic umbrella and this necessarily implied certain reciprocal obligations. Consequently, during my last two weeks in London more of my briefings than normal were in FCO departments, especially in Cultural Relations. The core of my British Council brief was to engage energetically in setting up a separate cultural centre outside the embassy (as envisaged by the 1978 Cultural Agreement), but as will be seen, this project fell victim to the 1979 Thatcher cuts and it took another ten years (and a bloody counter-revolution) before it could be realized.

Our preparations reached a climax in mid-September when Sarah and Louise went back to Sherborne, but the previous weekend had seen us doing a crazily spontaneous dash by shuttle to Glasgow, at the invitation of the Shirley-Quirks to stay a night in Fitzroy Maclean's hotel, Creggans, on Loch Fyne. A few years earlier John had bought some land for tree planting under a private forestry scheme, and the excuse was to see how the plantation was doing. The conifers were about two feet tall. We went looking for the site some 15 years later, long after John had sold it, but could not identify it.

At last we set off, with Jessica aged nearly seven squeezed into the middle of the back seat, surrounded by my cello, boxes of apples and overnight bags, and we made our first night stop in Canterbury ready for an early crossing from Dover to Ostend. It was almost a case of 'set a course east-south-east and keep driving': we spent the second night in Brussels and the third in Wurzburg, followed by two nights in Vienna with Klaus and Helga Ziegler, formerly of the Austrian embassy in Kuala Lumpur and now back in the Austrian foreign ministry. We then carried on, but just across the Hungarian border we were beguiled by a notice no musician could ignore — Haydn's birthplace signposted as only four kilometres off the main road. We found that the simplicity of the wheelwright's house had been beautifully preserved. In other respects, however, crossing from west to east is unnerving for the first time; Diana and Jessica registered a distinct lowering of spirits, brought on (as expected) by witnessing the gradual deterioration in the state of the countryside. Our stop in Budapest was with our colleague of the time, Tom Stones, in the fine vaulted house allocated to the cultural attaché, high on the Buda side overlooking the river and Pest beyond. Crossing our last border we reached Cluj-Napoca in northwestern Transylvania for the seventh night, and late the next evening we were welcomed by Richard Timms in the spacious second-floor flat at Aleea Alexandru 5, Bucharest. He had arranged two handing-over parties on successive evenings, one for the educational and scientific contacts and the other for the cultural ones, and on the fourth day he left.

What was the state of affairs in Romania in the late 1970s? And what did our mentors think we should be trying to do? The ruling Partidul Communist Roman indulged in an annual celebration of 23 August 1944, the date for which they claimed the credit for deposing the Fascist dictator Antonescu and changing sides in the Second World War. In fact it was the young and courageous King Michael who had taken the immense risk of arresting Antonescu personally when faced with the inevitability of the Red Army advance and the Russian takeover of his country. At this moment the communists were very few in number and were incapable of doing what they subsequently claimed to have done, but Stalin used the same techniques of intimidation and subversion that were effective in the other satellite states of eastern Europe and by 1948 the King was obliged to abdicate. For 17 years, until 1965, the standard policy of decimating the intelligentsia was pursued: out of 130,000 imprisoned only 25,000 emerged alive. (A distinguished professor of economics, Dan Hurmuzescu, was one such survivor whom we knew.) The deal with the Russians in the mid-1960s was that Ceauşescu could follow a pseudo-independent line in foreign policy provided he maintained strict internal security. (The Hungarians chose the other option of relatively loose internal control but supporting the Soviet line in foreign relations.) The West proceeded to bolster Romania as a thorn in the flesh of the Warsaw Pact. President Nixon visited Bucharest and the Americans opened their only library in eastern Europe, the Israelis opened their only embassy in eastern Europe, and — sad to relate — we British invited Ceausescu and his wife for a state visit and entertainment by HM the Queen. This was largely in return for a multimillion pound contract for British Aerospace to supply BAC 1-11 aircraft and spares for TAROM, the national flag carrier. There was also a curious plan for the Romanians to build them under licence and sell them to the Chinese.

The afterglow of this exercise in Anglo-Romanian fraternity in the summer of 1978 was still being nurtured when we arrived in the autumn, but the royal involvement with a regime of dubious credentials had been viewed very equivocally in Britain. An article by Bernard Levin in *The Times* entitled 'And how is your family, Mr Ceauşescu?' documented the 13 members of his family occupying government positions. Decline from the heyday of the mid-1970s had already begun; hard currency loans had encouraged the overdevelopment of industry at the expense of collectivized agriculture and, in the 1980s, the population was deprived of food so that it could be exported to earn the hard currency needed to repay the loans. The events of 1989 were not even dreamed of.

The Manchester Royal Exchange Theatre Company

The British Council occupied a few rooms in a temporary building, best described as 'a shack in the embassy compound', but more colourfully mentioned by a visitor as 'portaloo premises', a phrase which offended the sensibilities of some colleagues in London but which served the useful purpose of shocking them into some grasp of the true situation. We had little to be proud of, but the challenge for me — once the hope of money for a cultural centre had been abandoned — was to develop a proudly-labelled BIBLIOTECA BRITANICA in what there was. Outside the physical constraints our activity was subject to control by the bureaucracy of a fiercely totalitarian state, requiring us to renegotiate a cultural exchange programme every two years. My participation in doing this in London in January 1979 for the 1979–81 programme enabled me in due course to obtain much better terms when repeating the task for 1981–83, by which time our leading colleagues, both from the FCO's cultural relations department (CRD) and from the British Council, had changed. We were designated as the agents for the British side, so on the ground in Bucharest we dealt with the relevant Romanian bodies.

The State Impresario Agency of Romania (ARIA) had agreed with my predecessor to host three performances of Shakespeare's *Winter's Tale* by this Manchester company as part of its London-organized drama tour. Within less than a month of our arrival, hardly having found our feet, we were faced with the logistical demands of such a tour — and we remembered the Watford Palace Theatre Company in Kuala Lumpur only too well. Neither the choice of play nor the venue were entirely to our taste. There had been a disastrous fire on the main stage of the National Theatre, so only the smaller stage, the Sala Mica, was available, although the foyer was serviceable. Such was the thirst for live theatre from the West that tickets were sold out the day they were first offered.

By arrangement with the Office for Exhibitions, a didactic display prepared in London depicting 'The Age of Shakespeare' was mounted in the foyer. It helped our publicity, as did a well-timed issue of the embassy's colourful periodical, *Panoramic Britanic*, depicting the company's home stage, constructed like a moon-landing module inside the old Royal (cotton) Exchange; but a family crisis occurred during its preparation when an unstable sculpture toppled over and caught part of Jessica's foot on the way down. Her leather shoe saved the instep from worse injury, but the cut needed emergency stitching in conditions of very dubious hygiene, and with no anaesthetic beyond my sympathetic cooing. That was a most inauspicious beginning, but worse melodramas lay ahead.

Audiences were appreciative and all seemed well, but the cast was in deep trouble. During the second night some members questioned whether one young actress playing a small part was fit to go on. The efforts of the company manager, John Grant, to resolve her problems that evening degenerated into hysterical outbursts which disturbed the whole of the Hotel Minerva. A Romanian doctor attempted sedation and an understudy was called for the third and last night, but by that time the patient had become so violent and abusive that her friends in the cast had to operate a roster to watch and control her.

A succession of *Salvarea* doctors of the Romanian ambulance service could make no firm diagnosis. Withdrawal symptoms were assumed, but they could not be sure what drugs she had been on and each successive injection failed to knock her out. The day of departure became a nightmare. We enlisted the support of HM

170

Consul to ensure that the local British Airways manager knew the score. The pilot might be reluctant to take a potentially violent passenger, but if so he needed to face the likely consequences of leaving her behind — indefinite incarceration in a Romanian psychiatric ward!

We had planned a relaxing farewell buffet lunch in our spacious flat for the whole company, in spite of having to borrow most of the equipment from our defence attaché neighbours in the flat below, James and Ann Wilson (our heavy baggage from Malaysia was delayed). The company duly assembled *en route* for the airport and they all did their best to conceal the tension caused by the actress. She had to be held down on our spare bed by relays of two men (for strength) and two women (for sympathy). After each 'shift' we noticed some in tears taking refuge on the balcony. Then we summoned a fifth doctor and yet another ambulance for the final run to the airport, trusting that this time a 'cocktail' of sedatives would keep her quiet. We managed to get her through the system, thanks partly to diplomatic privilege, without too many questions being asked, but the airport authorities did make our little group of embassy officials remain with them in the control tower until the British Airways Trident was well away and showed no signs of turning back.

Some weeks later we learnt that the company had sat close round the patient and sung boisterously to drown her complaints, but that other passengers had hardly noticed. We also heard that her father had been so shocked on meeting the flight at Heathrow that he had suffered a mild heart attack. But a happy ending did emerge some years later when we realized that the whole episode had produced no long-term damage. Our young actress had begun to appear on television.

Learning the ropes in a new parish
To work from within an embassy wearing two hats, both as cultural attaché and as British Council representative, and to work on the far side of what had been an Iron Curtain but had become more of a currency and information barrier, was a salutary experience, bringing home to me (and most who do it) the serious risks then inherent in such acute discrepancies between the two

halves of Europe. It was a time bomb quietly ticking away and being ignored by many people necessarily preoccupied with Africa, Asia and the Caribbean. Few in the Free World had any understanding of the day-to-day problems of ordinary people on the other side, and the few resident foreigners who had had the experience found their accounts regarded with some incredulity.

Getting to grips was a three-stage process. First, who's who among the colleagues? Next, who's who in which institutions and organizations in Bucharest? And finally, which people and places needed our attention in the country at large? In the 'portaloo' my closest collaborator was Jenny Garland, assistant cultural attaché, and we relied for support on just two Romanian ladies — the librarian Cornelia Ionescu and our secretary Aura Vlad. Half way through my time Jenny was replaced by Theresa Kassell and, after a prolonged battle, it was accepted that running a library single handed was nonsensical, so we got a second and later a third assistant. Across the courtyard in chancery was HMA Reggie Secondé (later Paul Holmer), and those who filled the posts of head of Chancery (a designation more recently abandoned in favour of deputy head of Mission), first secretary, defence attaché and commercial counsellor. Many will be named as close friends later. Additionally, we also relied on the consular and administrative staff on the ground floor for many essential services, and these we enjoyed in the form of hidden benefits, so distorting the image of our budget if viewed simplistically in London. The cost of separation had to be estimated.

The principle enshrined in the exchange programme was that of reciprocity, but to apply this in practice between unequal partners was not simple. The inequality of Britain and Romania need not be laboured; it was a factor in almost every form of cooperation, especially in the movement of people. The desire was to avoid the transfer of hard currency, so that the sending side paid an airfare and the receiving side stood the onshore costs. The programme provided so many man weeks of short-term visits and so many man months of longer-term study in each direction. Under this scheme, we had a handful of British lectors in Romanian universities and a trickle of postgraduate research students, all operating under conditions that required us to provide (outside the formal

172

Home-made punt on the Cam. BN punting with (back to camera) Roderick Fisher and Mary Elspeth Milford, and (facing camera) Erica Greenwood and Peter Greig, 8 June 1954.

Alhaji Ahmed Tijjani Malumfashi, MBE, Senior Livestock
Superintendent, Northern Nigeria, 1958.

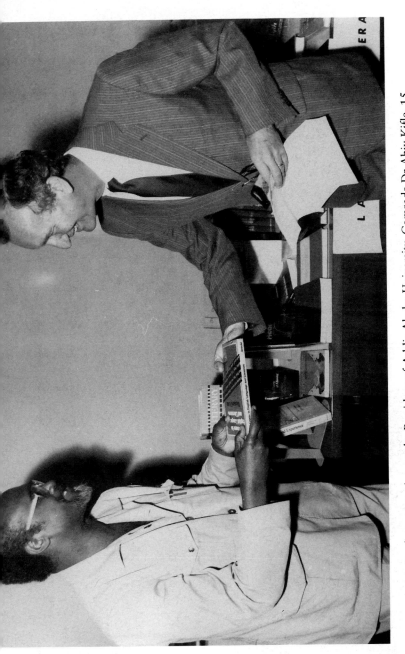

Book presentation to the President of Addis Ababa University, Comrade Dr Abiy Kifle, 15 December 1988.

Annual Staff Lunch-party in Addis Ababa, Ethiopia, on the day of the EPRDF take-over, 27 May 1991 (The whole staff plus the five who went to the Bank for the payday cash)

terms) various forms of support. There was a steady stream of academic visitors, coming or going for two or three weeks, seeking to impart advice or to gather information, and all were subject to being proposed and accepted (or vetoed) by the controlling Ministry of Education. Similarly, in the cultural field the Council for Culture and Socialist Education was obliged by the system to apply ideological criteria when considering a proposal. It was our standard practice to provide some sort of entertainment, reception, drinks party or meal for visitors and their hosts and new contacts roughly once a week. In this way, several of the Romanian officials were regularly in our flat and became as friendly as their constraints would allow, but all invitations were monitored by the Party cells and the Securitate, and only a very few Romanians were 'licensed' to invite us into their homes. As our invitations were often intercepted and held until after the event, we adopted the habit of sending two to each person, one to a home address. The recipient would then at least know and could take the initiative in seeking permission to attend.

At the London end of this network, besides our own HQ and the FCO, we provided 'overseas arm' services for the Great Britain East Europe Centre (then in Knightsbridge) and acted as a long stop to sort out last minute muddles or non-communication for Royal Society and British Academy visitors. It is a fairly widespread view, not just when dealing with eastern Europe, that 'we prefer to run it directly ourselves' until things fall apart and then 'Auntie Council will help us back onto the rails'.

Having made introductory calls on most of the significant people and places in Bucharest, the third stage was to begin a series of familiarization trips to the provincial centres. A day trip to Piteşti was encouraged by Dr André Bantaş who held a part-time post as head of the English department at the Institut Pedagogic, now incorporated into the Higher Education Institute. We took a book presentation of 60 volumes of much needed reference works and teaching texts which had been unaccountably held up for almost two years. The transfer of our Age of Shakespeare exhibition to Turgu Mureş gave me an excuse for a night in the centre of Transylvania, remembered chiefly for a sudden drop in temperature to −18 °C, forcing me into a panic purchase of a sheepskin-lined hat of distinctly Germanic design, and which remains serviceable to this day. More important was an 18-hour day in Iași, the old capital of Moldavia, where Tim Williams was our lector needing a 'pastoral' visit. This was done by taking the night train in both directions — a recipe for appreciating one's own bed on the third night! Finally, a much shorter day return by train to Craiova was squeezed in before Christmas to see how our newly-arrived lector, Tony Bakes, was settling into the university's modern languages department. The Museum of Art there is in an exceptionally fine French baroque-style building of 1908 vintage. It housed the Polish government in exile taking refuge *en route* for London in 1940, and in 1944 Tito lived in it while planning the liberation of Belgrade.

Excursions to Cluj and other points northwest had to wait until the new year, but by the end of 1979 we could claim to have covered most of my parish except the Danube delta area. It was certainly a considerable privilege to have the freedom to travel throughout such a very varied and beautiful country, sadly misgoverned though it was. The great crescent of the Carpathian Mountains dominates the geography, and for many centuries it constituted the barrier between Christendom and Islam, between the Habsburg and Ottoman empires. The naturally attractive features of river, forest and high grassland were enhanced by many examples of architectural excellence, including the fortified churches of Transylvania, the painted monasteries of Moldavia and the wooden churches of the Maramureș border country. Nor could the many Roman and Hellenistic remains be overlooked. Of closer personal significance was the style of city buildings, especially in Bucharest, which had been laid out with broad boulevards at the end of the nineteenth century and along which public premises and private mansions under mixed Franco-German influence had been built.

Domestically, this was very much to the advantage of foreign residents able to use the leverage of hard currency payments, and we were no exception. Our embassy had for many years rented a block, better described as three single-storeyed houses on top of each other than as flats: the bottom one was allocated to the commercial counsellor, the middle one to the defence attaché and

174

the top one to culture. They had been built by an Armenian exile in a vaguely baronial style, probably in the 1920s, so it was ironic that of all our postings our best accommodation should have been in Romania, and we stayed in the same place for all three years. (The only other posting where we did not have to move for some reason was in Ethiopia.) So when Sarah and Louise arrived for their first Romanian Christmas (by Swissair this time) they had plenty of warm space to appreciate, although not much equipment, our heavy baggage being still untraceable, apparently lost somewhere in central Europe, but eventually found shunted into a siding, covered in snow and delivered unharmed four months late.

Lieutenant Colonel James Wilson, in the middle flat, was also a lay reader of long standing and was filling an interregnum by running the services in the BISERICA ANGLICANA, the curious English church built in red brick a short walk from the embassy compound. It was therefore natural for me to be expected to rehearse an embassy-based choir for my first of three annual carol services. By the third year we had introduced some stringed instruments and mixed a short section of Schutz's *Christmas Story* in with the carols. This arose from our friendship with Reinhardt Kraus, a German diplomat and fanatical violinist who was very keen on *hausmusik*. Another member of our group was Mary Ann Ignatius, who was in charge of the American library; but it was a couple of professionals, Ivan and Marianne Kauntz-Jakobovitz, joining us on violin and cello, who provided a breakthrough. Subsequently, we were able to perform Vivaldi's very sensuous setting of *Stabat Mater* in the German Lutheran church, with Diana singing the solo mezzo-soprano part accompanied by a string quartet and double bass — these were professionals who found my amateur conducting skills acceptable. We also sang with the Lutherans in one or two German-language performances, but the scope for unofficial music was otherwise very limited.

The importance of being squeaky clean
We experienced no culture shock comparable to that in Japan, but the move from Malaysia to Romania did shock me into realizing how little of the British Council's received wisdom and well-tried orthodox working practices were being applied in eastern Europe.

Successive incumbents seemed to have been allowed to shelter within an embassy and use the false excuse of abnormality. Given that the diplomatic umbrella was indispensable for getting any work done at all, the other differences from a normal British Council role had been overplayed. Hence my determination to make the Bucharest office catch up with the rest of the organization by emphasizing the two hats principle, namely that if you played your cards carefully you could get the best of both worlds rather than the worst of each. Hence also the introduction of our own letterhead modelled on that of the commercial section, the drafting of properly forthright aims and objectives seven years after the rest of the British Council had accepted them as mandatory, and the merging of embassy and British Council stocks of documentary films ten years after the policy had been agreed.

Surrounded by an ideologically hostile regime, however, it was necessary for personal conduct to be much more circumspect than in an open society. Cultural work may be regarded as innocent and its practitioners to be without any secrets worth divulging, yet it is common knowledge that competing intelligence organizations are constantly on the alert for opportunities to blackmail any individual who commits either sexual or financial indiscretions.

The grey area of currency dealings was the subject of a strictly-worded embassy circular — grey because there were three or four 'currencies' in use: the Romanian lei (exchangeable at the official rate, or at two and a half times that on the black market), the US dollar (illegal for Romanians to hold), gold-wrapped Kent cigarettes (in packets of 20 or cartons of 200) and bottles of whisky. The official line was that on no account should any of us offer Kent or whisky as payment for goods or services, although the odd packet or bottle was allowed as necessary inducement or due appreciation. Whatever other privileged people might do, we the British, the Americans and the Canadians would remain squeaky clean.

An incident that showed how difficult it was to be consistently pure occurred embarrassingly soon after this edict had been issued. Each year on Remembrance Sunday in mid-November, a ceremony was held at an Imperial War Graves cemetery beside the main road a little way beyond the airport near Snagov. The graves are those of 80 Allied air crew who lost their lives in the raids on the Romanian oilfields in the summer of 1944. After the ceremony a small gathering would take place in the defence attaché's flat and, on this occasion, we had just begun to wonder why some colleagues were missing when news came of a road accident. No injuries were sustained, but on the return journey a car in front of Donald MacLeod, our head of chancery, had braked so suddenly that he had collided with the back of it, whereupon Sandy Hardie, first secretary, in the car behind had collided with Donald's rear end, so he was damaged front and back.

Now, the MacLeods were due within two weeks to drive back to London on leave and transfer. How could the car be repaired in time? A backstreet respray could be arranged, of course, but only by accepting the necessity to pay with 12 cartons of Kent. (It should perhaps be said that gold-wrapped Kent had no definite monetary value; they could not be had for lei, but were only obtainable by those with access to hard currency, so they were effectively priceless.) A year earlier we had ourselves been advised to give a carton of Kent to the doctor who sewed up Jessica's foot, and we very willingly did so. It was also widely accepted that to place a packet of Kent on the table when taking a seat in a restaurant was a useful way of ensuring that the waiter gave you as good a service as he could manage. Of an entirely different order was the criminal offence of exchanging hard currency for inflated numbers of lei, and we had to warn our many short-term visitors of the dangers from touts on the lookout for unwary foreigners — and of the dangers of being entrapped deliberately by eager Securitate agents.

Opportunities for rest and recreation
Controlled access to Romanian society tended to drive the international community in on itself, especially dependent families who were less free to travel around the country. For short breaks we were fortunate in being able to use the embassy's alpine-style villa at Timiş, high above the pass leading northwards from Sinaia through Predeal to Braşov. The mountains were good for skiing in winter and offered exhilarating hill walking in summer. Timiş often accommodated two and sometimes three families at a time, but even up there we had to guard our conversation for fear of

being 'overheard' — the title of a hitherto unpublished Peter Ustinov play. Visible from the veranda were two rocky peaks, one each side of the pass, which provided attractive climbs for keen walkers. Times taken to conquer Piatra Mare and Christianul Mare were competitively recorded in the Timiş book.

In Bucharest there was a rather dilapidated diplomatic club in an otherwise pleasant suburban setting where swimming and tennis were available, together with grassy areas for picnics. It was said that the golf course had been closed after a visit from one of the more puritanical of the Soviet leaders who had declared the game to be ideologically unacceptable. Also in Bucharest, however, there was plenty of opera, ballet, theatre and concerts to test the critical faculties. The dead hand of party allegiance rather than artistic excellence tended to repress standards on the musical side (we gave up attending orchestral concerts because the conducting was so utterly uninspired), but the theatre was of a very high quality. Musicians had a transferable skill, which could be sold abroad, but actors were much more language-bound.

> *Riddle*: What is a Romanian string quartet?
> *Answer*: A Romanian orchestra that has been on tour in the West.

'Defectors' in cold war terms, who should more charitably be described as voluntary exiles, were either admired and envied for their courage and determination or vilified as traitors. As we shall see, the desire to escape from totalitarian state control and the hardships of daily life extended to our own staff. For foreigners with a reasonable grasp of the language it was, however, possible to enjoy such memorable productions as Liviu Ciulei's *Furtuna* (Shakespeare's *Tempest*) with Prospero in a laboratory technician's white coat, and Alan Ayckbourn's *Absurd Person Singular*, translated as *Plurarul Englezesc*.

Valuable though these distractions were, it was important to plan a total escape for a week or two every six months or so. Our first such excursion was in April 1979 a few days after Sarah and Louise had joined us for the Easter holidays. We combined John and Miranda Villiers's offer to use their villa on the island of

Andros with an invitation from Tris and Joan Russell (of Kuala Lumpur and Forglen) to join them on a chartered fishing boat for a trip round the Cyclades. The Villiers family had built their Villa Fellos during a posting in Athens. John had also been my predecessor but two in Bucharest, and later became director of the British Institute in Southeast Asia, which he moved from Singapore to Bangkok.

We travelled *en famille* and were nine hours on the road from Bucharest to Sofia, where a night stop enabled me to see some embassy staff known only by telephone, and 15 hours on the road from Sofia to Athens, where two nights gave all of us a breather and a solid day of sightseeing. Without a word of Greek, we had been instructed, when reaching Gavrion by the ferry from Rafina, to go into the grocer's shop and utter the magic formula '*Kyria Miranda*' — abracadabra, it worked and we were given the keys. As arranged by telex between Kuala Lumpur and Bucharest, on our third day the Russell family turned up in the motor sailing vessel *Ionnis*, which they had chartered with skipper and crew for $US 300 a day. The voyages to Mykonos and back to Tinos, including a run ashore on Delos, provided memories that are unlikely to be erased until, if ever, we return to those parts.

Five months later we took further 'local leave' for the more serious purpose of improving Jessica's schooling, flying back to London after the summer holidays, when Sarah and Louise had to go anyway. Since our arrival in Romania, Jessica had been attending the only available English-medium school, the American-run International School of Bucharest. We knew Dos and Peggy Johnson, the principal and his wife, not only because my duties included *ex officio* membership of the school board, but also because Jessica was in Peggy's class. Potential embarrassment arose when a precocious little girl came home saying she was not learning very much, which meant that we had to face the need to minimize the re-entry problem (from which Sarah had suffered when returning from Japan) by arranging for her to board at home at the tender age of less than eight years old. Happily the Johnsons were wise enough to understand our problem and Godstowe girls' prep school in High Wycombe was an excellent if emotionally painful solution for the first few terms.

179

By this time we had decided we needed a second car to increase Diana's mobility in Bucharest, so we spent a week driving a new one on a second trans-European journey. We varied the route this time by taking a southern sweep, beginning with the Portsmouth–St Malo ferry, and spending the first night in Saumur, followed by our favourite Loire château, Villandry, and then Chenonceau *en route* to Charolles. The third day took us via Cluny and unhappily through the fume-laden 11 kilometre-long Mont Blanc tunnel to Bergamo. Pressing on (no luxury of two-night stops this time) we took a short break in Padua, crossed into Yugoslavia and stayed in Rijeka. A poorly insulated room gave us a bad night in Belgrade, and our last day of travelling was by an ill-mapped, sparsely signposted and unnerving route to the Romanian border near the Iron Gates (Drobeta Turnu Severin), reaching Bucharest late in the evening.

Making sure that London kept Romania in view
The Romanian musical establishment honoured its hero, George Enescu, with a festival every three years, and the 1979 one was in full swing when we returned. The Gabrieli Brass Ensemble was in town to participate under our auspices, and the soprano Sheila Armstrong with accompanist Martin Isepp gave a recital. She had also been booked to sing in the last night performance of Beethoven's Ninth Symphony, but her fee for the recital was outstanding so she phoned me for advice. It was not surprising that ARIA was reluctant to part with any of its precious dollars, but Sheila said quite firmly, 'No money, no sing on Saturday'. That morning we went to the pavement outside the ARIA office for me to witness the counting out and handing over of a wad of dollar bills. The soprano soloist in the choral symphony undertakes an unrewarding battle with the forces beneath her, so we went to the concert to admire her unrelenting struggle. Two years later the centenary of Enescu's birth in 1881 was celebrated with an extra festival, but by then the Romanian economy had declined so much further that not only hard currency but its own money was so scarce for support of the arts that it proved impossible, despite prolonged negotiation, to clinch any British representation at all — except Julian Bream at the eleventh hour (see end of this chapter).

180

Meanwhile, more central concerns demanded attention. Earlier in the year a blizzard had prevented a visit by the President of France — the pilot overflew the airport, took one look at the horizontally driving snow and headed for home — thereby aborting all the elaborate preparations for a state visit. The same storms delayed my efforts to get to London (Swissair obliged on the third day) to take part in the renegotiation of the cultural exchange programme for 1979–81. On the first day these talks took place in the dignified surroundings of the old India Office council chamber, but on the second we adjourned to the British Council boardroom for a session which lasted until 9.30 p.m. John Morgan, head of the FCO's CRD, led our side with Peter Prescott for the British Council and Sally Bird in support. The need to attend a few meetings of the Joint Commission on Science and Technology the following week gave me the excuse for a weekend in Totnes and, before flying back, the extra days provided the chance for a quick overnight stay with the Harrisons in their snowbound house in Bramerton near Norwich.

Two years later the disarray in the Romanian ministries caused the postponement of the talks until late May, long after the beginning of the year in which financial provision had to be assumed for continuing the programme. It was Bucharest's turn to host the talks and our side was led by John Macrae, then the new head of CRD, with Graham Coe and Michele Saward for the British Council. At one moment Domnul Brad, the Romanian cultural attaché in London, attacked us (in fact me) for allegedly obstructing a particular visitorship that had been proposed. His story was so wide of the mark that I felt forced to intervene somewhat hotly and say 'I am sorry, Mr Chairman, but Mr Brad's account of this incident is a travesty of the facts' and was happy to be reassured by John Macrae afterwards that it was sometimes necessary to be outspoken.

These government-level discussions were not adequate, however, to ensure that our work in Romania benefited properly from the expertise of colleagues in the specialized departments of our headquarters; and in any case it was received wisdom that we should pioneer (as much as the system would allow) outside the formal terms of the programme. So, in my first year we secured a visit from Ken Churchill to survey the teaching of English literature in the universities; Derek New came from Accommodation Services to look at all the buildings on offer for what we still sanguinely thought was a real possibility of setting up a cultural centre; and the jovial, pipe-smoking Dr John Compton came to scrutinize our staffing arrangements, which in turn depended on the views of Patrick Villa from Libraries Department about how to revamp our information services. Our series of 'visiting firemen' was completed when Jack Phillips took a glimpse at us from a Personnel angle, and Rex Lee came to report on language teaching as a complement to Churchill's work with literature. In this way there was some prospect of gaining recognition for expanding needs and of living down the assumed inapplicability of normal British Council practice.

During this time we also 'fielded' such characters as Iris Murdoch and her husband Professor John Bailey who were on holiday to spend the royalties from the published translations of her novels, the soft currency payments being nontransferable. Anxiety made me tackle a few of her books for the first time, but over dinner she preferred to stick to her professed interest in comparative university administration. A happy by-product, nonetheless, was my realization a year or two later that her philosophical writings, especially *The Sovereignty of Good*, were the key to what her storytelling was about. Sir Eric Berthoud also came in the hope of recruiting a pair of Romanian pupils for Atlantic College and generally to promote the ideals of the United World Colleges, but the Ministry of Education was sceptical and unreceptive.

When Diana flew home in late May for the annual commemoration at Sherborne, leaving me in charge of Jessica, she came back with my mother who spent a very full month with us. Beginning with a weekend at the Timiş villa, we contrived a figure of eight tour which enable her to see much more of the country than we had hitherto done, and the combination of business with pleasure gave her a good insight into how we went about our work. Jessica's term finished in mid-June, so all four of us could travel together. The crossing point of the route was the attractive old Habsburg border town of Sibiu where we stayed at the end of the

182

first day, having successfully located Stelian Ogrezeanu's pottery workshop in Horezu and seen the Cozia monastery. When checking into a Romanian hotel the first thing to do is to find out where the disco or nightclub rhythm will be throbbing and then to secure a room as far away as possible. A high noise level is also favoured in the restaurants and is often presumed to be a means of neutralizing any listening devices, but it can kill any desire to converse normally. The Boulevard Hotel was no exception and made our dinner with Professor Bogdan quite difficult.

The highlights alone of this journey would make a long narrative. The turning point in the northeast was Suceava and in the northwest Cluj. A single watercolour done by my mother during a midday picnic stop captures the atmosphere of a meadow at haymaking time in the alpine surroundings through which we passed. We entertained Dr Farkaş from the Institute of Medicine and Pharmacy in Turgu Mureş, and reached Suceava's Hotel Arcaşul for a two-night stay at the weekend. The painted monasteries of Upper Moldavia (or Bukovina) are rightly famous, but our personal preference was for the plain peacefulness of Dragomirna. After a quiet Sunday, picnicking near its lake and sketching its architecture, we gave dinner to Mr Borjoi, the dean of engineering at the Institute of Higher Education. Next day we headed west-southwest through the high grasslands of the Bistriţa mountain range, carpeted in magnificent wild flowers, and reached Cluj for another two-night stay. Most significant for the future was our first meeting with Alexandra Rus, director of the art museum, and her husband Vasile Rus Batin, who later made a bas-relief carving on oak of four of our family, based on photographs taken by Dr Tiberiu Graur of the ethnography museum. We also saw an exhibition of Eugen Tâutu's work. He later dedicated a picture to me (paid for, of course) which now hangs by our dining table. Returning southeastwards, we explored Alba Iulia, passed Sibiu again, then went via Fagaraş Castle and Braşov to a last night in Timiş.

Collaboration with other foreign representatives
A working environment in which most of the foreign community felt alienated from the party-dominated intelligentsia, while making strenuous attempts to build genuine friendships with the few

Romanians who could afford to risk it, provided a strong incentive for sharing the burden of providing a view of the rest of the world as free of distortion as possible. Changes of staff in other agencies could therefore be as significant as changes among ourselves, especially among our American friends in the United States Information Service (USIS), and among others in the Service culturel français, the Goethe Institute, the Italian Cultural Institute and the Canadian embassy. Our French colleague, for example, was André Michel, accredited as scientific counsellor and a man of strong physical presence, like a mixture of General de Gaulle and Maurice Chevalier. Our USIS colleagues, Alvin Perlman and Hank Zivetz, could be immensely reassuring. When, for instance, the quality of my relationship with the Ministry of Education was queried by a London visitor, they simply shrugged their shoulders in despair. Enough said.

Contrary to the public misapprehension about cocktail parties and the diplomatic round, much useful business was done during national day celebrations when you could usually find someone you had failed to catch on the telephone. It was Mr Erni, the Swiss Ambassador whom we had known previously in Malaysia, who spotted Diana across a big room in the Chinese embassy and shouted — 'Madame Dubonnet!' in his surprise. When we heard that the Crown Prince and Princess of Japan were due to make a state visit to Romania we managed to convince their embassy that we really did know Prince Akihito and Princess Michiko personally, and were duly invited to meet them in Bucharest. (By a similar coincidence we saw them again nearly ten years later in Finland.)

In teaching English, the worldwide official policy was one of close collaboration rather than competition with the Americans. Our common interest was the mutual intelligibility of English and the avoidance of extreme variations. We did our best to dovetail our programmes in Romania — there were about ten Fullbright-funded teachers in the universities compared with our provision for 'up to five' — but my attempt in a letter of October 1980 (addressed to the ministry with USIS support) to rationalize its geographical distribution according to expertise in literature, language or linguistics (and in the light of the existing skills of the

Romanian academic staff) fell on deaf ears. Even so, we somehow did manage to move our lector in Bacâu to a more rewarding post in Cluj. Better coordination was achieved with the annual summer school for teachers of English in Suceava, but that was sabotaged by the ministry after 1979.

It seems to be the ambition of all relatively small countries to secure the permanent presence of an institution sponsored by the United Nations. This can only be achieved through a process of fierce competitive bidding and political manœuvring, yet the Romanians had succeeded in getting Unesco to establish its European centre for higher education (CEPES) in Bucharest. We knew the Norwegian director of CEPES, Audun Ofjord, and he commissioned Diana to translate the French text of an 80-page document on 'Access to Higher Education in Europe'. She shared the dollar proceeds with Sue MacDonald, wife of Patrick, our new defence attaché colleague in the flat below, who did the typing.

In the second half of 1980 we valued the advice of our American colleagues in dealing with the consequences of 'defections' — either of members of their own staff or of sponsored travellers of various sorts who went to the West on holiday or to study and failed to return, usually applying for asylum and becoming voluntary exiles. They were used to it as a regular occurrence, but when it happened to us we were shocked by no less than five such cases in one year. Our librarian, Cornelia Ionescu, was the first to fail to reappear after her summer holiday. The Romanian control of passports and exit permits created a system of 'hostages', but with skill that could be evaded and Cornelia had managed to get her schoolboy son out with her. We heard that she was in Geneva, so it was a relief to be assured by my Swiss colleague that his country never sent such refugees back. In due course we heard that she was being very generously supported. Next, the embassy translator overstayed her leave and, thirdly, the telephonist escaped to Cyprus with her Austrian Airlines boyfriend. Most upsetting of all, however, was the realization that the commercial officer and his wife (the administration assistant) had driven to London in their own car, leaving their young children with the grandparents. They were the first to apply for asylum in Britain and were kept waiting for a year. My worry was how the authorities would react to my request for the recruitment of a replacement librarian, but our American colleagues assured me that any recriminations were most unlikely and that it would be treated quite casually as a routine matter. They had plenty of experience. In the event it was not entirely straightforward because the Office for Service to the Diplomatic Corps vetoed our first choice, refusing to give any explanation and causing distress to the temporary employee we had taken on.

A long mid-tour leave: swotting for A and O levels

Eighteen months after arriving we were entitled to catch up on some of the untaken leave due, so we planned to be at home for the Easter holidays and not to return until shortly before the children would be coming for the summer. Theresa Kassell had been with me for several months and knew the ropes well enough to act in charge, so, shortly after visits by a ballet duo (Maina Gielgud and Jonathan Kelly to dance with the local company) and the Lontano Ensemble (giving four concerts in Bucharest and three provincial centres), we took off westwards.

It was a nightmare journey. We had decided that the car that had originally been exported to Malaysia, had been shipped back to Britain and then driven to Romania (and had continued to serve us well despite being right-hand drive) should be changed. What we did not know was that a latent design fault would choose this moment to emerge and cause us to break down. After a first night in Arad near the border with Hungary, we called on Tom Stones and Claire Newton in Budapest and pressed on, but just beyond Tatabanya the engine suddenly lost power. We got a tow to the nearest hotel — ironically the Hotel Diana — and then remembered that Patrick MacDonald, our defence attaché, was in Vienna and could get us a spare petrol pump. Next day they came through and towed us to a garage, but it did not fit, so we had to accept the opinion that the existing pump would 'work all right now'. After a few miles we broke down again, got a tow back and then persuaded the garage, through Diana's limited German for lack of any Hungarian, to diagnose the trouble properly. The fibre mounting had allowed the pump to twist sideways and miss the camshaft which drove it. Late into the night they manufactured a thick plastic replacement, but by this time a blizzard (which we should have been comfortably to the west of) was blowing vigorously from the east. Diana took some convincing that the problem would not recur, but my watching the details of the work gave me confidence, so we set off in search of a bed for the rest of the night. The roads were deserted and the hotels all full with travellers wiser than us, but we had lost two days of our planned itinerary to London for appointments that mattered. Going on was dangerous but stopping was worse. We headed towards the Austrian border and crossed with relief in the early hours, but the first motel was full and not until 6.00 a.m. did we reach one where we could take a few hours' sleep, have the most welcome breakfast ever and go on towards Linz.

Reaching Nuremberg the same day and Lille the next, we crossed by hovercraft and offered a Sunday morning surprise to the Dover customs. Had we anything to declare? Yes, the car itself. How come? Well, it was exported five years ago to a non-European country and now we want to pay the duty so we can sell it. What is its depreciated value? You tell us! OK, but not here, in London. So on we went. During two days of calls on colleagues in the British Council's Spring Gardens offices we put the heavily laden car in the basement park, only to suffer the sting in the tail of this whole episode — the car had been opened by thieves who took a box of personal papers and Jessica's half size violin, but little else of value. The same day we collected the girls from High Wycombe and Sherborne and reached Totnes — 1933 miles from Bucharest. For the next month we depended on Potty Granny for peace and quiet while Sarah and Louise worked in preparation for their exams.

With the children back at school we set about recovering our Bourne End house from our American tenant. He had kept the heating at a tropical level, which had not done our furniture any good, but more seriously he had allowed the telephone to lapse; and the exchange was short of lines, so it could not be restored in the short term. This meant using the public call box on the corner for the rest of our leave and being embarrassed when asked for a number we did not have. Another month was devoted to domestic improvements, work which was rewarded by our securing a

Japanese family as tenants during our second tour in Romania. Then it was again time for the annual Sherborne commemoration. After the Godstowe speech day we took Jessica for her half-term break for a week up and down the Oxford Canal in the Shirley-Quirk's narrowboat. The third month of leave saw us visiting and catching up with a very long list of friends and relatives, and in the first week of July we set off eastwards once again, this time choosing the Newhaven–Dieppe crossing, reaching Strasburg on the second night and staying with the Sandiford family in Munich on the third. After the next two nights in Graz and Belgrade, in contrast to the September 1979 route, we kept north of the Danube and crossed into Romania at the Bela Crkva border post on a fine afternoon, with sunny smiles from the guards, who welcomed us in a language they realized we knew.

Making the best of the most we could expect
While not wishing to relapse into a travelogue, the wrong impression would be given if the amount of travelling demanded by the job was understated. A cultural diplomat has to be seen and known in a country's provincial centres no less than in the capital, but at the same time the central facility of a library and an information service has to be developed. For a month in the summer of 1980, having come to accept the impossibility of executing earlier plans for a new centre, we closed to the public and embarked on a major refurbishment of our 'portaloo' premises, most significantly shifting a number of partitions so that my office could double as a projection room for screening films in the library, itself requiring a new layout of the shelving.

Although the public had to pass the Securitate at the embassy gate to reach us, and were liable to be questioned about their intentions on the way in and the contents of their bags on the way out, our clientele was increasing steadily. After a few test screenings we were sufficiently encouraged to announce regular series such as Bronowski's *Ascent of Man*, Clark's *Civilization* and Attenborough's *Life on Earth*.

Programming, receiving, accompanying and entertaining visitors continued to be a constant preoccupation and generally provided as much pleasure as pain. An example of a nice mixture was the visit of Sir Donald Logan, director of the Great Britain East Europe Centre. We arranged the customary drinks party, with dinner to follow, for him to meet a select group of Romanian academics in a relaxed atmosphere. Two days earlier, however, Robert Maxwell (the notorious 'bouncing Czech') had announced his presence in town by making a rudely demanding call to our Ambassador. We offered to include him in the drinks and he came; but being neither the guest of honour nor the centre of attention, he did not enjoy it very much.

Just after the summer upheaval Professor John Ferguson, who had given Diana away at our wedding in Ibadan 20 years earlier, and his wife Elnora came for a tour of Roman Romania. He claimed that Dacia was the only province of the empire to which he had not yet been, so in just under two weeks we covered 2000 kilometres. Eastwards on the Black Sea coast lies the port of Constanţa, or Tomis, where a statue of Ovid recalls his exile. By approaching on a southerly route we saw Trajan's monument at Adamclisi and, while going northwards to Tulcea, we picnicked in Histria, returning by the Hirsova crossing of the Danube to Bucharest. John preached a sermon in our church and then we went westwards, saw the Brâncuşi sculptures in Tirgu Jiu and stopped in Drobeta Turnu Severin for a visit next morning to the Iron Gates archaeological museum. It contains a scale model of Trajan's mighty bridge over the Danube (designed by an imperial servant from Damascus) and displays samples of the wooden piles preserved from the fourth century. Remains of the bridge's masonry abutments are visible at both the Romanian and Yugo- slav ends. We returned via the Bruckenthall museum in Sibiu and the fortified church of Prejmeer near Braşov. John also gave two lectures in Bucharest — one on 'Shakespeare and the Spiral of Violence' and another on 'The Classical Influence on English Poetry'. We saw them again in Istanbul the following year, but he died in 1989 in harness as president of the Selly Oak Colleges in Birmingham, where Elnora carries on much of their public work.

To keep our library in good shape and to benefit from the neces- sary professional advice, instead of someone coming from Lon- don, we had two successive annual visits from John Salter, who was based in Warsaw. Checking stocks and weeding are never very rewarding tasks, but a week supervised by an expert was valuable for our inexperienced new colleagues. John was also able to give a lecture in the Central State Library, and, to celebrate the end of his first week, we went on a day trip to the monastery at Câldâruşani, to Lake Snagov for lunch, and to the fine country house of Mogoşoaia.

In addition to the BBC's big 13-part series, we began experimenting with the relatively new genre of 50-minute documentary films designed for the standard television slot, showing them in our flat to invited audiences. Best appreciated were Peter Ustinov's history of Wimbledon entitled *The Great English Garden Party* and a live record of a British Council-sponsored brass band tour of Italy called *Arrivederci Grimethorpe*. There was a good audience also for the freshly made BBC Shakespeare plays, available on U-matic video tape.

It should have been no surprise to me at this point to get a letter from London saying — 'Your next post will be as director Films Department' to take effect in the autumn of 1981. 'Who? Me? Films? You must be joking' was my reaction. Hardly ever inside a cinema at home, this seemed absurd to me; yet in due course it proved just right for my next stint in London.

The BBC's The Long Search *and alternative Romania*
Before my time, but not long before it, a filming team had been all over the country, with the blessing of the Minister for Cults, to gather impressions of the Orthodox Church and its role in Romanian society. *The Long Search* was a survey of world religions made for TV by Ronald Eyre. He called Part 7 'The Romanian Solution', and in the 50 minutes available he was seen in conversation in village churches, in monasteries, in the patriarchate and in ordinary homes. At one moment he is eating with a family in the far north and he asks the head of the household:

'Is it true that you are a keen member of the party?'
'Yes.'
'Is it also true that you are chairman of the new church building committee?'
'Yes.'

'How can you be a good communist and a good Christian?'
'Because they are equally patriotic for a Romanian.'

Under the Ottoman Empire the Orthodox Church learnt that the price of survival was not to oppose, so it has a long history of passive collaboration — reluctant at times perhaps — with the secular powers of the day. In Romania one third of the pay of the usually Orthodox village priest (many Catholic and evangelical communities were not included) was derived from the communist state, another third from the contributions of the faithful and a third from the income of the church from the sale of candles, rugs and other products. As a whole, especially in rural areas, church-based economies constituted an alternative society, some examples of which we were privileged to see at close quarters.

The Orthodox Church did not provide a focus of opposition to the communist regime, in marked contrast to the Catholic opposition in Poland, and this goes some way towards explaining the more durable grip of the regime in Romania — and the slower recovery after the counter-revolutions of 1989.

The last quarter of Ronald Eyre's film featured Bishop Justinian of Cluj as his mentor, and we discovered that Justinian had never had an opportunity to see the finished work, although after the series had been transmitted to the BBC's domestic audience, two 16-millimetre prints of Part 7 had been provided, one for the patriarchate and one for the embassy to hold. So we explained to the Bishop that we could load our car with all necessary projection equipment and bring the film for him to see. We also knew that it was possible for embassy staff to arrange to stay overnight in certain monasteries if the request was channelled through the patriarchate. Remus Rus of the theological institute in Bucharest, who had an Oxford doctorate in theology and had been Ronald Eyre's guide and interpreter, was our intermediary in fixing this tour.

Louise and Jessica arrived for the Easter holidays, but Sarah, having left Sherborne, was doing a gap year, spending two terms as a junior matron in Lambrook boys' preparatory school followed by a spell of immersion in Italian at the British Institute in Florence. So it was just four of us who set off, from a Saturday to the following Thursday, to experience some extreme contrasts.

191

Both the Western and Orthodox Easters were two or three weeks away, so the lenten season caused Bishop Justinian to apologize for the frugal nature of the lunch he offered us, luxurious though it was. After lunch he was really delighted with the film. He was so pleased, not so much with his own role in it as with the colourful and impressive photography of the church settings, that (as we shall see) he encouraged others to demand a showing. Before becoming bishop he had been the abbot of Rohia monastery, where he had arranged for us to go after the weekend.

Setting off northwards with Constantin Bradea from the theological seminary as our guide, we left the car near Gherla to walk to a very unusual establishment only accessible on foot. This was the Uniate or Greek Catholic church of Nicula where a small workshop specialized in making icons painted on glass, a technique that requires the pigment to be applied in reverse order, the 'top' layer going on first rather than last. Reaching Rohia in mid-afternoon, we found a small community of only six monks and two nuns with a few lay employees hidden high in a remote and wooded mountain fastness, but with a library of 20,000 volumes. Justinian had obviously been a much loved father figure and only reluctantly released for higher duties in Cluj. Word had spread that the film depicted him well, so it was shown to a small gathering in their dining room after supper. Next morning Louise and Jessica were somewhat nonplussed to be offered *tsuica* (plum brandy) as a breakfast aperitif.

My official calls in Baie Mare gave us an excuse to see some of the celebrated wooden churches of the Maramureş region, especially Serdeşti and Plopiş — each rather more memorable than the interviews with the Committee for Culture and visits to the mineralogy and ethnology museums. A carburettor blockage (dirty petrol engine trouble) frustrated our intention to range more widely and we returned southwards through Cluj and past Aiud, reaching Rimeţ monastery two hours late on account of bad signposting.

Welcomed by Bishop Emilian of Alba Iulia and the mother superior, we found both him and Rimeţ a strong contrast after Justinian and Rohia. The latter was a saintly person associated with a relatively recent foundation, whereas the former was

192

inclined to be overbearing with his subordinates and responsible for a church and community dating back six centuries, claiming to be the oldest in Transylvania. It lies in a deeply secluded valley. The 60 nuns were in three categories — a third employed in weaving carpets for sale, a third in domestic and religious duties and a third in retirement. In spite of the late hour the film was screened in their kitchen for over half the nuns, the bishop and his staff. Next day in Alba Iulia (a hill citadel situated not far from the remains of Trajan's imperial headquarters) Professor Alexandru Popa showed us his archaeology museum and Bishop Emilian gave us lunch. Such are the privileges of itinerant foreigners among people thirsty for impressions of the West; and the film gave them a view of themselves as perceived by the West.

A few final flings and one daring dash

How can the foregoing features of work and life in Romania be summarized? How can batting on a wicket, stickier even than Ethiopia a decade later, be justified? Did we have any chance of penetrating, beyond discouragement by the bureaucrats, through to the long-suffering people struggling to maintain academic and professional contacts with the outside world? In reverse order the answers are: yes, we did circumvent the ideological obstacles in many small ways, which in aggregate meant that, yes, the innings was worthwhile and it was characterized by very cordial relationships in so far as risks could be minimized from the Romanian angle.

Nevertheless, Bucharest in midwinter could be extremely dismal. Early in our third year, Diana agreed with my spontaneous suggestion that a one-week excursion by El Al to Israel could give us just the right uplift required. Some friends in the Israeli embassy helped make up our minds and David Waterhouse, on a personnel tour from London, happened to change planes at the airport and give us the invaluable tip that the American Colony Hotel in Jerusalem was misleadingly named. Indeed, its unspoiled stone buildings and proximity to the old city made it ideal. In a spirit of wonder we visited quietly (because it was out of season) so many scenes of our historico-religious awareness since childhood. We walked in the Garden of Gethsemane and up to the Mount of

193

Olives; we hired a car and drove to Jericho and the Dead Sea coast, and climbed Masada; on the third day we were in Bethlehem in the morning and in Nazareth in the afternoon. Staying in a kibbutz guesthouse on the shores of Galilee, we found just one nun in the church on the Mount of Beatitudes and were thankful to be only imagining the press of people implied by the empty coach parks at every site. We enjoyed similar solitude in Capernaum and Tiberias, and on the way south were able to admire the Roman amphitheatre and aqueduct at Caesarea. Finally, back in Jerusalem, we managed to find our way to see the Chagall windows of the twelve tribes in the synagogue of the Hadassah medical centre. On our return to Bucharest we immediately listed what should be done on a second visit — and later found we had set a fashion for others wanting a winter break.

An opportunity to reciprocate Dos and Peggy Johnson's understanding over Jessica came to me when a pair of teachers at the American school tested our patience to the limit. Dos asked me as a board member to go with him to the couple's house and exercise every ounce of diplomacy to persuade them to leave. They had retired to their accommodation claiming to be too 'ill' even to discuss their problem, which had been debated by the school board the previous afternoon and a 'generous offer' of a face-saving nature been recommended. By repeatedly emphasizing their own true interests we gently succeeded in gaining their acceptance, and happily Dos thought that was to my credit.

The pace became hotter than ever during our last year with a steady stream of visitors ranging from a professional puppeteer to the curator of Norwich Castle museum and including Dr Derek Brewer, the master of Emmanuel College, Cambridge. He lectured on Chaucer and Malory. Another anticlockwise round trip was fitted in to visit people and institutions in Bacâu, Iaşi, Cluj and Sibiu (about 1500 kilometres) and we took a last chance of seeing the Danube delta's bird life, going with John and Dawn Willson for a rather too early in the season weekend. He had come as commercial counsellor to replace Colin Mays and they both became very good neighbours on the ground floor of Aleea Alexandru 5. Diana's annual visit home for the Sherborne commemoration and half term coincided inconveniently with the arrival of colleagues from London to renegotiate the cultural exchange programme, but my capacity for hospitality held up reasonably well. All the while we were arranging official presents of books and periodicals as our contribution towards alleviating the book famine.

On 1 July it became Britain's turn once more to occupy the presidency of the European Community (EC) for the ensuing six months. This meant my having to host the occasional working lunches for EC and NATO cultural colleagues at which we swapped valuable information about each other's problems. One example of useful nitty-gritty groundwork we achieved was a comparison of the allowances for scholars and postgraduate researchers, done before our separate negotiations with the Romanian side.

Some careful dovetailing of diary commitments enabled us to populate our spacious flat with the family and its friends for several summer weeks, including a car load with Sarah from her Lambrook and Sherborne days, Norman Routledge of Eton and King's, and our godson, Peter Shirley-Quirk. They all had to accept a deadline to go, otherwise we could not carry out the rest of our plan for a second holiday in Greece. We had known for some time that my mother would be travelling on the same Swan Hellenic cruise ship, the *Orpheus*, as John and Elnora Ferguson, he as one of the lecturers, and a rendezvous during their day in Istanbul seemed a practical idea.

By this time we had learnt that it was possible to get right through Bulgaria in one day and to complete the 500 mile (800 kilometre) run from Bucharest to Kavala in northern Greece by loading a reserve jerry can of petrol to avoid the need for Bulgarian currency. After five days in a beach bungalow on the island of Thasos we headed for the Turkish border along the coast road through Alexandropolis and reached our destination, where preferential rates in the Sheraton Hotel had kindly been arranged by Bill Hudson, our colleague in charge of the British Council's Istanbul office and library. Contact was made with the ship and we found that my mother, with her friend Christine Halstead and the Fergusons, were expecting us on board for lunch. The most memorable part of this excursion was our gaining admission, thanks to Bill Hudson's contacts, to the Florence Nightingale room in the corner turret of the Scutari barracks, across the Bosphorus bridge, and then the HQ of the Turkish First Army.

That autumn there was an historical colloquium in Iaşi, a history of science conference in Bucharest and a group visit to the Union of Architects very close together; but my final, most personal and risky contribution to the cause occurred in our last ten days. We had set up a British film week, involving the complex process of importing a bulky consignment of many reels of 35-millimetre prints, and had opened with *Chariots of Fire*. The actor John Hurt of *The Elephant Man* and Jack Gold, director of *Little Lord Fauntleroy*, had arrived. A duo from London City Ballet, Marion St Claire and Michael Beare, were booked to perform with the local company in the 3000-seat Sala Palatului, but a Party function had forced its transfer to a nearby 600-seat theatre, with only hours to reorganize.

Then news came that Julian Bream would arrive for an engagement in the Enescu Centenary Festival, hitherto without any British participant and arranged without our involvement. Not for long, however, since my presence at the airport to meet him was obviously desirable, if not strictly necessary, to back up the ARIA representative. On the way out there was evidence of an impending event — sure enough, the road was being cleared in preparation for Colonel Gaddafi's arrival to confer with Ceauşescu on Romanian–Libyan affairs. Mr Bream appeared in due course and seemed none too happy at being associated with British officialdom, although he needed me because the ARIA official had already gone when we came out to my car. The slip road leading south into town was blocked by stationary vehicles, but it was dark and my Talbot Alpine had a similar profile to the Romanian officially preferred Renault 18 cars. Telling Bream that his story was that he was due on stage in half an hour ('What? Isn't it tomorrow?') and determined to get into town somehow, my adrenaline took us down the northbound slip road, swung the car round with a protesting policeman hammering on the window, put my headlamps on full beam and accelerated down the middle of the deserted four-lane highway. No bullet in my back, but a salute from a startled guard as we passed the statue of Lenin.

Diplomatic numberplates are helpful and, although we left

Romania finally only six days later, there would still have been time to declare me *persona non grata*. Colin and Gertie Munro, who had long since taken over the head of chancery role from Donald and Rosemary MacLeod, and become equally good friends, particularly when able to share the Timiş villa, made sure we had a good sendoff. A Lufthansa flight direct to Munich took us once more into the 'decompression chamber' hospitality of our kind friends, Brian and Margot Hitch, he then being our consul-general in Bavaria. Handover notes for my successor, John Harniman, were compiled over a couple of quiet days otherwise spent walking in fine autumn weather, with a brief taste of the celebrated Oktober Fest and some sightseeing. We were then off to London and a new chapter opens.

12

London:
Films, Television and Video

In contrast to my London stint in the early 1970s, this posting, after six years altogether in Malaysia and Romania, gave me renewed responsibility for a worldwide service, with an even better chance of being a good gamekeeper than the narrower past of Malawi and Japan had provided. Previous knowledge of Arts was a help, but why films for one with no special liking for the cinema? The answer lay in the way the British Council used the short, documentary and didactic material which was its bread and butter, together with the occasional feature film. All that was familiar enough to me, and it was rightly assumed that my sympathies would be with colleagues in posts abroad who had high but often disappointed expectations of what they thought ought to be available. Among top management there was a conviction that the time was ripe for us to 'do more with films and video', but at all levels there was a communication blockage and a consequent ignorance, both of the legal constraints of copyright and of the customs of the trade. My own learning curve had to be very steep.

Poacher turned gamekeeper again
The literary academic, Richard Hoggart, in a report he wrote later on the British Council's work in the arts, quoted my description of

films as 'a Cinderella department in a Cinderella division', and my inheritance was not a happy one. My initiation in mid-December 1981 was at a meeting of the National Panel for Film Festivals (NPFF) of which the chairman, James Quinn, was not on good terms with my predecessor, Don Gillate. The NPFF had a curious history. It had been established in 1966 by the FCO and serviced by the COI until 1973 when the British Council took it on, but because it had never been integrated with us, the colleagues who did its business ('my' staff now) got no acknowledgement, not even a mention in official reports. Its subtitle was 'The Selection Committee for Short Films' and it had the job of viewing and recommending official British entries for the plethora of competitive film festivals all over the world. An air of demoralization prevailed; there was high staff turnover in the section and it was clear to me that radical reform would need all my energy and a great deal of tact and diplomacy. Happily, it gradually emerged that the then director-general, Sir John Burgh, had approved my appointment, believing in my capacity for precisely that. The friction engendered by the festival work was distorting the department's ability to respond to the more general and legitimate needs of the British Council proper and, in any case, the contribution of a film festival to our work in any one country was very marginal and often unnoticed. So we were in some ways going to have to fight the same battle that had been my job with Geoffrey Tribe seven years earlier, i.e. to bring our activity into line with an integrated policy. My previous observation of the workings of the advisory committees for music, drama and fine arts immediately became relevant.

There is no virtue in doing more than setting the scene in this way. There was pressure for confrontation and abolition, but my preference was for transformation and evolution. It took a year to get acceptance in principle, to expound the merits, to obtain Lord Brabourne's services as chairman, to appoint the members and to convene the first meeting of the Films, Television and Video Advisory Committee (FTVAC). In persuading the members of the NPFF to allow themselves to be transformed into the FTVAC it had been necessary to give an undertaking that a fair proportion of them would be invited to continue. This gave rise to a most uncomfortable meeting in the director-general's office. We had submitted a list of appropriate people, carefully balanced to include film makers, academics, critics and institutions, with seven names from the old panel. The director-general suddenly asked me 'If you had to nominate two of these, which would they be?' Taken aback and appalled, my credibility was on the line. Quick thinking was needed, yet my very halting response was to imply that if our moral obligation could not be honoured my resignation — hardly an applicable threat — would have to be considered. No more was said. All seven went on the list.

Scepticism concerning the value of yet another committee was widespread, yet the FTVAC quickly vindicated our belief that the circulation of the papers prepared for it and the minutes of its deliberations would begin to educate our colleagues in the realities of intellectual property and the minefield of rights. It also met a basic need in protecting a small and devoted but vulnerable group of specialized (not specialist) staff from ill-informed impatience with the constraints on its operations, and it provided a much needed link from the home constituency — the suppliers whose goodwill was essential — through London to our branches abroad — the consumers. At this time, too, the working environment was changing fast. Video was replacing 16-millimetre film and the proportion of television-inspired 'programmes' in whatever format was increasing. The moving image was on the move. For the first time, again, our work was being reported through the usual channels alongside that of others, and the extent of it caused surprise. Apart from the festival work there was a regular series of British film weeks, so the concept of film screenings as cultural events obtained a higher profile. The dual nature of our service gained recognition through the analogy of lending documentary films and videos as if they were books from a library.

In support of all this my personal priority was to get to know who was who among the professionals in the industry. Tony Smith of the British Film Institute (BFI) gave much encouragement, as did staff in the Central Office of Information and BBC Enterprises Ltd. Time was needed to learn the meanings of BFTPA, BAFTA, BUFTC, BISFA, BOTB and BBFC, not to mention SSVC, LIFS, IBA, ICA, NFA and NFT. James Quinn, whose chairmanship of the NPFF had dissolved, remained a close collaborator, and James Archibald's enthusiasm for producing his own updated documentary on contemporary arts in Britain, *Opus 2*, was infectious. Sadly, it lacked admirers when done and James died not long after completing it. On an entirely different scale was Brabourne's making of *A Passage to India* with enormous success. My being *ex officio* secretary to his chairmanship gave me the opening to ask to witness the excitement of viewing the 'rushes' flown overnight from location shooting in India, and to watch the shooting in Shepperton studios of the Bangalore court scene with David Lean directing.

It was also important for me to be seen by my staff to have first-hand knowledge of the ambience of the major film festivals they struggled to service, and the earliest opportunity was the Berlin international one in February 1982. Nine films of various lengths in two and a half days was my ration, and making notes of my views for reporting back was a way of showing that my critical faculties were developing. A month later Diana came with me to the Lille international one (she at my expense, of course) and my report on that contains details of no fewer than 35 films of very variable quality, viewed morning, afternoon and evening for two days. A short quotation is indicative: 'These occasions provide good opportunities for sharpening one's critical faculties and developing a sense of relative merits. There are occasional moments of pleasure, but there is no escaping the fact that watching films that are in bad taste or poorly made is hard work.'

My assessments ranged from 'very witty, clever and imaginative' to 'thoroughly nasty, brutal and noisy'. Shorts have no monopoly in this, so the next question was 'Why has the British Council hitherto never sent anyone to size up the feature-length films at the annual jamboree in Cannes?' James Quinn kindly guided me through the procedures and in mid-May Diana came with me (again at my own expense, of course) for a week in a self-catering apartment next to James and his wife. We saw 11 films in six days and held many useful conversations, not least with Barbara Dent from our Paris office who had plans for a British film fortnight. The BFI celebrated the fiftieth anniversary of 'Sight and Sound' with a dinner. Eyebrows were raised in London, however, when it was realized that 'Bruce had gone on a swan with his wife to

Cannes'. There was little appreciation in those days of what was a pioneering venture, raising our profile, so that only three years later, after my time, top management would go there to participate in promoting the British presence.

Domestic concerns during a home posting

We got home from Romania and into our Bourne End house just in time to take Sarah up to Durham University and install her in St Mary's College to begin her three-year degree course, combined honours in French and music. Then, in quick succession, followed Jessica's half term and Louise's half term, together with visits to Highcliffe and Totnes. That autumn we made contact with the Euro-Japanese Exchange Foundation, where our tenant had been studying, and made a donation of several of my books on Japan. We also visited the Harrisons in Norwich, the Fergusons in Birmingham and my sisters in Bosham and in Oldham.

By the middle of the following year Louise had come to the end of her time in Sherborne and, after much uncertainty, we had concluded that training to be a nurse would suit her best. In due course, St Bartholemew's Hospital offered her a place from January 1983, so meanwhile she worked locally in an old people's home. For summer leave we took her with Jessica and Potty Granny across to France, accepting an offer from Reinhardt Kraus (our German diplomat friend from Bucharest) of the house he had acquired while posted to Paris some years earlier. It was in the village of St Denis d'Authou in the area known as Le Perche, south of Normandy and north of the Loire, and not far west of Chartres.

Meanwhile, we were not neglecting music. Nick Steinitz ran a Music Camp weekend around Handel's *Theodora*, and we went to John Olive's celebration of his seventieth birthday with *Birthday Bach* at Shawford. Locally, we had the Wooburn singers to support and, the next year, Nick Steinitz did another opera weekend with Handel's *Semele*.

In the autumn we made another trip north, Sarah having decided to move out of her college and share with friends a very dilapidated miner's cottage nearer the centre of Durham. We stayed with Peter and Kay Orr in Guisborough (he being a former British Council colleague devoted to recordings of poetry and

202

drama) and did a bit of research into my Nightingale ancestors. Diana and Louise patiently accompanied me in searching several churchyards and cemeteries in the villages along the western escarpment of the North Yorkshire moors, and we were rewarded by finding no fewer that 15 gravestones with the same family name in Stokesley. By this time we already knew that my great-great-grandfather William had been recorded in the 1861 census as the head of a farming household in a place still marked on the Ordnance Survey map. We also knew that William begat George who begat John Leathley who begat Cuthbert Leathley who begat me. Sorting out the weatherworn inscriptions on the gravestones was not easy, since most of them were called William, Henry or George. The next year, however, it was possible by appointment to consult the Northallerton county records and obtain evidence that helped to make sense of the memorial stones.

We also needed to begin thinking about where Jessica should go after Godstowe. We visited Downe House near Newbury and Bryanston in Dorset, but eventually she opted to follow her elder sisters to Sherborne. Her violin playing had flourished and, when she competed in February 1984, they were pleased at the prospect of a third musical Nightingale and awarded her a music scholar-ship. The necessary common entrance had previously been obtained at the 13-plus level when she was not yet 12 years old and, although this was fully understood by Godstowe, when we took her to Sherborne in September there was an extremely upset-ting error in placing her in the fourth rather than the fifth form with her friends. This ruined her initial enthusiasm and the crisis was resolved only by my dropping all my office commitments for a morning and telephoning both schools to obtain urgent remedial action. It was the headmistress of Godstowe who got it put right because her reputation was at risk.

Boarding schools had around this time developed the habit of taking a full week for a half-term holiday in the summer term and, in the previous year, we had taken Jessica for a sailing adventure in Norfolk. This was especially popular because at that time she was enjoying Arthur Ransome's books. We started from Potter Heigham, went down the rivers Thurle and Bure to Great Yar-mouth, and up the Yare to spend the fourth night moored near the

Harrison's house in Bramerton. Chartering a 'Broads boat' with a tabernacle mast was a new challenge for me, requiring nice judgement in timing the lowering and raising operations. We made two very uncomfortable transits of the strong currents at the confluence of the rivers in Yarmouth, but survived to complete the return voyage in another three days.

For a summer break we went again to France, this time by the Plymouth–Roscoff ferry to a gîte right in the middle of Brittany, taking Potty Granny, Jessica and a school friend. Our base was near Carhaix, so a series of radial routes (for expeditions to the coast on alternate days) enabled us to go south to Concarneau, southwest to Quimper, north to Lannion and west to Douarnenez and the Point du Raz — the last of which in a strong gale looked distinctly vicious.

A happy event in midyear had been the celebration of Diana's parents' golden wedding with a surprise party in our house, preceded by Diana driving them up to Durham to visit all their old haunts. Her father was really delighted, but sadly he was to die just one year later.

Think-pieces by the dozen

The drafting and redrafting of policy papers became almost an obsession, bringing me closer to the life of a home civil servant than at any other time. One did not feel very close to the front line or at the sharp end of cultural relations when bound to a desk, a telephone and a dictating machine, but such toil is inescapable if the right framework is to be provided. It is also salutary to learn some of the techniques needed when seeking to influence the thinking of powerful people, both within Whitehall and in Westminster.

Each time our new advisory committee met, three times in its first year and twice in its second, a sheaf of papers had to be produced, the core of which was usually a solid piece of research or explanation of current practice, with recommendations for reform and improvement. My work with the controller of Arts in the mid-1970s, then Geoffrey Tribe, helped to ensure my happy cooperation with his successors, first Lyon Roussel and then Barrie Iliffe. The corresponding members of top management who supervised us were first Dr John Mitchell and then Trevor Rutter. As will be obvious, however, my initial ignorance was profound and my reliance for guidance and background knowledge on my immediate colleagues was complete. (This was rather more acceptable than thinking one knew all the answers.) John Cartwright, as deputy director, had built up an encyclopaedic familiarity with the world of producers, directors and actors in the feature-film field; Una Hurding, as head of Acquisitions and Festivals, quickly learnt her way round the very large number of 'independent' film makers seeking our help in getting their 'shorts' entered for the international competitions; and Ann Boggust was our Senior Acquisitions Officer with invaluable contacts among the makers of documentary and didactic programmes. Within two months of my taking charge, Lyon Roussel needed a six-page review of the role of films and video in support of our service to convince top management that we were on the move. Then followed three pages of argument setting out the case for transforming the NPFF into the FTVAC. Another six pages set out and made explicit a departmental policy, and 52 paragraphs of the *Operations Handbook* had to be revised and reissued. The British Council's Chairman, then Sir Charles Troughton, needed a four-page brief on the composition of the advisory committee, and the Arts and Office of Libraries in the Department of Education and Science (DES) required a statement of similar length on the importance of British film abroad.

The inaugural meeting of the FTVAC debated the department's current pattern of work and future policy towards international film festivals. Its second meeting considered its own terms of reference and scrutinized my paper on the acquisition of non-theatrical screening rights so thoroughly that the minutes ran to eight pages. A subcommittee later considered four possible ways forward, but could only recommend one as having any potential. The third meeting endorsed my very comprehensive paper on our policy in making acquisitions both for stocking in London and for sending abroad.

Meanwhile, the FTVAC had become aware of the multiplicity of bodies concerned with promoting British films abroad and of the absence of any coordinating responsibility, so an 'acorn group' of three was formed, which in turn led to two meetings with the Minister for Information Technology (then Mr Kenneth Baker) in the Department of Trade and Industry. It also led to a presentation on the committee's work to the British Council's board by our chairman, together with Derek Malcolm (critic of the *Guardian*) and David Puttnam (producer of *Chariots of Fire*), both of whom spoke eloquently and passionately in favour of our work. By the time of the fourth meeting in May 1984 there was already talk of launching a British film year to unite and galvanize all interested parties.

This detail is emphasized because the by-products were so important. The department was coming of age, holding its head high and being seen to be as devoted as any other to the British Council's interests. Any mystique there may have been was now being laid open and a true understanding was spreading both vertically (up and down the British Council) and horizontally (among our 'cultural industry' clientele and the creative professionals). In short, sniping was giving way to respect.

One 'law and custom' issue (which caused frequent heart-searching) was the question of the use by our overseas offices of the increasingly popular home videos. Since the 'intellectual property rights' were ill-defined and the small print text put on the sleeves by many 'publishers' in an attempt to restrict their use to 'the immediate family circle' was unenforceable, the problem required a completely fresh and radical approach. My draft of a four-page circular was sent for scrutiny by our in-house legal adviser in the full expectation of a prolonged wrangle. To my surprised relief, David Corcos sent it back with the simple comment 'OK. Representatives do after all have to live in the real world.' The effect was to devolve responsibility for observing the customs of the trade (and the law of copyright, which could not keep pace with technological developments) to our colleagues abroad and to abandon any attempt to monitor the supply of video material from London. One friendly recipient sent me a rare bouquet — so rare as to be quotable, whether deserved or not. He said 'What a pity all management documents cannot be as clear, as good-humoured and as easy to read.'

Getting back to the front line in under three years
Some colleagues in the globally transferable career service found themselves condemned to London for four of five years on each occasion. It was my ambition to move on in less than three years because the eight years from 1984 to my necessary retirement at 60 in 1992 was only just enough (more precisely seven and a half years) to be sure of two more postings, allowing for slippage and leave.

Opportunities for excursions continued to occur, however, and having visited Berlin, Lille and Cannes in my first year, some excellent reasons arose to go further afield in my second. The All-India Film Library in Bombay housed the biggest British Council collection outside London, and an invitation to attend India's ninth international film festival in Delhi was irresistible. Ten days devoted to these in mid-January 1983 were well spent. A flavour of the manner of organization is offered by this sentence from my report: 'The 16-millimetre screenings were held in the All-India Institute of Medical Sciences, which displayed a handwritten notice stuck onto a pillar saying TENTATIVE PROGRAMME.' Nevertheless, the daily panorama of Indian films enabled me to see three good, if rather long, recent feature-length ones. The British director, Lindsay Anderson, was chairman of the jury and his own film *Britannia Hospital* was among the six British ones competing. Film in India could be regarded as the opium of the enormous population, but television was then just beginning its inexorable takeover; this was the chief topic of my conversations in the high commission, in the British Council and with Mark Tulley, the BBC's long-serving Delhi correspondent.

Fulfilling a long-felt desire to travel on Indian railways, my journey to Bombay was in the *Frontier Mail* on its return journey from the northwest. It took exactly 24 hours, a day and a night, crossing the edge of the Rajasthan desert for half the time and arriving punctually. Some intensive discussion with all six of our staff concerned with the use of films — both as cultural events and as lending-library items — was followed by an unexpected bonus. Not far from our offices was the National Centre for the Performing Arts where an East–West music encounter was being jointly sponsored with the French and Germans. Peter Connell's party in his (the regional representative's) flat enabled me to meet many of the musicians taking part. Lyon Roussel had lived there and was glad to have a nostalgic photo of the flat, which has a view of the Gateway of India on the shore. Another well-received photograph was of the Brabourne stadium, our FTVAC chairman's father having been Governor of Bombay from 1933 to 1937.

The Moscow Film Festival had a long history of causing problems regularly every two years and the thirteenth, in 1983, was no exception. Difficulties invariably arose over the selection of the official entry; the buck was passed between several organizations at the British end and the Soviet authorities took every opportunity to make their own choice in spite of strong objections. Our embassy in Moscow naturally took a keen interest, so when enquiries revealed that the Ambassador, Sir Iain Sutherland was in London, clearly my best course was to seek his opinion on our suggestion that *Local Hero* should be our official entry. His first response on the telephone was 'I think I know you as Sarah's dad, don't I?', which was true, since our respective daughters were school friends and we had previously seen him in Athens. The upshot was his strong encouragement for me to check at first hand the film scene in Moscow, and an invitation to stay in the residence if a visit proved feasible. Meanwhile, we had arranged a special screening of *Local Hero* for two officials from the Soviet embassy in London who had raised no objection.

Though only four working days were necessary, with excursions available at one-third of the standard airfare if a minimum of six nights including a Saturday were booked, my journey began two days earlier and took in a familiarization trip to Leningrad. By travelling overnight on the *Red Arrow Express* it was possible to avoid two hotel nights and enjoy one whole day. The morning was spent on foot admiring the architecture, the afternoon with an Intourist excursion to the Pavlovsk Palace and the evening at the Kirov opera, followed by a walk back to the station in midsummer daylight — a foretaste of later experiences in Finland. All this was possible only through the strenuous making of arrangements by Michael Sullivan, the cultural attaché — at that time an FCO rather than a British Council appointee.

Besides viewing a very mixed bag of ten films there was much business in the British Council 'implant', the cultural section of the embassy, and a substantial by-product for me was retrospective enlightenment about many features of our recent three years in Romania. The satellite countries were subject to the imperial capital of the eastern bloc, so to have lived in one of them without being able to envisage the seat of power was quite a disadvantage.

True to form, despite the festival organizing committee's enthusiasm, the ideological censors rejected our official nomination of *Local Hero*, so the Ambassador decided in protest not to attend the opening ceremony; in his place he sent the Minister, David Ratford, and me. There was also a fuss over the entry for the children's film category, but what eventually confounded the Russian hosts was the gala screening of *Gandhi* in the place of honour on the last day, attended by HMA and Richard Attenborough, its maker. Overriding all other memories, however, was the view of the Kremlin across the river from my guest bedroom — bigger than the entire floor area of our house — whose last occupant had been the Foreign Secretary himself. On my return to London the usual criticisms were voiced (suggesting incompetence in our handling of Moscow), but this time they were silenced by my two-page statement, agreed with Lord Brabourne and others, setting out precisely what could and could not be expected.

Each autumn we had viewing opportunities without travelling far. The London Multi Media Market (LMMM) in September was followed by the London Film Festival (LFF) in November. Both the LMMM and the LFF had the advantage of being late in the season, and were in theory able to pick better products. My report on the twenty-sixth LFF of 1982 in a circular to colleagues abroad mentioned five new British features we would be acquiring, but saying 'The other films seen suffered from a variety of shortcomings ranging from the gratuitous exploitation of sex and violence to substandard film-making techniques.'

Following the success of *Chariots of Fire* expectations ran high, but my circular a year later said that only one offering was really good and that had been made for television — *An Englishman Abroad*, which depicted Guy Burgess (by Alan Bates) and Coral Browne (being herself).

Derek Malcolm, the *Guardian* critic and FTVAC member, was

209

appointed early in 1984 as the new director of the LFF. For the past two years he had been supported by us in attending the Durban Film Festival, which was both international and multi-racial. Derek was very keen that the devoted work of Mrs Ros Sarkin, the festival's director and a Progressive Party member of the Durban City Council, should be given plenty of encouragement, and Richard Watkins, in charge of our work in South Africa, agreed. A somewhat tortuous itinerary got me to Durban for 48 hours, to Maseru (Lesotho) for two nights, to Johannesburg and Pretoria for half a day each, and to Harare (Zimbabwe) for two full working days.

There was nothing cosmetic about this multiracial activity in Durban; Indian and Coloured attendances were increasing and special screenings were arranged in the African townships — the problem for the latter being transport. Two unexpected points of interest for me were visits to Gandhi's former ashram and to the township of Umlazi where a magnificent new technikon (local polytechnic) had been built with Urban Foundation funding.

Less expected still was an attempt to arrest me in Maseru. Our office and library there occupied quite elegant, purpose-built premises and, as my camera came out of my pocket, a local man in plain clothes asked me to come with him to the police station up the road 'for attempting to take a photograph of *him*.' My hesitant counter-suggestion was that we cross the road and discuss the problem inside with the boss. Brian Chenery knew the score and, while apologizing on my behalf, coolly explained that photographs were needed by London for publicity purposes. The plain-clothes man went on his way, but the apparent hypersensitivity probably arose from a recent incident with white South African soldiers. Lesotho displayed many features familiar to me from Malawi days, but Maseru was even smaller than Blantyre.

Although the British Council's base in South Africa was then in Pretoria, our joint film library was in the Consulate-General in Johannesburg where several hours were usefully spent elucidating the expected misconceptions among the staff. A working lunch with the Watkins family in Pretoria was so extended that Richard came close to missing my airport bus.

Our old friend Colin Perchard greeted me warmly at Harare airport and arranged fruitful talks with his library staff. The main topic, however, was the possibility of using the commercial chain of Rainbow cinemas as shop windows for British films, and relying on London distributors to provide 35-millimetre prints at trade prices, together with sponsorship in kind (free air freight) from British Airways and supporting documentation from us. Before flying home my final pleasure was to accompany the Perchard family to the opening of an extension to the nearby Jairos Jiri Rehabilitation Centre, designed by another old friend from Malawi days, the architect Jim Peto, who had also planned the conversion of our new premises from their previous use as a shoe factory.

Before setting off on this tour in southern Africa my hat had been put in the ring for a posting in the current year in accordance with an earlier postings preference form on which my curiosity about (indeed ignorance of) the Nordic area had been expressed. This had raised a debate about what sort of person should replace me — either a versatile generalist who 'knew nothing about films', the profession, the industry or the trade but who had the necessary experience to understand the point of view of colleagues overseas, or an expert in films, television and video who would need a long and painful indoctrination into the ethos of the British Council. Happily it could not be denied that there was a supply of the former sort, so my release was agreed and Finland accepted.

The sting in the tail of my time in films was an absurd incident over asbestos dust in our Portland Place building, which meant being locked out of our offices and film library for five weeks. Camping in temporary space in the Davies Street building, we struggled to contain the chaos that ensued from having no access to any records, commitments or film stock. Even our diaries were inaccessible — except mine, which had been extracted by stealth. We operated in shifts because there was room for only half my staff on any one day, and a single telephone had to suffice.

My swan song for the FTVAC and top management was a 12-page blueprint for the future on 'Developing the British Council's Work in Promoting Britain Through the Moving Image', which included a costed shopping list and set the stage for expansion.

211

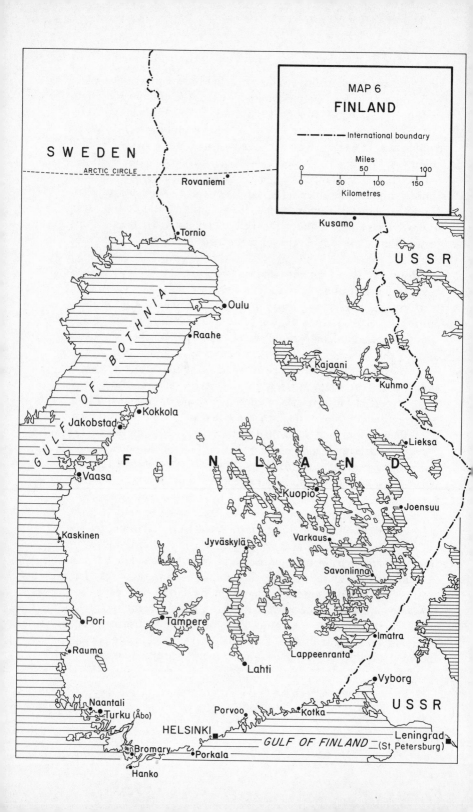

MAP 6
FINLAND

----- International boundary

Miles

Kilometres

SWEDEN

ARCTIC CIRCLE

Rovaniemi

USSR

Kusamo

Tornio

Oulu

Raahe

B O T H N I A

Kajaani

Kuhmo

Kokkola

Jakobstad

Lieksa

G U L F   O F

Vaasa

F I N L A N D

Kuopio

Joensuu

Kaskinen

Jyväskylä

Varkaus

Savonlinna

Pori

Tampere

Imatra

Rauma

Lappeenranta

Lahti

Vyborg

Naantali

Turku (Åbo)

Porvoo

Kotka

USSR

HELSINKI

GULF OF FINLAND

Leningrad
(St Petersburg)

Bromary

Porkala

Hanko

13
Finland at the Fulcrum:
The Bear in the Baltic

Preparations for Finland had to begin while we were still exiled from our proper offices; most of them were domestic and required much telephoning. Throughout our time in Malaysia and Romania we had let our house in Bourne End, but had lived there as a commuting base for the past three years of my London posting. It was quiet and had a good garden for my vegetable growing, but our children no longer needed a garden in which to play. What they did need was an easily accessible base in London itself, so we began the hunt for a flat. Unfortunately, the search coincided with a time when Diana was suffering from a short-lived loss of her customary energy, so many light summer evenings were spent by me chasing up leads and visiting potential homes. By mid-July we had attended Sarah's graduation ceremony in Durham and she was free to come with Diana to approve our selection of a leasehold at the falsely impressive address of 4 Emperor's Gate, conveniently near Gloucester Road tube. Two months later we managed to squeeze the contents of a four bedroomed house into this rather eccentric two and a half bedroomed basement flat, with an entrance and one room on the ground floor. Its chief merit was that it could in fact just accommodate our family of five, even if we were seldom to be together there at any one time. In due course it proved very difficult to sell, but that is another story. It had plenty of storage space, which is significant when needing to let a place during an absence abroad.

Clearing the decks for a Nordic adventure
Sarah had meanwhile been selected for a two-year assignment to teach English in Japan under what was then the newly-launched Wolfers or Japan English Teaching scheme, but which has since grown into the British English Teaching Scheme (BETS), providing hundreds of British (and other) English teachers for Japanese schools, funded by their Ministry of Education. Our old boss, Robin Duke, had been a member of the board that interviewed her. She went to a girls' junior high school in Mito, north of Tokyo, but the pupils were not very receptive, so she moved for her second year into the capital to work through an agency which provided English tuition for keen young executives in big companies. She flew to join us in Helsinki for her summer holiday between the two years.

Earlier in the year Diana had been listening to Radio 4 while doing the ironing and had pricked up her ears at mention of a sailing-cum-music weekend. Only 12 berths were available, but we booked promptly for this midsummer voyage from Ipswich to the Aldeburgh festival in Snape Maltings aboard the schooner *Stina of Sipoo*. Not recognizing the Finnish connection from the name, imagine our excitement when discovering books about Finland in the vessel's library. Exactly a week earlier — on the day the Queen visited the British Council's HQ in celebration of our fiftieth anniversary — news of our posting had come from Personnel. Sipoo is a small port east of Helsinki and the *Kristina* was elderly, wooden and previously used for coaling and as a church ship. Her bell had traditionally been used upside down as a font and the names of two children baptized in this way were inscribed on it. It was a blind date for us and the other ten passengers, but happy congeniality was assured by the common interest, even in very cramped quarters. We slipped downstream in the early hours of Saturday morning, sailed up the coast, caught the flood tide at the mouth of the Alde and reached Snape (after some very tight bends and going briefly aground) at the top of high water in time for breakfast. A wind quintet celebrated our arrival by climbing into

214

the rigging and playing from on high, and we remained moored there for two evening concerts. Disappointingly, on the Monday morning the skipper regretted that the wind was too strong to navigate safely on the ebb tide, so we missed the return voyage, having to retrieve our car from Ipswich separately.

We met our first Finns in Cardiff where the fourth in the series of British–Finnish mixed commissions was convened in late September 1984. This was a relatively relaxed arrangement (under the benign influence of Kalervo Siikala) to review the progress of cultural cooperation every three years, not at all like the renegotiation sessions with the Romanians. It was especially valuable for both parties to have a preview of each other in the presence of my predecessor Andrew Payne. Hospitality was arranged by Hugh Salmon, in charge of our office in Wales, and included a civic dinner in Cardiff Castle, formerly the property of the Earls of Bute and consequently adorned with portraits of the Crighton Stewart family. We also visited Atlantic College at St Donat's where the principal, Andrew Stuart, was a former ambassador to Finland and where several Finns held scholarships under the United World Colleges scheme.

Throughout October Diana came with me three times a week for an introductory course in the Finnish language which, unlike Swedish which is Germanic, has precious little in common with anything recognizable to a western European eye or ear. Our lady teacher also gave us our first lesson in the regional variations of physical appearance among Finns, saying 'Look at me. I'm from Karelia. See the shape of my eyes? I'm a fair-skinned Mongolian.'

As the countdown to departure reached a climax so too did our anxiety about Louise's health. Her training at Bart's to become a state enrolled nurse had been going well, but in her second year repeated infections and too frequent antibiotics were getting her down, yet my enquiries revealed that there was no adequate pastoral care for the inhabitants of the nurses' hostel, and the nurse tutor disclaimed any responsibility beyond the teaching role. Even so, she knew there was a problem because Louise's sick leave record had caused her to threaten to put her back into the previous class. An ENT consultant had recommended a tonsillectomy yet nothing had been done. As parents of an adult we

215

seemed to have no standing, even in this student/trainee situation. Eventually my plea of urgency in the light of our imminent disappearance was effective, but the operation was done just one week before we had to be off. Suffering from a lot of postoperative pain, Louise's plight was really distressing. We comforted her in the flat over the weekend, but had to rule out any postponement of our complicated journey and had to leave her back in her cheerless hostel, all of us feeling miserable. The one hope we had was that she could go to Potty Granny in Totnes for some recuperative care as soon as she could face a train journey. In due course we heard that we had been right to make a fuss; Louise's health improved beyond recognition and, soon after her visit to us in Helsinki the following March (including her twenty-first birthday), news came that she had passed her exams.

Having bought a small Volvo 340 with a left-hand drive and Scandinavian specifications (you cannot turn the lights off when the engine is running), we set off by an overnight ferry from Harwich to Esbjerg, driving the next day right across to Copenhagen. One of my motives for trying to get this posting was my complete ignorance of this part of Europe, so now we had the chance to become familiar with three of the four capitals, leaving Oslo for another time. We stayed two nights with William Brown, who was in charge of our work in Denmark and had earlier been my predecessor in Kuala Lumpur. One of his dinner guests was Dr Harald Fugelsang who turned out to be a close friend of John Anderson, the ophthalmologist brother of Robert, both of Shetland fame. The Louisiana Museum of Modern Art commanded our admiration, both for its content and its seashore setting on the way past Elsinore castle to the ferry across to Sweden.

A chance meeting with a Swedish researcher at a King's College dinner in Cambridge two months earlier had elicited advice on where to stop over in central Sweden; he had unhesitatingly recommended the Gyllene Uttern (Golden Otter) Hotel as the ideal halfway house. It was indeed peaceful and rural, on the shore of Sweden's biggest and most central lake, near Granna. In Stockholm our man in charge was John Day, known from our past in London. We had been warned against using the ferry to Helsinki on a Sunday night because of potential rowdiness. It was bad enough the next night, but the delay gave us an opportunity to attend the Remembrance Day service in the English church, which evoked memories of both my mother's brothers who had been lost in the Second World War. We also inspected the raised hulk of King Gustavus Adolphus's wooden warship *Wasa*, which had sunk on her maiden voyage while still in the harbour, probably from the same design faults that sank our King Henry VIII's *Mary Rose* off Portsmouth; and we lunched in John's flat. His office was right inside the British embassy behind bullet-proof glass defences, which had been made necessary because of a terrorist attack on a nearby diplomatic building. The most surprising discovery for me during the night crossing to Helsinki, however, were the lights on the navigation marks, which changed colour as we passed them. There are technical reasons for this, peculiar to the tideless nature of the Baltic.

First impressions and plunging into 'joulu'

David Kirwan, the assistant representative, greeted us on the quayside and whisked us quickly from the customs shed to an embassy lunch party, our arrival by chance having coincided with one of their regular leavers and joiners' functions, so we were immediately 'on show' to all our British colleagues. Although welcomed as members of the team, we did not have (as in Romania) any diplomatic status: the British Council paddled its own canoe in a separate office and library within walking distance. In fact, wherever one needed to go in central Helsinki was a walkable distance. Trams, buses and very efficient taxis did not always save time.

Our house, on the other hand, was a substantial bus ride away, in the suburb of northern Tapiola. All previous representatives had lived in pleasantly spacious flats near the centre, but my predecessor had had very bad luck with leases and had been obliged, towards the end of his time, to rent a house he knew would be none too convenient for any successor. Fortunately for us, he had made this abundantly clear on paper. Although we were in no mood to make changes immediately, before unpacking very much baggage it was necessary for me to telephone the Finnish owner, temporarily working on contract in Dar es Salaam in Tanzania, to find out how soon he was intending to come home. We had barely

217

six months' grace. The second domestic task was to collect an extra set of four wheels for the car. It was compulsory to have studded tyres fitted by a certain date each autumn and to revert to ordinary tyres by a certain date in the spring. Each time we did this — eight times in four years — we were glad of the slickness made possible with eight wheels.

While the word *joulu*, the equivalent of our English yule, is used to describe both the month of December and the Christmas festival, the students begin celebrating with *pikku joulu* (little yuletide) in mid-November. The dismal surroundings and falling temperatures at this time of year make it generally beneficial to begin the party season early and, for most of December, a steady series of afternoon receptions in offices serves to raise people's spirits. These *glögi* parties (on mulled sweet wine with nuts and raisins) turned what would otherwise have been a gloomy time to arrive into excellent opportunities to meet all the right people. By Christmas proper my initial familiarization was well advanced.

Finland in 1984 was still enjoying the benefits of a symbiotic relationship with the Soviet Union, analogous in some ways to Hong Kong's service to China. Finland exported industrial products in return for raw materials, especially fuel oil and low-grade timber. Much of the trade was by barter rather than exchanging currencies, but within five years the new Russia needed payment for oil in hard currency at just the time when Finland was finding it more difficult to earn it. Recession and unemployment has since hit them hard. In our time, however, self-confidence in the Finnish way ran high. The contrast between this thriving market economy in northeast Europe and the struggling command economies of southeast Europe could hardly have been greater. Helsinki and Bucharest are nearly identical distances eastwards from London, yet worlds apart. Whereas the Romanian regime had succeeded in building up the illusion of independence in foreign affairs, the Finnish people had actually fought off the Russians twice in living memory, and their government took great care to maintain its neutrality on the fulcrum between east and west, particularly in balancing cultural influences. Hence the American Centre, the Alliance Française, the Goethe Institute and ourselves were balanced by four eastern bloc centres run by the Soviets, the East

Germans, the Hungarians and the Poles. The Italians and Canadians were also active, as were the Czechs, but without upsetting the balance.

In this context the British Council's role was concentrated in the traditional fields of running a library and information service, supporting the movement of teachers and students in both directions, bolstering the teaching of English throughout the Finnish system, and engaging in as much cultural activity as possible. Everything depended on collaboration with, and often contributions from, local officials and institutions. When my one excellent British colleague, David Kirwan, introduced me to our handful of Finnish supporting staff (two librarians, two secretaries, an accountant and a clerk-cum-messenger) it was a severe shock to discover that Inger Honkeranta, designated as my secretary, had been absent since my predecessor had left and was more or less refusing even to come in and meet me. So my first challenge was a psychological one. If there is anything that a new man needs most it is the help of a reliable secretary. Messages were sent saying that she need have no fear of such a gentle new boss as me, of all people, but it was several weeks before she could be persuaded to appear.

Inger's problem was obscure and it baffled us. She was a valued member of staff with a long history of energetic service, but was in a minority of one in being the only Finn of Swedish origin among us. We learnt what we could of her background, but failed to understand whatever it was that steadily eroded her health until one morning, in the fifth month since my arrival, she came in clearly unfit for work and, after a delicate interview with which David helped me, we had to suspend her. The symptoms seemed to suggest withdrawal from something, but what? This time her mother was persuaded to come and fetch her, but a long period of sick leave followed, during which time her work was being 'carried' by others. The circumstances were reported to London and discussed with the embassy, but action lay with us. Drinking was only a small part of the problem; the roots were deeper, but treatment with a specialist in alcoholism did improve matters. More than a year later, during which time we had all known that any relapse implied inevitable dismissal — even the heavily protective Finnish labour law recognized the due process of final written warnings — we reshuffled duties among our three lady assistants and that helped. The end of this long story was a surprise — almost a shocking one, the relief was so great. News reached me one summer day that Inger was in hospital after an emergency appendectomy and, having visited her promptly and seen her transformation, my faith in human nature was strongly reinforced. She never looked back and all was not only forgiven but joyfully so.

My second challenge was simply the climate. The tropics had tested me over many years in various places, but having to cope with arctic conditions was new, apart from very brief moments in Austria and Romania. In the first week of January 1985 the temperature fell one day to –17 °C, on the next to –21 °C, then to –25 °C and stayed there for six weeks, which surprised even the Finns. It was just my luck to be set an endurance test so soon. My Romanian fur coat came in handy, but the Transylvanian hat had to be replaced with a bigger and better one, and my lined German farmer's boots did well; but the wait for the bus at the end of the lane each morning was only tolerable with padded ski trousers (salopettes) over my office suit. Then there was a ten-minute walk from the bus station to the office; this was good exercise, but had to be done at a carefully regulated pace. If one walked too fast too much freezing air would be taken in too quickly and icicles would form round one's nose and mouth; if one walked too slowly one would not be kept warmed by the effort. A curious form of panic begins to take hold if you feel the back of your head is not keeping warm.

First time round the changing seasons

The Inger episode illustrates all too well how concern for our local staff always took a high priority, even if it could normally be expected to be more necessary among the long-suffering Romanians or Ethiopians than among the relatively prosperous Finns. Turning the climatic conditions to advantage was important for our own welfare, so the winter was not far advanced before we took lessons in cross-country skiing (or langlauf, as it is known in some parts). This is very good exercise and, unlike downhill skiing, needs relatively light clothing because of the heat generated. If the temperature is much below –15 °C, however, the Finns tend not to ski for fear of the wind-chill factor on the head. In our second winter, by which time we had moved from Tapiola to Haukilahti, we could walk to the shore and ski on the frozen sea around the islands we sailed past in the summer. In this first year the inshore ice was more than a metre thick, so the ferry to the island of Suomenlinna just off Helsinki harbour, for example, was replaced by a bus route on an official 'road'. One's car insurance cover was valid for such roads, but not for other places where one might misjudge the strength of the ice. One of our party tricks was to take incredulous visitors out onto the sea and invite them to take a photograph of the car alongside a navigation mark.

As elsewhere, we were into the musical scene pretty quickly. The very fine Lutheran cathedral dominating the tsarist imperial-style architecture of central Helsinki has a semidetached annexe on one wing, which is used as the Anglican church and served by an official chaplain to our embassy. An informal group known as the St Nicholas Singers roped us in and, before long, the organist Paul Dillingham (a teacher of English with a Finnish wife) shared its direction with me. Nearer the heart of genuine cultural integration was our welcome into the Kamarikuoro Cantemus, the Sibelius Academy's chamber choir, which was very professionally directed by Matti Hyökki. As the only foreigners in it we had a problem understanding his instructions in rehearsals, but were paired with kind helpers, mine being Tom Salakari, a very competent tenor, who whispered English translations to me. Fortunately, the Finnish language has a strictly phonetic orthography, so singing in it did not present problems for us — unless at high speed, of course. In any case much of the repertoire was in Latin or German, except when we found ourselves plunged into making a video recording of boisterous folk songs for Yleisradio television. These were in due course transmitted for *Vappu*, the 1 May student madness that celebrates the end of winter.

The Finnish–British Society, of which all British Council and embassy staff were ex-officio members, was another centre of social activity. Ever since the immediate postwar period there had been a network of Finn–Brit teachers of English based in the

221

society's local branches and supported by the British Council. Times had changed and the numbers had shrunk, but the expectation of our involvement was very much alive, and the Helsinki centre ran a programme which included amateur dramatics. We enjoyed its productions of *Oh What a Lovely War* and *Whose Life is it Anyway*, which were too soon for Diana's involvement, but she later played leading roles in Galsworthy's *Escape*, in Shaw's *Pygmalion*, and in a version of *Alice in Wonderland*.

The transition from winter to summer can be quite startling, but that year it was wishful thinking to expect *Vappu* to mark Finland's transformation from an Arctic to a Mediterranean society. Yet between late May and mid-June an enclosed, introspective culture suddenly gave way to an open, extroverted one. As one of my letters said, 'The grey-white monochromatic frostbound environment, from which warm-blooded life requires continuous protection, suddenly gives way to a fertile polychromatic ambience of blues and greens; man and beast emerge to bask in the warmth, the open air markets thrive, the boats bring the harbours alive and Finland displays her alternative character.' Winter means work and survival; summer spells relaxation. Teaching institutions close on 31 May and by the time of the Midsummer Eve pagan sun festival most Finns have already left for their sauna huts, boats and islands.

May was the month for naval visits and, as it approached each year, our defence attaché friend, Lieutenant Colonel Bill Collings, would be biting his nails while trusting that the sea ice would melt in time. HMS *Fearless* was a rather old vessel, but HMS *Diomede* the following year and, above all, HMS *Bristol* and HMS *Euryalus* in our last year, were fine examples of the best of the Royal Navy. We enjoyed the privilege of parties on board and of the chance, quietly at home, to entertain their skippers Captain West and Commander Cardale, along with their 'quack', Surgeon Commander Cunningham.

This stimulated thoughts of sailing and summer music festivals, but first (as in Romania), having taken stock of the office and library — somewhat gloomily, it must be said — and having encountered the whole range of key contacts within the Helsinki 'establishment' by the turn of the year, it was necessary to visit provincial centres and to show the cultural flag. The Tampere Film Festival gave me an excuse for a day trip for a first look at the Manchester of Finland; a Finnish–British meeting took me to the small port of Rauma on the west coast, and an internal flight to Jyväskylä (in the central region) provided a view of one of the younger universities. James Took, my London boss (the controller of Europe Division) came on a visit. This coincided with a press conference in advance of a tour by the London City Ballet and with a party for the seventy-fifth anniversary of the Finnish Library Association. He is a keen ornithologist (his book on the birds of Cyprus has been reprinted), so our friend Matti Gustafsen, a long-serving official in the International Relations section of the Ministry of Education, arranged to take him for a weekend to the well-known nature reserve of Kusamo near the northeastern border. We flew together as far as Oulu near the top of the Gulf of Bothnia and were entertained by Professor Mannerkoski, the energetic Rector of the newish university.

The final and most important of these initial visits was to Turku, the original capital of Swedish Finland known as Åbo, in the southwest corner of the country. This needed three nights away to do it justice, so Diana came with me by car and we made a thorough exploration, including a first look at 'boaty' places such as Naantali, Ruissalo and Tamisaari. As well as meeting the Rectors of both universities (Åbo Akademi being the Swedish one) and other academics, this marked the beginning of our friendship with Professor Nils-Erik Enkvist and his wife Tua, and led in turn to our meeting Gottfried and LaVonne Gräsbeck.

As the summer gathered pace everything began to happen at once. The London City Ballet came for an extensive tour, giving three performances in each of the main centres and two each in Lahti and Jyväskylä. They opened in Helsinki just before we had to fly home for the annual jamboree at Sherborne. Diana stayed on, but my journey back was just in time for the first of three concerts by the Kamerate of Köln, which we had co-sponsored with my German and Italian colleagues for European Music Year. Then, in Diana's absence, the deadline for a decision on our housing forced me into abandoning our fruitless hunt for a central flat and committing ourselves to a modern *rivitalo* (row house or terraced condominium) in the suburb known as Westend, or Haukilahti, some 12 kilometres out to the west but on a much better bus route than Tapiola. Our neighbours there had meanwhile begun the characteristic operation of blasting a cavity in the bedrock for the building of a house on the next-door plot, so when Diana came back her ears were assailed at regular intervals all day and we were happy to move a month later.

Summer music festivals and chartered sailing yachts

David Kirwan had a tightly scheduled series of seminars on his plate including one for textbook writers, one on drama in education and a third on English literature, which was timed to mesh nicely with the annual Lahti writers' reunion to which Malcolm Bradbury and Christopher Bigsby had accepted invitations. Held during the white nights of high summer (8 June to 8 July), this meeting specialized in all-night parties. We dutifully put in an appearance at these seminars, but had to confess that we kept a closer lookout for the many British musicians who were coming, with or without one of our travel grants, to perform during the season. The first opportunity was in Naantali where Barry Tuckwell (horn) played one of the Mozart concertos with The Netherlands Chamber Orchestra in the priory church. On the return journey we made a detour to Paivola where the Helsinki Early Music Society had engaged James Tyler to give lute lessons.

Immediately before the packers came to prepare for our move we had a long weekend visit from James and Ann Wilson (our former defence attaché and lay reader friends from Bucharest days) then posted with NATO in Mons, Belgium. Almost at the same moment our old musical friends Nick and Wendy Roles turned up for a medical conference in Tampere and, after a very lively dinner party (in which we included Bill and Jenny Collings for the military and medical connection), they took off for a visit to Leningrad. A surprise call from the airport on the eve of our move announced their premature return; the flight they had been booked on did not exist and they were starving. Par for the course, we thought.

Our next musical excuse was a quick flight to Savonlinna, the Swedish-built castle in the central lakes region, used for an opera festival every year, where the British baritone, Donald McIntire was singing the name part in *The Flying Dutchman*. The Finnair excursion stipulated a minimum stay of 24 hours, so we took a couple of short boat trips nearby and at last satisfied my curiosity about seaplanes. My father had flown very primitive ones in the First World War and my flying lessons in Kuala Lumpur had stimulated an interest. A local pilot was offering ten-minute trips for a small sum in a Cessna 206 with floats, so the chance had to be taken. The takeoff technique required one float to be skewed out of the water to reduce drag and help to obtain flying speed. The decision to 'land' again could not be taken without checking the proposed water lane for potential obstacles. This visit was also the genesis of a little plan to come back next year by water — see below.

Work in the office, with a staff reduced by seasonal leave, was closely focused on squeezing award letters, or the authority to issue them, out of London. There had been many changes since my previous involvement in our scholarships system when in Japan. Not only had the concept of a scholarship unit been abolished, but the cash equivalent had to be augmented from other sources so that more could be done with less money, and the terminology had been adjusted to take in the FCO's own offering of study awards. At the turn of the year we had convened the usual group of Finnish academics and a representative of the Ministry, under my chairmanship, to interview and select the candidates. The successful awards this year ranged from postdoctoral research in bioengineering for a paediatrician to the vaguest sort of training for a translator. The new flexibility was fine in principle, but in practice it entailed months of agonizing uncertainty, hectic communications (or lack of, which was worse) and some very invidious assessments of need in relation to family circumstances, which tested our tactfulness to its limits.

There were also some high-powered visitors around. Mr Speaker Weatherill charmed our staff when he visited the library; Mr Robert Dunn, MP and parliamentary undersecretary, spent four intensive days as the guest of the Ministry of Education in visits and discussions; and Baroness Young, FCO Minister of State, sent me a nice letter of appreciation after being shown our establishment.

A sailing holiday looked very attractive and enquiries had led me to Nautic Centre, a clearing house for people with underemployed boats wanting to make a little money. Bill Collings was a keen sailor and had taken me out in Helsinki harbour several times in his day boat. But our benevolent Ambassador, Alan Brooke-Turner, had taken up sailing his own small cruising yacht and, when he heard of our intentions, he asked Bill — 'Do you think Bruce knows what he is doing?' Bill's answer must have been equivocal because HMA clearly wanted to satisfy himself at first hand, so he invited Diana, Jessica and me to join him and his wife for a Sunday morning spin. The weather was not auspicious, but we set off from the Lautasaari marina and he handed me the helm after a few minutes. Before long it was evident that we were heading into a fog bank and, on my requesting advice, he said we should take a bearing on the last mark astern and keep going — 'proceed with caution' is the usual phrase. After some pressure from Mrs Brooke-Turner, and among the sounds of other vessels, we used the engine to turn round and follow a reciprocal course, successfully finding the mark we had left behind. Then a wind blew the fog away and out we sped with Alan thinking of increasing sail, whereupon Hazel uttered the inimical remark 'Oh, let's not have the spinnaker: it creates such agro!' Seldom a truer word was spoken, and we retreated back to the mooring to eat our sandwich lunch in the rain.

Next day was the official opening of the International Federation for Vernacular Languages' conference, but between this and a big party in our office for its participants on the third day, we managed to savour the delights of the Kuhmo chamber music festival by flying to Kajaani, spending two nights in a self-catering flat and attending five concerts in one day. Jane Manning (soprano) and Robert Cohen (cello) were among the British performers, and thus began our long friendship with Kuhmo's founder and director, Seppo Kimanen and his wife Yoshiko Arai, who leads the Jean Sibelius Quartet of which he is the cellist.

Within three more days, during which Sarah joined us from Tokyo, we were off to Raisio marina and aboard our chartered Targa 101, a ten metre (33-foot) sloop-rigged yacht, the biggest and best of all the ones we had in four years, but sadly abused by previous charterers and a little intimidating for a first time skipper in strange waters. She sailed quite beautifully, but the agents had failed to repair the sea toilet properly and the gas bottle gave out on the second day. We had the inevitable minor adventure; Diana slipped and fell between boat and shore when landing and was rescued by a startled Finn in his pyjamas, and our propeller became entangled in a neighbour's mooring rope, which required a diver to release it. But we had only one patch of bad weather, learnt a lot about the Western Archipelago, navigated our 12-metre mast nervously under a bridge with 15-metre clearance, and reached Naantali by water. Approaching a landing stage for a lunch stop near Rymattylla church, Sarah leapt ashore but began to descend through some rotten timbers. When given the shouted instruction to 'take a turn' rather than try to hold the mooring rope in her hand, she countered with 'Daddy, I'm 23 and not stupid!' — a remark which has continued to raise a laugh for many years.

The Turku festival had invited The Sixteen and the London Baroque for two concerts, so we went for a weekend and heard them perform Bach's *Mass in B minor* in St Michael's church (a Lars Sonck design he wished had been bombed) and some earlier works in the cathedral. The Endellion Quartet impressed everyone with its 'fantastic playing' in the suburban St Henry's church.

My second sister Jenny Bain arrived for a short holiday while Sarah and Jessica were still with us, and was somewhat bemused to step straight into our house-warming party for 97 people. During her stay we managed a day trip eastwards along the coast to Haiko Manor and Porvoo, partly by boat, and later visited the Galen Kalala museum, the city art gallery and the village museum on Seurasaari. The Helsinki festival opened, and our long-running negotiations with Mrs Savola and her husband, in charge of Finland's national theatre, to bring over our National Theatre production of *Animal Farm* reached fruition. The text of the satire was well known to most Finns, for whom the risk of totalitarian subversion was quite close to home, and all four performances were sold out. This was an 'out-and-back' export made possible by a gap in the company's diary resulting from a cancellation. Being not part of a Drama and Dance Department multi-country tour, the budget could benefit from excursion air fares and the timing did not depend on any other country's convenience. Such an arrangement worked well a few years later for the English Brass Quintet coming to Ethiopia.

More excursions to provincial centres

In Kuopio there was another moderately new university (which had developed out of a teacher training institution) and the sequence of interviews for such visits became fairly standardized and easily arranged over the telephone by a secretary. One would see the Rector, then the library, and spend most of the time in the language centre, or the specifically English department if there was one. In Kuopio it was also important to see Kari Kujanen, a young lawyer who was chairman of the Federation of Finnish–British Societies. This time, too, some correspondence had led me to the home of the Lehtimaki family whom my eldest sister Sheelagh Bridgman had known in Riyadh, Saudi Arabia, while my brother-in-law Mark was working there. She had taught one of the daughters the violin.

The Rectors of both the university and the technical university (or *korkeakoulu*) in Tampere (a paediatrician and mathematician respectively) were visited to expound what services we offered and to encourage them to put forward candidates or to ask for support. On this occasion Professor Sandy Cunningham was checking the arrangements for a ten-week exchange of students from his University of Leicester.

Joensuu was another 'seat of learning' in the central lakes area, rapidly equipping itself with the facilities required by a self-respecting community. The university already had both an English department and a language centre; it had just opened a new concert hall and library, and the old boys' grammar school had been turned into the town's art gallery. The Protestant and Ortho-dox churches faced each other from opposite ends of an avenue named, not surprisingly, Kirkkonkatu (Church Street).

Back in Helsinki, Kai Forsblom, the owner of a commercial gallery with a very astute view of the market, was opening an exhibition of Allan Jones's works with the artist present. The prints on show gave a fine impression of sensitivity to the flowing lines of the human figure, and we were glad to obtain one at a suitable discount and to have it framed in Kai's wife's Turku workshop. We provided a buffet lunch for the interested members of the local artistic fraternity.

Vaasa is a west coast port halfway up the Gulf of Bothnia opposite Umeå in Sweden. The university needed visiting and the Swedish Club had invited me to give a talk. Better than talking, however, was my use of the British Council's own documentary film called *Have Culture Will Travel*, which gave a very well balanced view of our global coverage and was especially salutary for such a sophisticated audience. They needed to know about our work in delivering development aid, for this helped explain their place in our order of priorities — tactfully indicated as not as high as they might have liked. It was used again to good effect both for the Helsinki Finnish–British Society and in the embassy itself for colleagues there. The Ostrobothnian museum in Vaasa is of special historical interest because of the connection with Marshal Mannerheim's leadership in 1917–18. Next day in Oulu the AGM of the Federation of Finnish–British Societies was combined with a dinner to celebrate the fiftieth anniversary of the English Club, and then an overnight train took me back to Helsinki.

While Diana had flown to London to be with Jessica during the Sherborne half-term week, it seemed wise to complete my coverage of the provinces before the winter advanced further and to go eastwards to Lappeenranta and Imatra on the shores of Lake Saimaa near the Russian border. Such reconnaissance was essential for the planning of itineraries for performing groups or visual exhibitions, unless one was to be entirely reliant on second-hand knowledge. In this case it was useful sooner than expected, for the Scottish Chamber Orchestra (SCO) came on tour early in the following year. As well as the usual call on the Rector, the language centre and the university library, there was time to see the Southern Karelia Museum, the art gallery, the public library and a fine new concert hall. At this point it should be mentioned that the Finns had been unable to decide which town in Karelia should be favoured in the bid for higher education, so all three — Kuopio, Joensuu and Lappeenranta — had been encouraged to develop interdependent specialisms.

Pori had once been a significant west coast port, but the fine

customs house had been turned into an art gallery. Our ambassador had accepted an invitation to open an exhibition in the public
library to commemorate the fortieth anniversary of the Pori
English Club, and my journey was to accompany him, also for the
dinner in the Swedo-Finnish Club. All these club celebrations
helped to keep alive the valuable work done by the Finnish–British
Society teacher/secretaries of the past and to minimize the effect of
the dwindling numbers now available.

The experience of handling the selection for fellowships and
other awards in January 1985 convinced me that we should bring
everything forward by a month and do it again in December, so
getting the initial processes for 1986/7 done before Christmas.
Another compelling reason was to benefit from David Kirwan's
knowledge of the field before he was replaced by Paul Docherty,
who was due to arrive early in the new year. One more innovation
was to have our own *glögi* party in the library, as a vehicle for
publicizing our services and reciprocating hospitality.

1986: a year of surprises, new people and new places
News of the SKOP Bank having bought the Bensow building did
not at first seem very momentous, but on the very day we were
holding a big office party for the handover/takeover of my assistant representatives, David and Paul, a stranger walked into the
library unannounced and casually informed the staff that we had
six months' notice to quit. It seemed odd to me that he had not
asked to see me, the man in charge, nor had he come bearing a
letter containing polite regrets of inconvenience; but perhaps that
was just the Finnish way of doing business, we thought. The British Council had been model tenants in Eteläesplanadi 22a for 26
years, and we had just installed a new internal telephone system
and a telex machine.

Only a month later John Salter, our library adviser who had
previously visited us in Bucharest from Warsaw, came with a consultant from Coopers and Lybrand to carry out a prototype cost-
benefit analysis of British Council library work, using us as guinea
pigs. It was eventually recognized in London that we had been
'very ill-served' by this exercise, but at the time we felt vulnerable
in the light of suggestions that we ought to be marketing our

library as if it were soap powder and that it was discouraging for the public to be faced with bookshelves when entering our premises. Struggle as we did during that week to get onto the same wavelength as our outsider, Paul agreed with me that we could find no common ground in basic philosophy. It seemed that we were assumed to be mad long-haired artists, whereas we viewed him as a mad short-haired executive. The ethos of public service broadcasting seemed to us relevant, but that was dismissed as value-judgemental. So much self-justification was required, and our library staff so bewildered by it, that some midnight oil was burnt in my study at home to produce a four-page essay entitled 'Notes Towards an Operational Philosophy for the Helsinki Library'. This was not unlike the paper on the VSO's operational philosophy written more that a decade earlier, with the same morale-raising purpose.

Happily, the manner in which the SKOP Bank had conveyed their intentions was belied by their subsequent interest and concern in catering for our needs. They were renovating a building round the corner, which would be ideal for us but would not be ready for two years. Would we be prepared to move within the Bensow premises from the third to the seventh floor on a temporary basis and then move again early in 1988? We cast about for alternatives to the contemplation of a double move, but found none and before long came to terms with the prospect of using the first move as a convenient preparation for the ultimate one. Nevertheless, our office and library accommodation problems did divert our attention from proper work and unavoidably became an obsession for two full years. Our landlords in due course proved extremely considerate. They constructed internal layouts to our own specification and to a very high standard without asking for any financial contribution at all, and this alone made the double move worthwhile.

As a light-hearted diversion Diana came with me to a local boat show where we spotted a small sailing dinghy of the plastic bath-tub type. We fancied keeping a dinghy near our house for occasional inshore pottering between the times when we might be chartering bigger boats for offshore voyages. The Finnish system, we discovered, was that before owning a boat you had to have a mooring allocated and that could only be done by the sailing club in whose catchment area you resided. So we soon became the only foreign members of Westend Sailors, whose appropriate official then showed us which landing stage we could use. Then we ordered the boat.

The power of critics became clearer than ever when a journalist in the *Helsinki Sanomat* assessed the SCO as 'one of the best in the world'. On the morning of their concert in Helsinki he published a rave review of their performance under Jukka-Pekka Saraste in Joensuu a day or so earlier. In a flash that evening's concert was sold out, and they did not disappoint anyone. We had a very lively buffet supper for all of them in our snowbound quarters and next day they finished their tour in Turku.

Paul Docherty had taught English for six years in Spain and had spent a year at Strathclyde University taking a B.Lit. degree before joining the British Council's career service and coming to us in Finland. Once he had settled in we thought of taking a little leave by asking our friend, Terttu Jares, in the nearby Finnair booking office to fix us a personal package tour of Spain. Paul's advice was invaluable and we took a lozenge-shaped route round Andalusia, staying in *parador*s in all but one place. To arrive via Madrid at Malaga airport at midnight and then wake up in the Parador Golf within the sight and sound of the unfrozen sea was a most invigorating tonic for the winter-weary. The countryside we drove through from Granada to Cordoba and on to Seville was blessed with almond blossom, and orange-laden trees lined the streets.

On our return my first duty was to pay my respects to our new Ambassador, Justin Staples, who had previously been posted in Bangkok. Having benefited from his predecessor's interest in sailing, it was a happy discovery to find that we shared a common interest in music, and we enjoyed the embassy's strong support in our work throughout our time. Quite soon the idea of using a local band to play in the residence garden during the Queen's birthday party celebrations became a firm invitation from me to the Töölö Brass Band to take on this 'honour'. The band was duly appreciative, but as we had no money (or disliked the idea of paying cash) we suggested the reciprocal device of using one of our travel grants to entice Ray Farr, a well-known British brass players' coach, to come and train it in preparation for entering a European competition. When the time came in mid-June this enhancement of the Queen's birthday party caused it to be voted the best in memory.

The Kamarikuoro Cantemus was unfortunately dissolved for lack of support from the Sibelius Academy's student members, but several singers continued to be known to us who occasionally supported the church-based St Nicholas Singers mentioned earlier and the Finnish radio chamber choir, the nearest approximation to a professional group in a country where choral singing tended to be strictly amateur but of a very high standard. One such friend was Matti Kilpiö, a lecturer in Helsinki University's philology department. Another was Nikki Vaskola, the administrator of the Yleisradio choir, who had been instrumental in getting John Aldiss to coach it for a week and to guest-conduct a concert. Matti not only had a rich baritone voice but he was also a keen viola player, so we sought his advice (and that of Seppo Kimanen) when Jessica said she needed us to buy her a decent viola. We visited Taskinen's workshop in Espoo and heard that a French maker was in town. Eventually, we had an evening of string trios, punctuated with supper and the testing of three short-listed violas — a big Polish one, a very new Finnish one and a French one that had won a prize in Tokyo. The choice was both amusing and agonizing, and the French won. It was during a similar chamber music session that Matti had endearingly said to me, 'It is obvious, Bruce, that you *have had* a good technique.'

Having seen *en route* to post the circumstances under which our colleagues in Copenhagen and Stockholm worked, we were very pleased when Peter Thompson in Oslo agreed to host a meeting for the four of us to 'talk shop' comparatively. James Moore decided not to come from Denmark, but John Day from Sweden did attend. My lasting impression was the essentially Atlantic atmosphere of Norway, in contrast to the Baltic context of the other three Nordic states, though one should not forget Iceland as the fifth. Our office in Oslo had one very rare characteristic; its local staff were not Norwegians but resident expatriate Britons, and its library had been dispersed some years previously. We were lucky to be able to squeeze in a visit to the Viking ship museum.

A very unexpected requirement to find the Helsinki equivalent of Moss Bros and hire full evening tails arose from a virtually compulsory invitation from Professor Inna Koskiniemi to escort her to the Turku University *promotio* ceremony. It was a solemn academic occasion held once a year to celebrate new appointments and grant doctoral degrees. A service in full regalia was held in the cathedral, followed by a feast in the castle. Inna Koskiniemi had been one of the earliest holders of a British Council scholarship from Finland and was especially anxious to maintain the connection. The concern was mutual, of course, and it was a privilege to oblige.

Another surprise was my mother breaking her ankle. She had been planning to visit us, having previously managed to come and stay in Malawi (with my father), in Malaysia (when widowed) and in Romania. The minor mishap occurred just two months before the journey was due, but she was determined to stick to her plan and my sister Sheelagh was luckily able to make herself free to come with her. The bones set quickly but she could not have travelled alone. They arrived a few days after Diana returned from her annual trip to Sherborne, during which time our plastic sailing dinghy had been delivered and my tasks of preparing its equipment (sanding and varnishing unfinished timber items) had made good progress. We still needed a light boat trolley, however, to get the vessel from our veranda to its designated mooring place. It also had to be registered with Westend Sailors and that required agreement on a name. There was no hesitation this time — it had to be the Finnish word for Nightingale: *Satakieli*, which means 'a hundred tongues'. As in Japanese, flames = tongues = songs. In the evening of the day the Töölö Brass Band had entertained the guests at the Queen's birthday party, we held a small launching ceremony, but Potty Granny could not manage to pronounce the boat's name as the bottle of fizzy water was poured over the bow.

It was time for the Naantali festival and this year the ECO was giving two concerts under Ashkenazy's baton with a day off in between, so we planned an early evening waterborne party for them. The only vessel with no previous commitment was booked by telephone from Helsinki in good time, but the skipper of *Zaida*, a motor fishing vessel in style, would not confirm anything in writing — a Finnish habit that never failed to put me on edge, except that one did learn to respect the my-word-is-my-bond principle. Cases of wine brought with us from Helsinki were cooled in our hotel's cellar and we enlisted the help of our friends Peter and Tessa Harborne, he being head of chancery in our embassy, to muster the orchestra on the quayside and to man the bar. We waited patiently at the appointed hour, fearing the rapid development of a British Council-inspired fiasco, but at precisely two minutes past six o'clock we spotted the profile of *Zaida* rounding a headland. Simultaneously, the ambassadorial Rolls-Royce arrived with Justin and Susan Staples and, with the skipper's agreement, we hoisted a Union flag. Although it is technically illegal in Finland to fly any but the Finnish flag, we presumed we would get away with it in abnormal diplomatic circumstances until we noticed a marine police launch coming our way. Quite soon, to our relief, we saw that it was more interested in preventing another boat from exceeding the speed limit. The two short trips between the islands were so much enjoyed that a similar arrangement was repeated two years later. Potty Granny and Sheelagh were with us throughout, and we also fitted in a visit to the museum of Vaino Aaltonen's sculpture in Turku.

To coordinate the availability of a chartered boat with the booking of opera tickets in Savonlinna and timing the voyages out and back presented a nice challenge. We managed it by taking a ten-day charter from Imatra and going northwards on Lake Saimaa for four days, spending three in Savonlinna and returning southwards over the last three days. Louise joined us for a three-week summer break and, though the Finnexpress 741 with three berths was the least satisfactory of all the charters we had, it served our purpose adequately. Navigation was scarcely different from being out in the Baltic, except that the water was brown rather than green. There was less traffic, but more hazards from log rafts; some idyllic anchorages, but fiercer storms with less warning; and surprisingly deep water in some places, with overhead cables to watch. The *vierasvenesatama* (guest-boat harbour) in Savonlinna was a short walk from all facilities and gave us a fine view of the rowing regatta on arrival. Tickets for the dress rehearsal of *The Magic Flute* were the best we could get, but we also took a bus to

Retretti, the amazing under-rock complex of halls and galleries, where the British conductor David Shaw and tenor Philip Sheffield were performing in Britten's *Rape of Lucretia*. Moored alongside us was a Finnsailer 34 whose owner said he had 'been to London last year', taking 30 days each way and enjoying a week at St Katherine's Yacht Haven near the Tower of London. Our paltry distances, by the way, were roughly reckoned as 148 kilometres up and 131 kilometres back, say 280 kilometres altogether.

Jessica arrived in time to come with us to Kuhmo again (for twice as long as the year before) where the Lindsay Quartet led by Peter Cropper was in residence with a British Council subsidy. Seven chamber concerts in two days is a strong musical tonic. Another British group, the Equale Brass Quintet, was performing in the Lieksa brass week but could only be reached (to check on the propriety of our travel grant) by taking an overnight train to Joensuu, a bus to Lieksa and then, a short night after the concert, another bus and a flight back to Helsinki. Another rapid excursion was necessary to hear the distinguished British organist Gillian Weir give a recital in Lahti. The music critic Seppo Heikinheimo wrote his review on a laptop word processor at the back of the church and then transmitted the text by modem and telephone in his car direct to the *Helsingin Sanomat*, thus gaining a whole day on any competitors. This was my first experience of such technology.

A second charter in the same summer could be thought excessive, but we had an invitation and it required as tight a plan as the Savonlinna one. Could we go westwards from Helsinki on a Thursday, reach our destination for a Saturday night and be back in Helsinki by Tuesday evening? The reason for trying was that my colleague in Warsaw, Dick Alford, would be staying at the summer house of a Finnish diplomat, Jukka Valtisaari, with their respective families, for their wives had become friends in Oxford. Jukka, who had done his military service in the Finnish navy, asked me to bring my charts to his office in the Foreign Ministry for a briefing on navigating to his place, which was well off the marked routes. He tried to reassure me with 'My brother has done it many times in a boat very like the one you will have, so just follow these pencil marks and you'll have no trouble — but keep a sharp lookout for *that* rock!'

Jessica's school friend Clare Jory came with us in our chartered Sunwind 27, a neat four-berth boat, and a strong east wind took us by the end of the second day to within striking distance of our turning point, the Hanko peninsula, and our destination beyond. Hanko is littered with rocks and obstacles, but concentration got us through, only to face a battle with the now contrary east wind and eventual arrival in failing light at an unpopular moment when Jukka had gone into his sauna. After a peaceful night in Oby, we were given an alternative route back into the main channel, slithering over one submerged rock, and were happy to leave Hanko astern once again.

The day after our return Kai Forsblom opened a Hockney exhibition, the Helsinki festival began and the Medici Quartet required our attention. A more serious preoccupation, however, was a project inherited from my predecessor. Though a tour by the King's College, Cambridge choir would find me in the right place at the right time, the problem of funding it with sponsorship and the apathy of our agents meant that it would have been wiser to have cancelled it several months earlier. For personal reasons and because our friends the Harbornes knew Stephen Cleobury, the director of music at King's, we could not bring ourselves to do it. At the root of the Finnish failure to support the tour was a basic misunderstanding of the nature of professional cathedral choirs in Britain. Because the singers were boys and young men it was thought to be a youth choir and nothing we could do or say could correct this. Despite the strong choral tradition in Finland there does not exist any comparable, full-time ecclesiastical establishment. Happily, however, my appeal to companies with British interests revealed that Olli Sallantaus, managing director of ICI in Finland, was a lifelong enthusiast of King's. He agreed to underwrite a large proportion of the Helsinki concert, and Matti Merikallio of English China Clay offered further sponsorship.

With less than a week to go before the choir's arrival it was evident that, outside Helsinki, there had been virtually no publicity and no tickets sold. My determination to stir things up required a day trip each to Tampere and Turku, in both places obtaining local radio interviews and personally distributing posters. (In the middle of all this, a day trip by air to Rovaniemi

237

on the Arctic Circle was necessary to support Lord Shackleton's attendance at the second Arctic film festival.) Eventually, the outstanding quality of the singing was recognized, especially by the handful of experts who heard it, and reasonable audiences ensured that the tour could be regarded as an artistic success. But it was a financial failure and a shock to King's, which is rightly accustomed to being warmly welcomed and understood in central Europe, the United States and Japan, or wherever the Anglican musical tradition is familiar. For me, it had to be confessed, it was an embarrassing (but perversely enjoyable) misjudgement. Our guests certainly had a good time, and Diana managed to organize no fewer than three parties in 24 hours.

Hard on their heels came our deputy director-general, Roddy Cavaliero, for a four-day programme which included a civic lunch as the guest of Mrs Kaarina Suonio in Tampere town hall. When she left the Ministry of Education she had hinted to her former staff that they should route plenty of visitors to Tampere, so Matti Gustafsen in International Relations remembered to do so. Roddy won her heart by uttering a most memorable and hyper-diplomatic toast, which was 'Here's to Tampere; second in size but first in culture.' He went on to Warsaw and the report on the whole of his whistle-stop tour of the Nordic area produced recommendations which, to comment on, would break my rule of no axe-grinding.

A serious shock late in the year was news of the death of Diana's mother, Nana Herdman. She had recently turned 80 and the gravity of her heart condition seems to have been underestimated. We felt exceptionally sad that she had been exerting herself to redecorate and hang new curtains in happy expectation of our coming home for leave at the end of the year. A compassionate journey was arranged for Diana to fly the following day, but the week she had to be away was that of the final rehearsals for her role as Mrs Higgins in *Pygmalion*, so after the funeral all she could do was lock up the house and hasten back, leaving it for our later attention. Shaw's play was put on exceptionally in the Swedish theatre, a privilege for which the amateur performers had to thank Jack Witticka, the theatre's Anglophile director.

Now came the moment for the long-contemplated move up four

floors within the Bensow building. For the past six months we had been in intermittent discussions with SKOP Bank about layout and specifications. We had carried through an initial weeding of the library and made detailed plans for fitting ourselves into less space, getting rid of the accumulated junk of 26 years in the process. Dismantling and reassembling library shelving is very strenuous work and we were fortunate in being able to employ the members of a basketball team to carry the books up the stairs, such things being too heavy to put in lifts. We needed all of five days for the job. The salutary nature of this halfway house can be appreciated from the figures — formerly we occupied 390 square metres, now it was 330 and it would eventually be only 300. Once this was done we had two colleagues from London to embark on installing the software for our ICL Quatro 49 computer system, designed for running the British Council's BOS Finder information retrieval equipment. This required much hard thinking about the right codes to invent for the range of attributes we envisaged.

Sickness among some key singers obliged me to cancel plans for an Advent carol service, which had been intended as a variation on the usual and which allowed for our impending absence. At the same time we became increasingly worried by the gap in the usually regular letters from Sarah who was on her way home from Japan via an extensive tour of China, Tibet and Nepal with two friends from BETS. Letters from China had reached us weekly, but it later transpired that a letter from India had been lost. One feels utterly helpless during long silences with no remedy short of search parties. It is hard to recall any greater sense of joyful relief than the moment when we telephoned Potty Granny in Totnes and heard her say that she had that very morning received a postcard from Sarah in Delhi.

With the annual church bazaar out of the way, Paul Docherty helped me get the fellowship selection procedure launched for my third time; we held a second *glögi* office party; and, after a vigorous countdown, we began our mid-tour leave by loading our car onto the Finnjet ferry for Travemunde (near Lübeck) and relaxed in the luxury of a commodore-class cabin.

Ten weeks' winter leave and a trip to Malta
Julian Andrews in Amsterdam had a VIP on his hands so we were

unable to call and see the British Council's splendid canal-side base there, being happy instead to spend longer gazing at Van Goghs. An overnight ferry took us from the Hook of Holland to Harwich, and we were in our flat on the fourth morning after leaving Helsinki. To get to Sherborne for their carols and to collect Jessica on her fifteenth birthday we made an early start, ending the day in Highcliffe to take stock of the house-clearing task ahead of us. Back in London a few days of debriefing visits in HQ were mixed with tackling the many domestic jobs at 4 Emperor's Gate, for which there had been no time during the rush of moving and departure two years earlier. All five of us had a happy Christmas with Potty Granny in Totnes and then hurried back for Sarah to begin a temporary job selling shirts in Harrods' sales.

A phone call from Paul Docherty in Helsinki for a spot of advice served to remind me that one is at no time completely absolved from responsibility when on leave, and this was confirmed by Eddie Rayner's request, as my new boss following James Took as controller, for a two-page statement of the state of play in Finland, duly drafted and typed at home.

Another week of 'improvements' in the flat was followed by the really depressing task of sorting and disposing of all Nana Herdman's personal and household things in Highcliffe. Enormous accumulations of clothes, hats and shoes had to go to whatever charity we could find; Louise came to choose some furniture and the rest was labelled for Totnes, London or sale. The bungalow was a 'very desirable retirement home' which could have been kept as an investment and let, but without any prospect of proper local supervision for the next five years at least, Diana decided to instruct Pearsons to sell.

Sarah's twenty-fifth birthday was celebrated with a buffet for her friends in the flat and, having exchanged our less than satisfactory small Volvo for a new Peugeot 309, we went north to visit Diana's Aunt Sallie in Whickham and my third sister Phillida and family in Delph, Oldham. A bright and crisp winter day was enjoyed around the Kielder Dam in Northumbria and a similar day walking near Saddleworth. Duty then called again for me to make a day trip by shuttle to Glasgow with David Fuller from Fine Arts Department to see Robert Saunders, the director of the

Paisley museum with its special historical collection of British studio ceramics. These talks eventually bore fruit a year later when an exhibition toured Finland. We managed to squeeze into the day a quick glimpse of Macintosh's Glasgow School of Art and some time in the Burrell collection. Another combination of leave and future work was seeing a matinée of *Twelfth Night* performed by the Cheek by Jowl Company in the Donmar Warehouse. Declan Donellan and Nick Ormerod brought their production to Finland, with Drama and Dance Department's blessing, three months later.

A latent desire to revisit Malta as an adult lay dormant in my subconscious, but it surfaced whenever a possible opportunity appeared. Now, 35 years after my adolescent naval experiences, Diana fancied a bit of sun in mid-February and we booked a one-week excursion. Grand Harbour and Valetta seemed familiar but relatively deserted, and my memory failed utterly to lead us to where the British Institute had been. Even so, by hiring a small car we covered much of the island in two days and then thought about Gozo. This smaller and more agricultural island had always been beyond my reach when in the navy because of the ferry timings, but now we found the Cornucopia Hotel and based ourselves there for two days of walking in rather stormy weather. Only three years later we were in Malta again, enticed once more by Brian and Margot Hitch's hospitality, he having by then been appointed British High Commissioner.

We celebrated our twenty-seventh wedding anniversary with another buffet in the flat: we took Jessica on an inspirational visit to Cambridge, which included lunch with the Cleobury family and the inimitable evensong; took Louise with us for a day in Norwich with the Harrisons; and arranged for Sarah to live in the flat, sharing it with Sabine who had been in Japan with her. Then the journey back to Finland began with a drive to Purfleet and embarkation with our car on the ro-ro Finncarrier vessel *Arcturus*, one of the four ships on regular passages through the Kiel Canal run by the United Baltic Corporation. A strike in Rotterdam diverted us to Antwerp for a day of restowing the cargo, almost all of it in containers, and consequently what should have been a daytime passage of the canal happened disappointingly at night. The first sea ice of small round pieces like lily leaves occurred at the north end and, as we progressed up the Baltic, they became bigger and closer together until finally we were ploughing noisily through very solid ice.

A third year for consolidating the innovations

Accustomed as we were to being beyond easy reach of home, we found it strange to be able to travel so frequently — whether officially or privately — between our post abroad and our base at home. The children's holiday visit scheme provided us with three return airfares each year for Jessica while she continued in full-time education up to the age of 21. All other journeys had to be privately funded, so we were happy not to be on the other side of the globe when making contributions for Louise to visit us, or paying for Diana to be with Jessica for half-term weeks. Sarah was by this time in her first proper job as an exhibitions officer with the London Chamber of Commerce and doing a lot of travelling in connection with trade missions.

The first visitors after our return were three members of the Society of Education Officers, forming a delegation under the Analogue Country Visits' Programme, funded by the DES. They were generously hosted by their Finnish counterparts and this time (being the third in the series) they focused on financial delegation to schools, a topic very close to current concerns on both sides.

As mentioned in Chapter 11 on Romania, there is strong competition among smaller countries in bidding for the privilege of permanently hosting a United Nations agency. My old Sri Lankan friend from Cambridge days, Lal Jayawardena, was appointed the first director of the World Institute for Development Economics Research (WIDER), a branch in Helsinki of the UN University in Tokyo. Imagine our mutual pleasure in having the opportunity to entertain Robin Marris, whom Lal had invited to offer guidance on WIDER's own progress and who had supervised both of us in economics while at King's.

The system of postings preference forms was explained in connection with our move from Malawi to Japan, but it was always possible for Personnel to spring surprises, as had happened when Cape Town was dismissed in favour of Kuala Lumpur. Now, however, while presuming to be allowed to stay happily in Finland, it became evident that my name had gone forward to become director of Music Department in London. It took me a page and a half of close argument to plead for mercy on the grounds that my next post would be my last, that by the time of next year's departure from Helsinki ten years in Europe (even strange bits of it, including films) would be enough, and that a return to the tropical world was my best bet. Several months elapsed before the danger passed, and it was the turn of the year before a call from Personnel indicated that 'the best solution to their jigsaw' would be for us to go to Ethiopia. Allah be praised!

A ruthless weeding of our library stock now had to be launched, and it had to be done mostly by Paul and me. In the first move we had taken upstairs with us most of the 15,000 items, but there was only going to be space round the corner for 10,000 at the most. We devised 'weeding criteria', or principles of weeding, and wrote *Principles of Management, Stocking and Weeding* for the guidance of our library staff. The Finnish library system — public, academic and institutional — was highly efficient and well funded, so our task was a narrowly focused one to supply information for the specialized minority wanting material in English about Britain. All other material was better housed closer to the user in departmental and research libraries. To bear all this in mind while facing a 'bay' of six or seven shelves required constant mental reference to a long list of relevant factors — and then a decision: to keep or to discard and, if the latter, who should have it. Later in the process we sent some 5000 books across to Poland where the information famine was acute.

A summons to attend a three-day meeting in the Cambridge office gave me the opportunity for a short weekend in Totnes by flying to London two days earlier than required. The assembly of a small number of representatives had been decreed in an attempt to persuade us that the newly introduced system of activity analysis (which meant staff time accounting) should be taken seriously. My mind was open, but at the end it closed more firmly than before in favour of cheating. Granted that our work is labour intensive and that staff time is the biggest item in the budget, it does follow that the time any one member spends on any one task has to be recorded so that the FCO, ODA and other sponsors can know what they are funding. The basic flaw in 'activity paralysis', however, was its insistence that only office time should count. Without provision for recording the very high proportion of work done (especially abroad) in the evenings, the picture produced was grotesque — and worse, would lead to false conclusions. So we went on cooking the books. My total of analysed hours regularly produced a percentage of 130 or 140 of the official hours available. What price distortion?

We did no chartering in 1987, but were content with our plastic sailing dinghy in local waters. The risk of being becalmed on fine evenings made me buy the smallest available outboard motor as a precaution and, on the same day as the Queen's birthday party, we had a small launching party as before. But our immediate neighbours, Ulf and Bettina Koivula, who had lived in Leamington Spa for several years while he had been based in Birmingham for his paint company, had been 'sailing people' until their small children made it less easy. For a few years they kept a powerful motor cruiser in Naantali and they invited us to come with them to Marienhamn in the Åland islands between Finland and Sweden. There was just one weekend we could all manage, but it fell right in the middle of the fortnight when we expected Peter and Pat Harrison to be staying with us, and six plus could not be accommodated. The solution was to book the Harrisons on one of the big ferries from Turku to Marienhamn so they could do the same journey at the same time. It worked brilliantly. To sail this out and back needs at least ten days; we travelled at an alarming 21 knots, weaving in and out of rocky obstacles, and spent just one night *en route* each way. Meanwhile, Peter and Pat had an experience of smooth efficiency and luxury they have frequently recalled with amazement. Our memory, too, is of the square rigged *Pommern* moored in the harbour and of a hired car taking us to Eckero where the Tsar's empire had its westernmost post office, built in dignified neoclassical style.

Another little scheme that worked was inviting John and Ann Day from Stockholm to spend a night each way on the ferry and come to lunch to meet the Harrisons, the common interest being Kisumu on the shores of Lake Victoria in western Kenya. Peter had opened our branch there in the 1950s and John had left it in local hands in the 1980s. There was also some 'shop' talked in my office.

John Olive of Beckington, our one-time neighbour and Shaw-ford opera conductor, came to stay for ten days. We found excuses to take him to Naantali and Turku for a few concerts, and to Tampere for the opening of our major exhibition of 'British Paintings and Sculptures from the 1980s' in the Sara Hilden Art Museum, duly performed by HMA Justin Staples and Mrs Kaarina Suonio.

Only once did any of our travelling children go astray and that was when Jessica fell asleep in the wrong train out of Sherborne, waking to find herself by the sea instead of at Heathrow. Conse-quently, she did not appear off the British Airways flight we were meeting in Helsinki. The Finnair desk would not tell us whether she had been rebooked on their passenger list without permission from the police — whom we preferred not to bother. The British Airways' station manager was nevertheless able to help us by quietly accessing the Finnair computer to reveal her name, and she did indeed turn up, safe but a little tearful, three hours later.

Another summons from London took me to a four-day con-ference on libraries, information and books at Cumberland Lodge in Windsor Great Park. My original recruitment benefactor, Robin Twite, was by then the controller and was speaking much civilized sense in the face of so many misguided colleagues who were reluctant to recognize the distinction between measuring quantities and judging qualities. My contribution was minimal, but described some of our reforms. Again, a two-night visit to Totnes was possible before flying back to Helsinki.

For a change we decided to spend a whole day driving to Kuhmo, but recent absence from the office meant taking a great deal of paperwork with me. The Chilingirian Quartet was billed to play Tippett, Howells, Rawsthorne and Vaughan Williams in four separate concerts — a more than adequate excuse for my presence. We took with us an old singing friend, Gill Collymore, who is also Louise's godmother. Then, halfway through our five-night stay, she flew home from Kajaani and was replaced as our guest by Allison Pickard, a colleague from Music Department on a familiarization tour. The Chilingirian Quartet also played Elgar in a fifth concert, in Lentiira church, and the same afternoon we drove on to Lieksa where the Fine Arts Brass Quintet was performing. Allison had a good run for her money because on the way back to Helsinki we saw the Valamo monastery, Kerimäki church and Savonlinna.

The switch back from summer hours to the winter routine on 1 September signalled the beginning of an eventful autumn. By that time my personal score of weeding sessions (of several hours each) had reached 14 and, as our stock of books dwindled, so did our inputting (ghastly word, but unavoidable) of records to our computerized retrieval system gather pace. The preparation of paper for the fifth Mixed Commission meeting had required much midnight oil and telephone discussions with Patricia Wright, our desk officer in London. Our reward came when Matti Gustafsen, leading the Finnish side, congratulated me on producing a plain and honest brief, instead of the anodyne 'bureaucrat-speak' which invariably fudged what really needed to be discussed. Jessica left for school on the same flight that brought the British delegation, led by Nick Elam, head of the FCO's CRD, and Eddie Rayner, our controller, supported by Professor Bill Mead, a geographer, and Dr Michael Branch, the director of London University's School of Slavonic and East European Studies. We all flew to Kuopio for the two days of talks and more points were scored by our ordering a Finnish menu when it was our turn to entertain.

Then came the highlight of the Helsinki festival in the form of the City of Birmingham Symphony Orchestra (CBSO) under Simon Rattle. They had the temerity to play three Sibelius symphonies (numbers 5, 6 and 7) in one programme. The Finlandia Hall audience gave them a standing ovation and immediately after their second concert we gave them a party (the whole orchestra, not just the principals) in Paul Docherty's flat. With a substantial number of Finnish musicians we totalled 165 guests, and got part funding from Brian Rose as chargé d'affaires in the embassy. Veijo Varpio, the festival's director, maintained seriously that the CBSO had given the finest performances he had ever heard in that hall.

Russell Drury, our librarian in Warsaw, came over for a week to survey the results of our weeding and to tell us which discards would be useful in Poland. It actually takes about two hours per 'bay' of six shelves to weed conscientiously and, by the end, my time (nearly all at weekends) spent doing this added up to 49 hours spread over 19 sessions — an average of two and a half hours per session. Paul's contribution must have been similar. At this point SKOP Bank had finished construction work round the corner in Erottajankatu 7, so we were able to begin showing it to our more sceptical colleagues and to begin planning the details of how we were going to fit ourselves in. Several more months were to elapse — in fact the entire winter — before the final fitting out could be finished and our second move given a precise schedule. It was all too much for Pia Sundell, our senior librarian, who saw her empire being decimated and could not be persuaded that streamlining was essential to survival. Her resignation was hardly surprising, yet the attempt by her new Finnish employers to demand that she join them precipitately had to be resisted, and she agreed that a three-week period of handover was the minimum needed to round off 17 years of valuable work. HMA Justin Staples came to witness our farewell presentation to her.

Fourth-year crescendo and climax
The British fascination with and liking for Finland and its people is mutual, partly because the Finns see us as only slightly less cold and reserved in manner than they are. Personally, for Diana and me, our Finnish friendships have been some of the warmest we have made and our final months in their country were correspondingly both frantically busy and sad. Without sharing their interest in vodka, we did acquire a taste for their 'champagne' made from white currants.

The Programme of Inservice Training for Language Centres (PILC) went into its second year under Paul Docherty's guidance, and he had also been maintaining the series of summer courses for teachers which David Kirwan had run. PILC was linked with staff visits from Birmingham University, and academic visitors with British Council travel grants were frequently engaged for the other seminars.

Now that the advocates of culture-free language learning had been routed (our own Dr King being the chief apostate), there was fresh enthusiasm for British studies, so we launched discussions and Paul began planning the first of an annual series of major British studies seminars. They have been patronized by hundreds of Finnish teachers, have been fully self-financing and (although now biennial) the sixth will be held in 1996. Our first, entitled 'Understanding Britain Today', was chaired by Roger Sell in his new role as professor of English at Åbo Akademi. Finnish patronage was emphasized by Kalervo Siikala's opening remarks as head of international relations in the Ministry of Education; and Dr Eino Lyytinen, who had been a British Council scholar in the 1960s (and was soon to become the first director of the new Finnish Institute in London), surveyed the radical changes in British society over 25 years. Several distinguished speakers from Britain dealt with Thatcherism, the media and the arts.

Weeding books was relatively simple; the final countdown to our removal involved hours of agonizing decisions when weeding music records (did anyone want anything but cassettes?) and speech records (let's give them to the university), disposing of all our 16-millimetre films (were any of them of interest to the Finnish film archive?) in favour of stocking only video cassettes, and ensuring that our own archive was reduced to essentials. Then it snowed all night and, on 29 February 1988, it snowed all day too. The electricians and plumbers were still around in Erottajankatu, but Victor Ek's men and three vanloads using 308 boxes got us down from the seventh floor of Bensowtalo and up to the second floor round the corner. As with the previous move there was a tendency to ease off by Friday, so a staff harangue was necessary to decree that 'no desk work is permitted until the last box is empty', an achievement we then celebrated with some bubbly.

Suddenly Diana was struck by a third bereavement in four years; first her father, then her mother and now Sallie Herdman, her sole remaining close relative. Aunt Sallie had been to visit us in the previous year and had seemed as vigorous as ever, but died, like the others, in her eighty-first year. News came, as two years earlier, just as Diana was involved in a play, but Louise was staying with us and was due to leave within a few days, so she went straight up to Whickham and then reported to us by telephone that she had managed to arrange for the funeral to be delayed for two weeks. Jessica, too, went home halfway through her Easter

248

holiday to take up her place as one of the NYO's viola players, and simultaneously a summons for me to attend a meeting in East-bourne (about libraries in Europe — yet again) had to be acted on, so another weekend in Totnes was possible. As trains on a Maundy Thursday seemed likely to be booked up, the British Airways' desk at Helsinki airport was able to sell me the last seat on a flight from Gatwick to Exeter, a journey which was memor-able for its sunset. An unexpected bonus of all this travelling was our ability to attend the wedding in Bosham church of my nephew, Barnaby Bain, my sister Jenny's third son. Diana rejoined me in Helsinki a week later, having been with Louise up to Whickham to sort out the house and arrange its sale.

We staged the official opening of our new premises some two months after moving, and were proud to have secured such a bright and airy environment for our staff in a Jugendstil block of some architectural merit, and to have re-equipped it with stylish new Finnish furniture. Both the French and Germans had moved into more spacious premises in the last two years; we had to be content with quality on a reduced scale. In any case, there was no doubt about the warmth of appreciation in the words of the Minister of Education, then Mr Taxell, who accepted my invita-tion to perform the ceremony with HMA in attendance.

The first move towards our departure was to find an early buyer for our little plastic sailing dinghy and this proved to be Captain Scott Wilkins of the US navy, assigned to the American embassy and introduced to us by Bill Collings. Before that, however, we had to make arrangements for a visit by our then relatively new Director-General, Richard Francis, whose *Who's Who* entry gave offshore sailing as one of his recreations. My telexed offer of a weekend on the water before his official programme had been accepted while he was visiting Malaysia. Now the problem was to persuade Nautic Centre to charter me a vessel at the height of the season just for two days. The VIP status of my visitor stimulated them to secure an example of the very latest in Finnish yacht design, a Guyline 3800, which included an automatically retract-ing fin on the keel for the avoidance of rock damage. She was owned by one of the Donner family, and had only recently com-pleted her maiden voyage.

Bill and Jenny Collings had agreed to make up our crew and the plan was to go through the Eastern Archipelago and spend the Saturday night in the lagoon of the island called Byön, where the Enkvists (see above) had their summer hide-out. The director-general arrived in time for dinner on the Friday evening and we had a fair wind next day for the seven-hour voyage. It was an idyllic evening — with two dinners, one on shore and a second on board — giving the director-general the chance to talk with probably the best-known Swedo-Finnish academic of international standing in the field of languages. The return voyage took us nine hours in a stiffening breeze and quickly revealed that our visitor's recreation would have been better described as ocean racing. (Less than a year and a half later we were to receive him in Ethiopia and charter an aircraft for him, but with no offer of a turn at the wheel.) His official programme included an interview with the Foreign Minister, Kalevi Sorsa, who had been Prime Minister before a recent election and shift in the coalition spectrum. Bringing him to our new premises on the day he went, an acutely embarrassed me had to explain that overnight our landlords had without warning removed every single door for, they said, some repainting. His cool comment was 'You do realize, don't you, that you are occupying a very insecure building.'

This occurrence illustrated a strangely cavalier attitude of the SKOP contractors who continued to come and go, supposedly fixing one thing or another, long after we as tenants could have expected the privacy of 'quiet enjoyment', and to have been consulted as to convenience. In spite of appropriate remonstration we were without doors for a whole week.

We had survived four winters, so with gentle persuasion Personnel agreed we deserved four summers and would not have to leave as soon as originally proposed. We were determined to use this last chance and do as the Finns do at midsummer — take off by water. Because of the congestion of events, Justin and Susan Staples gave us a month in advance the most generous farewell party, which included music by the Helsinki Junior Strings and some part-singing (with ourselves) organized by Matti Kilpiö. My speech of thanks not only reviewed four years of many happy memories but also had to address the incredulity of most of our

250

Finnish friends over our equanimity at the prospect of going, of all places, to Ethiopia. In short, the explanation was in terms of the British Council's dual concerns — both cultural and philanthropic.

We had decided to charter a Sunwind 311 with five berths for a full fortnight but to change our crew at half time. My third sister Phillida and brother-in-law David Shipp arrived two days before Louise and we embarked together from the Airisto marina on mid-summer's eve. On the second day we reached Naantali for a concert by the Nash Ensemble with Sarah Walker, and then began preparations to entertain the SCO in the manner of the ECO two years before. Graham and Ann Hand arrived in their French-built 825 *Rosalind III* (he having replaced Peter Harborne as head of chancery). Diana had performed a naming ceremony for them earlier, using the royal invocation, 'May God bless her and all who sail in her.' They moored alongside us in time for the SCO's concert with Barry Tuckwell. Cases of wine were cooled in Roger Sell's family house nearby in Raisio and the *vesi bussi* (no prizes for translation) ordered. We were spared the nail-biting wait of two years before and were back in time for the Gabrieli Quartet's concert, again with Barry Tuckwell. We heard the Lindsay Quartet, the fourth British group in the festival, in Merimaşku church. Then a fine sail in perfect conditions brought us to the island of Iniö for one night and, on returning to Naantali, it was time for the changeover. Diana drove to Helsinki to see off Louise and the Shipps, and came back on 2 July with Jessica and with Sarah and her latest boyfriend, Nigel Clark.

In this second week, as in the first, we had breakfast in the cock-pit every day and enjoyed unbroken weather, sometimes with too little wind, but managed to explore some fresh parts of the west-ern archipelago. Within a day of our return Sarah and Nigel went on a trip to Leningrad where he contrived a suitable ambience in which to propose to her. Brian and Margot Hitch then arrived from Stockholm, so when the couple returned we all celebrated their engagement together. Sarah reported having expressed sur-prise that Nigel should still want to marry her after being 'cooped up in a boat with the parents for a week'. Their wedding in the following year is another story.

As Brian and Margot took off in a hired car the tall ships began to assemble in Helsinki harbour, among them the British sail train-ing sisterships *Winston Churchill* and *Malcolm Miller*. All too soon our successors arrived (Graham and Joan Coe), Jessica left for another NYO session and the packers were organizing a split consignment of baggage, some for London and some for Addis Ababa. We stayed for a few nights with Peter and Aileen Lehos, having a common interest in music and children of a similar age; and after moving to the quayside Hotel Palace enjoyed a last evening with Paul and Karen Docherty, discussing with her mother, Mrs Leithead, her years in Ethiopia. Dr Charles Leithead was someone we were later to know had been a much admired creator of the medical faculty at Addis Ababa University.

The Finnjet ferry took us once more in commodore-class com-fort to Travemunde and Lübeck, but this time we headed for Hamburg in order to see Glynne Stackhouse in our offices there. He very soon took up the post of director of music, the one that would have been a disaster for me to have accepted. By taking a ferry down the Elbe estuary and across to Harwich we effectively completed the circuit begun four years earlier with our crossing to Esbjerg in Denmark. We were in our flat in Emperor's Gate by teatime the following day.

Berber
Atbara

Atbara

Kassala

Wad Medani
Gedaref

Sennar

SUDAN

Blue Nile

Metema

L. Tana

Bahir Dar

Debre Mark'os

Blue Nile

ETHIOPIA

Nek'emtē

Ambo

Gambela

Gorē

Jima

Sodo

Ārba Minch

L. Ābaya

Gīdolē

SUDAN

Juba
due west on
White Nile

KENYA

L. Turkana
(L. Rudolf)

Moyale

E
R
I
T
R
E
A

Keren
Mits'iwa

ĀSMERA

Ādī Ugrī

Ādwa
Āksum

Ādīgrat

Mek'ele

Gonder

Debre Tabor
Woldiya

Desē

Debre Birhan

Āwash
ADĪS ABEBA (ADDIS ABABA)

Debre Zeit

L. Lagano

Shashemene

Awassa
Wondo Genet

Goba
Robe

Dirē
Dawa
Hārer

SAUDI ARABIA

R
E
D

S
E
A

YEMEN

Assab

DJIBOUTI

DJIBOUTI

SOMALIA

Hargeisa

MAP 7
ETHIOPIA AND ERITREA

—·—·— International boundary

Miles
0   100   200

0   100   200   300
Kilometres

14

Ethiopia and Eritrea: Civil War and Counter-Revolution

We were glad to be home in time to attend a promenade concert in the Albert Hall by the NYO in which Jessica was playing her viola. She went to Amsterdam with it the next day to give a concert there, but complained of hunger on her return, the supporting arrangements having been a little inadequate.

Amharic language and a trans-Atlantic excursion
After my obligatory day in our HQ being debriefed about Finland and submitting to an initial briefing on Ethiopia, we went to Oxford to meet Stephen and Pippa Sandford (née Norrington), she being the current head of the Sandford English Community School in Addis Ababa, and he being employed by the International Livestock Centre for Africa (ILCA), also in a suburb of Addis Ababa. Curiously, this was in fact not our first meeting, for on 12 August 1961 we had sung in the choir at their wedding, conducted by her brother Roger. More of the school and music later.

The Dartington Hall summer school of music had begun its second week when we reached Totnes to stay with Potty Granny for nearly a month. Diana had decided that Ethiopia was going to be her chance to indulge in horse riding, and it would be wise to learn the rudiments in the calm of the Devon countryside first. My riding skills had certainly rusted almost to extinction in the 30 years since Northern Cameroon days, so a few refresher lessons for me and a noviciate for Diana were duly arranged in a local riding school. Nigel and Sarah came for a weekend to make preliminary enquiries about organizing their wedding, which was going to have to be pretty well set up before we went to post, on the assumption that we would fly home from Ethiopia for it, probably only very briefly. St Mary's is a fine church in the centre of Totnes and within a short walk from Granny's house, but the Rector agreed that Berry Pomeroy church, also in his charge and only two miles out, provided better space.

The usual master classes were on offer at Dartington Hall and, at one time, it seemed possible for me to benefit from observing how Diego Masson set about supervising his trainee conductors. There was a very worthwhile selection of scores under discussion, but so little attention was paid to the observers that the idea had to be given up. Instead, there were other opportunities with Ian Partridge and the veteran William Glock. At that time the summer school was facing financial problems, but it has since been turned round by the skill of Gavin Henderson and now runs for five weeks, followed in recent years by a literary week known as 'Ways With Words'.

Ato Mesfin Abebe was assigned by the School of Oriental and African Studies of London University to give me lessons in Amharic. We managed to fit in 20 morning sessions (and plenty of homework) in the autumn. Remembering my experience with Japanese, my concern was more with the ability to read than to speak, and indeed the table of syllabic symbols used to write Amharic has a similar structure to the *kana* syllabary used in Japan — without, of course, any similarity in actual design. Mesfin had been a senior member of staff of the former emperor, Haile Selassie, and had consequently been in voluntary exile since the revolution of the mid-1970s. Knowing that negligible time would be available for any private study after taking up new responsibilities, my aim was little more than to acquire a minimal degree of word recognition. For example, we think of Ethiopia as a word of five syllables; in fact it really has only three — Y-tio-pya. Some of the vocabulary has Arabic origins and some words were familiar to me from the Hausa of Nigerian days. The Hausa *beit-el-mal* is a house of money, or treasury; the Amharic *addis megeb bet* is a new eating house, or restaurant. A learner of Swahili would probably have a similar experience.

The four months from late July to late November constituted a longer gap between posts than we had ever had before. We were in danger of exceeding our leave entitlement, so in addition to the language instruction my duty time was increased by signing up for some other forms of staff training. The first was an equal opportunities workshop, which left me wondering about unequal people and inverted discrimination; the second was a development project appraisal week in Eastbourne's Short Courses Centre, which offered indoctrination to reveal the bureaucratic requirements, not only of the ODA but also of the World Bank and similar agencies; and the third was a two-day introduction to our own new financial system, which was making strenuous efforts to be user friendly. Recognizing the opening presented by more time than usual, however, Diana agreed that this was the moment for me to take her across the Atlantic for a first visit, my own having been in the year we met, nearly 30 years before.

Our two-week tour was a rich combination of people and places, set up at short notice by telephone. Flying into Toronto, a bus took us to Guelph, Ontario, to stay with our ex-Malaysian friends, Professor Marian and Audrey Soltys. His expertise in veterinary microbiology was still being used by the university, which had originally grown out of a veterinary school. On a very fine autumn day we did a round trip with them via Hamilton to the Niagara Falls and back through the small town of Niagara-by-the-Lake. A bus to Ottawa took us to stay with a Canadian diplomatic couple known from Bucharest days, Brian and Kate Dickson. His father was a judge of the Supreme Court of Canada and, despite his absence, we were treated to a tour of the court building. In his room stood a recent present from a visiting delegation of judges from the Soviet Union: it was a small brass statuette of a man, perhaps a blacksmith. My interpretation of it surprised the official who was our host, but there seemed little doubt that it was symbolic of beating swords into ploughshares. Kate took us for a memorable walk among the autumn leaves of

257

the Gatineau Park and we strongly admired the glass architecture of the new national gallery, balancing nicely the nearby Victorian Gothic of the parliament building.

Thence we flew to the wrong airport in Washington DC, but eventually made contact with our hosts, Alvin and Ellen Perlman of Winchester, Virginia. They had been in the US embassy in Bucharest and shared our musical interests. Their local choir was rehearsing Rachmaninov's vespers. Al lent us his car for an exploration of the Shenandoah valley and the Skyline Route, and we walked two short sections of the Appalachian Trail, a 2000-mile track which runs from Maine down to Georgia, and has a central office at Harper's Ferry. Another bus then took us to Fairfax, Virginia, to stay with Khaw Yen Yen, our Kuala Lumpur singing friend, and Hilary Kressel, the American diplomat whom she had married. She was having difficulty getting appropriate work; all that her gynaecological expertise could get her was a job in pathology. A flight back to Toronto enabled us to spend our last night with my Cambridge contemporary, Colin Tilney (now a world-class harpsichordist) in the surprisingly rural house on the urban tramway system, which he shares with Bill Emigh.

Back in London there was no shortage of DIY jobs in our flat and we needed to decide on arrangements for our next and final period as absentee owner-occupiers. Sarah's friend Sabine had been replaced as her sharer by a Norwegian postgraduate student — Imperial College was a short walk away — but she had no new sharer in view. This offered an opportunity we were anxious to take. Louise had continued to work at Bart's for a while after qualifying as a state enrolled nurse and had then moved to its satellite hospital, St Mark's. She was living in rather unsatisfactory conditions in Forest Gate, east London, and being worn out with night duty, causing us concern about her general wellbeing and safety. Eventually she agreed to let me hire a van and, with the help of her boyfriend Ralf Sealey, we moved her over to our side of London and installed her to share with Sarah. The two sisters have very different temperaments, but at least for an indefinite (even if possibly short) period it seemed the best solution. She also had a different journey to work, but by this time she had given up general nursing and got a job as theatre nurse to Bill Jory (father of Jessica's school friend, Clare), an ophthalmic consultant who was pioneering refractive surgery in his Harley Street clinic.

Our impending return to the developing world — or the tropics, which is my preferred if old-fashioned description — meant a renewed interest in the activities of such charities as Oxfam and Save the Children, so my briefing included visits to both their central offices. VSO, too, had withdrawn from Ethiopia when the revolution occurred and had been unable to re-establish a programme, so Dick Bird and Myra Green explained the state of play to me. Also, there was news that the Minister of Overseas Development, Mr Chris Patten (now Governor of Hong Kong), had just returned from one of many visits to Ethiopia and had seen the queues of students outside our library in Addis Ababa. A call to his private office in the ODA explaining my status as representative-designate quickly secured for me a brief interview.

On a farewell trip to Totnes we fitted in an excursion to St Ives, taking Potty Granny with us and visiting many of her old haunts, including the Pedn Olva Hotel where she had stayed as a young bride in 1929. The heavy rain did not detract from our enjoyment of the Leach pottery and the Hepworth museum, and we have since returned to see the Tate of St Ives.

Then we flew to Rome.

The Italian connection and later influences
Awareness of Mussolini's imperial adventures in the 1930s, his desire for a continuous new Roman empire from Libya to Somalia, and its frustration by British-led forces in the Abyssinian campaign of 1941 was one reason for wanting to have a look at Rome; another was our curiosity about one of the few capital cities of Europe we had never yet visited. Also, since the abolition of sea passages, it was normally desirable to interpose a few days of disconnection between one world and another when going by air to a new post after hectic preparations, or when going home for leave after a similarly exhausting countdown.

Nigel Hudson in Addis Ababa had said he did not want to leave before the last day of November, so we planned to arrive for a one-week handover. This gave us time for three days in Rome, the first of which was spent walking and sleeping, the second sightseeing the obvious places, and the third included a call on Malcolm Hardy in the British Council's literally palatial premises, followed by a night flight by Ethiopian Airlines. My predecessor had been enjoying his third stint of work in Ethiopia and therefore knew and was known by everybody. He had taught in the General Wingate School in the mid-1950s, in the university in the early 1960s and then, after a 20-year gap, was posted by the British Council in 1985. A hard act to follow, except that, as our Ambassador wrote, 'jobs can be done in different styles with just as much effectiveness'. The challenge very quickly became one of collaboration with the embassy in a constant battle to prevent our London masters discounting the needs of Ethiopia just because its regime was politically distasteful and likely to be limited in duration. The experience of living and working among Ethiopians did inspire considerable faith in their resilience, and in a vision of a better future beyond present troubles; but it was not easy to convince others that long-term optimism was justified.

The physical state of the country and its linguistic, educational and religio-cultural condition derive from its very chequered history. Its first foreign language was French, until the Italian invasion of 1935, then English (first British and later American) followed by a brief flirtation with Russian, but it has settled on English again despite a serious decline in the standard of it in schools. So the country could be characterized as Anglophone, yet not in the Commonwealth; located in the Horn of Africa, yet strongly influenced by the Arab world, and, paradoxically, a Christian island in an Islamic sea. Because of its peculiar xenophobia, it is often discounted, despite being the third most populous country in Africa after Nigeria and Egypt. Throughout the post-Second World War period, up to the revolutions of the mid-1970s, the personal and autocratic rule of Emperor Haile Selassie had been generally beneficial, though corrupt and archaic in its latter stages. Genuine and effective development had moved much of the country into the twentieth century, but its terrain was unalterable and more of an obstacle to communications than anywhere. The young army officers under communist influence who instigated the ideological terror and blood-letting of the mid-1970s continued to misrule the country on Marxist–Leninist principles for 15 years, yet the surviving Amhara public servants kept the state running and, as in other parts of Africa, political conviction was very shallow. With memories of Romania uppermost, we found little to surprise us in the totalitarian bureaucracy. Its transplanted form was actually milder and we noticed a curious parallel in the way the Orthodox Church could retain its power. Party members of course could not be seen in church, yet a steady adjustment towards the eventual counter-revolution went on throughout our three years.

The intellectual atmosphere of the capital, Addis Ababa, was much more cosmopolitan than most outsiders imagined. The Emperor had persuaded the Organization of African Unity (OAU) to put its headquarters there rather than in Nairobi, and bigger still was the UN's Economic Commission for Africa whose building occupied a prominent site. Out along the old Asmara road was ILCA, and on the other side of the city was ALERT, which stands for All-Africa Leprosy Research/Rehabilitation and Training. Added to these, the World Bank, the European Community Development Fund, the United Nations Development Programme and other multilateral lending agencies had offices and there were bilateral representations of all sorts; every African country had an embassy because of the OAU, and most other countries of West and East had embassies as good centres for Africa watching. A consequence of all these institutions was a very broad range of resident expatriates and a richly varied international community. Another consequence was a need for schools to cater for the children for whom the Ethiopian government could not provide education in an appropriate medium, English being by far the most popular, followed closely by French and Italian. English-medium schooling has always been close to the heart of British Council concerns, but seldom with any financial input. There is more to tell later about my role as an ex-officio member of the board of the Sandford English Community School.

Being well informed in order to be informative
Jessica's instant reaction, when told of our posting, was 'Oh, but you will starve' — which was hardly surprising as a reflection of the media images of a war-torn country gripped by drought and

261

famine. Disasters there certainly were in the mid-1970s and mid-1980s in the low-lying desert areas of the northeast, but these were not representative of the state of the whole country. The high grasslands of the west-central and southern parts can attract rain at any time of year, and the altitude of 7000–8000 feet (2500 metres) tends to ensure moist and fertile conditions for much of the year. Fruit and vegetables, many of a temperate type, grow abundantly in and around Addis Ababa and did very well in the garden of our bungalow, which had been rented by the British Council for the past 25 years.

As in Romania and Finland, my earliest tasks were to get to know my staff; next to visit relevant institutions in the capital; and then to undertake a series of familiarization tours to the provincial centres. We are often asked about the frequency of postings and how long or short a time can be useful or justified in one country, the usual criticism implied being that we are moved just when we have learnt most about a country. There is, however, a psychological pattern which needs to be taken into account, as does the need to move around to gain a variety of experience in a hierarchical organization with a graded career structure. Nor can the central control afford to leave one person in a nice place at the expense of another in a nasty place. To my mind, in any case, the most significant aspect is one of a natural rhythm in the annual cycle of working; in your first year you are finding out what needs to be done, in your second year you carry out your reforms, in your third year you reap the rewards of the hard grind — and if you face a fourth year you begin wondering what next. Some people may stay five or six years in the same post, circumstances differ, and there is no universal pattern; the chance to prolong my stay never came my way. A further risk is that of one's judgement being undermined by emotional involvement in the fate of the people being served, a state of mind which comes easily in a first posting (as mine in Nigeria) but which is less likely in second and subsequent posts where life and work take on a longer perspective. It is also difficult to write dispassionately about one's last post, but the effort to maintain detachment must be kept up.

My emotions were stirred, nonetheless, not so much by the publicity given to the general plight of Ethiopia as by the relative neglect (despite the efforts of several predecessors) of the conditions in which our staff were expected to work. The compression of our offices and library into an apartment block, ill-adapted from its original purpose and in a run-down part of the city, was bearable for British-based staff for a few years at a time, but our many long-serving and devoted Ethiopian colleagues had to put up with it indefinitely with no prospect of improvement. Most neighbouring countries — Sudan, Kenya, Malawi, Zimbabwe — had purpose-built British Council centres, as did South Africa and Namibia, so we decided to campaign for a long-term building project, although my preoccupation with premises in Finland had made me wary of plunging in yet again. The chief obstacle is short-term 'prioritization' in capital funding, whereby the long view is distorted under political pressure. Progress was made with a site and a plan but no money agreed during my time.

Another aspect of local staff conditions was, however, actually improved after 17 years of intermittent negotiation. In the absence of a global pension scheme of any sort, each British Council establishment had to make its own arrangements, except that a non-contributary minimal (almost insulting) one-off gratuity was payable on retirement. With strong support and pressure from the embassy, which had twice the number of local staff as us, we set up a joint provident fund which, as the years go by, will bring about a decent improvement. The many years of abortive work had frequently ground to a halt, even regressed, when staff had been moved among the approving authorities in the FCO and the Treasury in London. It was an energetic embassy colleague, Hugh Morgan, who enabled us to 'cut the cackle'.

My own assistant was Nick Taylor, the only other British colleague in the office, with whom responsibility for some 35 Ethiopian staff was shared. This was a much larger team than my Finnish one, but there was scope for delegation to senior members such as Ato Mulugeta, the chief librarian, Ato Tesfaye, his deputy, Ato Tsega, our education officer, Wzo Achemyelesh, our accountant, and Ato Hailu, our administration officer. Up in Eritrea, our branch library in Asmara was run by Ato Gebrehiwot with only four or five staff to help him. More of that later. During 1989, Nick Taylor was posted to London, Andrew Hadley came temporarily to replace him, and then Rosemary Arnott came as his permanent replacement.

Outside the office, however, we had responsibility for several more British colleagues. The Black Lion Hospital incorporated the medical faculty of Addis Ababa University, which had been set up in the 1970s by consultants from Britain as heads of departments. The connection was kept going by our provision of travel grants for no fewer than 12 external examiners each year. After much argument by our Ambassador, the ODA had eventually agreed to fund the development of an orthopaedic sub-speciality in surgery by supporting a retired consultant, Reggie Merryweather. He was succeeded in turn by Ginger Wilson, Brian Madden and Geoffrey Walker, all nominated through the good offices of the profession's charity, World Orthopaedic Concern (WOC). The endless supply of cripples and child victims of polio requiring treatment was increased still further by wounded soldiers, yet there was so far no qualified Ethiopian orthopaedic specialist. Our second medical colleague was Leslie Whittaker, a retired consultant in radiology (a necessary support for other disciplines) who engaged in a long-running battle to keep equipment in working order.

Closer to the British Council's normal concerns was the ODA-funded Key English Language Teaching (KELT) project, which employed three, then four and eventually five experts on contract. The project coordinator was Oliver Hunt and, like the others, he was officially designated as KELT adviser to the Ministry of Education. His own work included writing teaching materials and textbooks for junior college use and running 'workshops' for teachers. The basic need to reform the teaching of English throughout the system arose from the poor methodology that had been introduced by the East Germans, as surrogates of the Russians, in support of ideological infiltration.

Our second such colleague was Dr Rod Hicks in the university's Institute of Language Studies, where he supervised MA courses and Ph.D. research, and wrote teaching materials for several levels. Norman Pritchard, the third KELT adviser (later known as English language teaching officers, ELTOs), worked on producing radio and TV programmes in the Educational Media Agency, so keeping alive the British connection with an institution we had created and staffed with educational broadcasting officers from the mid-1960s. A fourth member of the project team had been envisaged, but my predecessor had rightly refused to allow recruitment because of the impossible housing situation. This did ease during 1989 with the gradual release of houses back to private ownership, so Andrew Brigham came to fill the vacancy in the Curriculum Institute. Finally, after a project review visit had endorsed the programme, a fifth member, John Atkins, came in January 1991 and joined Rod Hicks in the university to concentrate on the teacher training aspects of the reformed materials.

Finding and servicing accommodation for these colleagues and their families was a persistent worry for our overstretched office. This is mentioned because the logistical infrastructure is easily taken for granted, but is an inescapable factor 'at the sharp end' both of cultural bridge building and philanthropic aid delivery. Indeed, a full welfare safety net had to be provided, up to and including the emergency medical evacuation Rod Hicks needed when the local Swedish clinic failed to diagnose the cause of a mysterious and painful swelling. St Thomas's in London did, and he was back in two weeks.

Familiarization with the institutions in and near the capital took the usual form, with priority given to the places where our out-posted colleagues worked. As many as ten separate book presentations were lined up for delivery and speech-making, several of them for the KELT project, and half were done by Christmas. The ODA-funded Book Presentation Programme ran for five years and distributed about £290,000 worth of books before being transformed into a new Books and Information Aid plan. This extended series of donations — some 20 institutional libraries were invited to make their own selection of titles each year — was a significant and highly valued contribution to the alleviation of the book famine, a phenomenon common to all countries with soft, nonconvertible currencies. Government control of hard currency allocations invariably puts 'food for the mind' low down the list, a tendency exacerbated in Ethiopia by military demands.

The first year anywhere encourages a 'do anything once' syndrome, but a glance at the map shows that it was necessary to stick fairly closely to a deliberate plan if excursions were to cover the whole country in reasonable time, and that meant an almost complete coverage during 1989. The year was action-packed regardless of external events, but the counter-revolutions in eastern Europe served to accelerate an already changing scene in Ethiopia, and were ultimately to inspire the dramatic change of regime we were to live through two years later. Asmara in the north was of first importance to us, but at our first attempt Ethiopian Airlines aborted the flight because of fog at the far end. When we got there the next day Gebrehiwot confirmed that visibility had been down to a few yards, so the story was not as unlikely as we had thought. The then president of Asmara University was the very charming Dr Tewolde Berhan who, with his English wife Sue Edwards, gave us dinner in their home. They had met studying in Bangor, North Wales, where arid zone agriculture was a speciality. Sadly, within a year the noose tightened, the city was besieged and their position became untenable.

We visited the northeast (Harar, Alemaya University of Agriculture and Dire Dawa) in February; the northwest (Bahar Dar and Gondar) in July; the southwest (Jimma) in October; the south (Wondo Genet, Arba Minch and Awassa) in November; and the west (Ambo and Nekempte) in December. Only one place in the southeast (Robe, beyond the Bale mountains) had to wait until March 1990. Activity by the 'rebel' forces in the mid-north regions prevented any attempt to go beyond Gondar into the Simien mountains, or to Aksum; and not until the end of the war, late in 1991, was it possible to go beyond Dessie up to Mekele and through to Asmara overland. That is another story.

Keeping the human spirit buoyant in adversity

Meanwhile, against a background of constant political change and shifting military fortunes, we had to recognize that the more severe the difficulties of daily life became the more important it was to keep up a normal routine in mundane matters and to maintain a spirit of optimism in other-worldly concerns. Some time in the previous autumn, Pippa Sandford and Colin Battell had jointly asked me what would be my choice of music to conduct around Easter time. We had arrived just in time to join the Motley Singers in their Christmas performances, so had some idea of the forces

266

available. Taking account of the Ethiopian desire to perpetuate the legend surrounding the Queen of Sheba, my wish was to perform Handel's *Solomon*, especially as an excuse to do it had evaded me since first hearing Sir Thomas Beecham's sensuous recording — a present from the staff in Japan. The singers numbered 35, of whom a few could be persuaded to take solo parts, and a little ferreting out of instrumentalists hiding their talents produced an expanded string quartet led by Peggy Florida, an English–Canadian diplomat. We mustered two flutes and used the organ for other wind parts, but could not aspire to the standards reached in Malaysia. Both the military bands in Addis Ababa were moribund for lack of inspired training. Some of the double choruses had to be simplified, but we tackled most of the score uncut and the well-known story proved popular. Even so, the lack of Ethiopian participation made the exercise far less rewarding than we had become used to, and in the longer run we put more effort into drama in English, which had a more immediate appeal.

The Addis Ababa city hall stands at the top of the long rising sweep of Churchill Avenue (never renamed, as totalitarians have a habit of doing) and was opened by HM the Queen in the 1960s, invited by the Emperor. It contains a 1000-seat theatre, and Abate Mekuria was its keen and adventurous director. It may seem that a country in which civil war was likely to reach a climax fairly soon would not be fertile ground for a touring drama company, yet the risk was reasonable provided we kept it small scale, and London offered us the Cherub Theatre Company consisting of just six people. We had slight reservations about yet another production of *Twelfth Night*, but it proved to be a very original and highly exportable version, beginning with a merry-go-round and keeping up such a vigorous style throughout that the company suffered from the shortage of breath associated with the altitude of 8000 feet. One actress asked for honey for energy and was duly given a pot of high-quality local produce. The local acting fraternity was very impressed and we filled the theatre three nights running.

The Italian cultural institute was, like the National Theatre, an example of rather boring Fascist architecture of the 1930s, but it had good film-screening facilities and, in the interests of European solidarity, the director was keen to have his auditorium used year after year for the annual Eurofilm festival, organized in rotation by the cultural attachés of the relevant embassies, usually in May. The 1989 one was interrupted when the army generals in the north staged an unsuccessful coup while Mengistu was visiting the German Democratic Republic. The 1990 one was notable for our contribution of the latest *Henry V* film, and the 1991 event was interrupted in the middle of our screening of *Memphis Belle* by the Italian consul dashing in to announce an impending curfew following Mengistu's escape to Zimbabwe earlier in the day.

The Ethiopian Wildlife and Natural History Society had a strong multiracial following and organized many Sunday expeditions to forest reserves, to climb the many challenging mountains visible from Addis Ababa (many rising to over 10,000 feet) or for quieter flora and fauna observation. We went on several climbs, but more often we took advantage of occasional weekends in one of our embassy's two camping houses on the shore of Lake Langano, one of a series of Rift Valley lakes, about three hours steady driving south on a tarmac main road. Diana bought a half share in a Laser sailing boat when the owner left the country, and Oliver Hunt helped me rehabilitate a derelict Mirror sailing dinghy found on the embassy scrapheap. The lake was 12 kilometres wide and there were very few other vessels around, so one did not venture far out alone; but we did once make a voyage with the two boats together to the northern end where the hot springs bubbled up, and subsequently learnt that David Marler, our colleague who had been the original builder of the Mirror some 20 years earlier, had boiled eggs there. The chief merit of the lake otherwise was its reddish-brown alkaline water, which made it disease-free for swimming. Cormorants in abundance, the occasional pelican, some kingfishers and a solitary fish eagle were supported by the limited underwater life: but the land birds were the pride of Ethiopia, making it an ornithologist's paradise — more plentiful and colourful than can be readily imagined. They could also be large and noisy, as we learnt two years running, when a pair of Egyptian geese nested in our garden, producing no fewer than 12 chicks the second time. Hammerkopf birds also nested in a forked tree.

An alternative to sailing, tennis or walking, was riding. The 80-acre British embassy compound was one of a string of similar sites granted by Emperor Menelik II in the early years of the century to the 'powers' of the day. The order in which they were established is still reflected in the numerical prefixes to the registration plates on diplomatic vehicles — 01 for Italian, 02 for French, 03 for British, and so forth. All in the same area of the foothills to the north of the city, these compounds, including the Russian and American ones, offer wide scope for gardens, plantations, large bungalows, spacious offices — and stabling for horses; plus, in the British case, a golf course, a small cemetery and now a miniature Euro-hospital. Between eight and ten energetic Ethiopian ponies were each 'owned' in turn by the shifting population of our embassy and we, in the British Council, were privileged to join. The cost was little beyond the pay of the resident grooms, and Diana's horse, duly transferred from a departing colleague, was exchanged for less than a quarter of the price paid for her English-made saddle. She enjoyed 'hacks' into the hills behind the compound several times a week, and nearly always on Sundays when the fourth of our orthopaedic consultants, Geoffrey Walker, turned out to be a qualified riding instructor. He set up jumps and indulged in dressage training, which culminated in a 'match' against the German embassy along the road. My involvement was restricted to the occasional 'riding picnic' and was reduced still further after being taken for an involuntary gallop by one of the friskier mounts. In any case, 'the bag' of official and private mail was supposed to come in on Saturdays and my deplorable workaholism made me prefer reading it on Sundays.

A family wedding in perfect conditions
As soon as the Cherub Theatre Company's visit was over, Diana flew home a week ahead of me to supervise the final preparations for Sarah's wedding to Nigel Clark in Berry Pomeroy church. On my arrival we drove together to Totnes to stay a week with Potty Granny and use her house as a base. Louise escaped from work in London and Jessica took two days out of her A-level countdown, the two making a pair of stunning bridesmaids, and Diana's special purple outfit with the unaccustomed hat was very impress-

ive. A more perfect English spring day than 20 May 1989 cannot be imagined and everything went wonderfully smoothly. Sarah had collected a very fine body of singers from Sherborne, Durham and London; the Rector of Totnes made an exceptionally sensitive and memorable address; and the wedding feast in the marquee on the lawn of the Old Rectory opposite was distinguished by Peter Orr's toast to the bride, some well-chosen wine with a good menu and the presence of a hundred or so family and friends, including a surprise arrival from Australia. We had met Nigel's parents, Frank and Joy only once before, and it was especially hard that Frank should be struck down with a fatal illness so soon afterwards. As is now customary, after a lull in the early evening, a band carried on the party well beyond the bedtime of the elders.

Back in London for a few duty calls in our HQ departments, a happy coincidence of timing enabled us to attend the annual musicians' memorial service in the city church of St Sepulchre-without-Newgate. An organization called the Friends of the Musicians' Chapel has a book in which the names of deceased musicians are inscribed, and my mother had arranged for my father's name to be so written. Consequently, we get a notice of the service each year and try to attend whenever possible. The four principal colleges of music in London take turns to provide a choir and organist, and the standard has been high each time we have been present. In this week there was a strike of the London underground in progress, so much walking from Kensington to Whitehall and to the City and back was required.

Even more convenient was our ability to attend Jessica's last commemoration at Sherborne. As a music scholar she was used to taking a prominent part and this year she had composed an amen for the abbey service, as well as singing and playing in two concerts. Earlier in the year she had applied to Project Trust to become a gap-year volunteer, which had required an initiative-testing journey to the Hebridean island of Coll for group selection procedures followed (for the successful ones) by a fundraising challenge. Prospective volunteers were asked to raise £2000 as a contribution towards the total costs. Jessica put on a concert with the willing support of her house mistress and other staff — charging 'charity' prices for admission and refreshments — and she also did a sponsored bicycle ride, so getting well over half the required sum. She had previously obtained an offer of deferred entry to the history degree course at Edinburgh University and when her A-level results proved more than adequate to meet their requirements there was much agonizing over the right course of action. By that time she had already gone to Namibia under Project Trust's auspices and eventually decided to stick to the Edinburgh plan. (See below for our visit to her in 1990.)

Before returning to Addis Ababa we began to make tentative arrangements for my mother to have a hip replacement operation. Her arthritis had become so painful that she had recognized the need; the alternative was to be reduced to a wheelchair far sooner than her otherwise very active life of pottery teaching allowed. It was done very successfully later in the year. Meanwhile, our return to post, through no fault of Lufthansa, turned out to be the worst air journey we ever experienced. Otto Benz, the manager in Ethiopia, arranged for the first of many later occasions to put us up overnight in the Steigenberger Hotel of Frankfurt airport, so obviating the risk of a fog-delayed connection from Heathrow missing the Addis Ababa flight at 10.00 a.m. Jeddah was the refuelling stop, after which we approached 'overhead' Asmara on a fine clear evening. Without warning we had turned, noticing the sun setting on the wrong side, and were told that there were no lights operating at our destination. Our immediate fear was that fighting had begun down there, but later learnt that a careless workman had severed a cable. Half the night was spent in the Jeddah transit lounge, followed by a return to Frankfurt. Then what? A bit of sleep, a flight to Rome for a seat on a second night flight, by Alitalia this time, to Jeddah again, and finally to Addis Ababa on Monday morning, having expected to be there on Saturday evening with time to recover before the next week began.

Some visitors are more equal than others

'Hasn't anyone told them that it rains in June?' This was the muttering we heard from the long-term residents in response to our invitation to a big farewell party in our garden for Nick and Emilia Taylor. Happily, we just got away with it; our lunch-time buffet was over by the time the first drops fell at 3.30 p.m. Nick had become fluent in Amharic and had made much progress in computerizing our office procedures, so was leaving a big gap while deservedly obtaining a posting on promotion to Educational Contracts Department in London. He came back a year later to negotiate with us the terms on which we should bid for a contract with the World Bank to supply lecturers to Alemaya University of Agriculture, and has since been posted to Cairo. His temporary replacement Andrew Hadley had been working on our Technical Cooperation Training desk in London, having joined the British Council after teaching English for several years in Istanbul, and very quickly established such an excellent rapport with our staff and our contacts that at the end of his four months we tried to keep him permanently. That was not to be, but the experience served him well and, in due course, he got a proper posting to Beijing.

In addition to the 12 external examiners for the medical faculty, each year the veterinary faculty down in Debre Zeit had three who came for similar purposes — to help the Ethiopian academics give appropriate gradings to their examinees, to offer advice on the curriculum and to run staff training workshops, which went some way towards compensating for the lack of access to current professional journals and other sources of information. We also tried to build up longer-term relationships based on more formal academic links, in this case with the corresponding department at Glasgow University, so that mutual interest could be maintained. The usual drinks party given by us at the end of their stay was a way of thanking their hosts for their hospitality. When Diana had to be in London to help Jessica prepare for her departure to Namibia, my capacity to entertain without her usual stage management was tested twice, at an interval of one week, when parties were needed for two batches of medical examiners.

Ever since the visit of Mr Chris Patten as Minister of Overseas Development (just before my time), the problem of the congestion in our library, and premises generally, had been on the agenda. One way of hiving off our secondary school clientele would have been the creation of a separate textbook reading room, and this idea was pursued vigorously for several months, but eventually abandoned in favour of expanding our bulk loan scheme to more than the handful of schools hitherto covered. The need arose from the plight of vast numbers of students trying to study for exams without any access to the necessary textbooks. The Ministry just did not have the hard currency to stock the school libraries. So we provided multiple copies of suitable texts, mostly English, maths and science — later very tentatively extended to more controversial subjects such as history — on permanent loan (a euphemism for outright gift) to special sections of each school library. Previously there had been a rationing system whereby each headmaster could nominate a limited number of his best pupils for membership of the library; now we would no longer accept school pupils for registration. We nevertheless included these student numbers in our library membership statistics, otherwise the figures would have been misinterpreted as a decline. Capacity among our crowded shelves was in this way released for the adult readers whom we needed to encourage.

None of these measures was a solution to our long-term need for decent premises, so our own architect, Roger Molyneux, visited us with a brief to weigh up the relative merits of the sites we had been offered by the Addis Ababa regional administrators in City Hall. The party comrades there were extraordinarily affable and assured me that both the city council and the party were keen on supporting our activities — such as might have been regarded as subversive by real hard-liners. The preference for renting premises whenever possible is a natural consequence of the desire for flexibility, yet Addis Ababa had become a city of arrested development, with no noticeable investment in buildings since the advent of communism in the mid-1970s, so the total absence of rentable premises forced the inescapable conclusion that if we wanted better premises we would have to build them. But did we have any prospect of getting the money? Not unless we had a plan, the catch being that making a plan required *some* money to initiate it. We found some and commissioned a firm of structural engineers to design a prefabricated building. When shown this, the comrades in City Hall teased me with 'What's this? We can't have the British Council accommodated in a *barracks*! We expect you to put up a building of architectural distinction which will adorn our city.'

In fact it was quite an elegant L-shaped design on two floors,

273

well satisfying our specific needs and well suited to the chosen site, which was near, but screened from, a main thoroughfare. The advantage of prefabrication would have been the avoidance of delay by importing all components in two containers duty free. The cost compared favourably with conventional building, the common element being stone, sand and cement for the foundations from local sources. The city planners said that our site was in a zone requiring a minimum of three storeys, but we got round that by suggesting a terraced garage and parking spaces.

In the middle of all this an invitation from the Marine Transport Authority (MTA) to visit Massawa came to me, and such a chance was too good to miss. The Port Workers' Club gave me VIP treatment and the MTA's public relations manager, Ato Negash Balcha, generously arranged for a cold box of fresh fish from the Red Sea Trading Company to fly with us back to Addis Ababa after a day of business in Asmara. Their interest in us arose from our patronage of ODA-funded training awards in port administration, and in the potential for supplies of books and English teaching materials. The only other port, Assab, was visited by each of my assistants in turn.

A further diversion came in the form of an archaeological seminar on Aksum, where the British-led excavations had been halted since the mid-1970s; but the results of previous work had just been published and the Nairobi-based British Institute was hoping to persuade the Ethiopian authorities to allow digging to resume. At one of the parties given to entertain the delegates, Professor Roland Oliver was heard to respond to a questioner about his work 'Oh, I invented African history!' — a remark which in a sense was at least partially justified.

Of more immediate concern, however, was our next visitor, our old friend from Malawi days and now our London boss as controller of Africa Division, Colin Perchard. The architects' report had surfaced just a week before his arrival, so he was able to check over the whole premises question on the ground. Our programme for him was otherwise fairly standard for such 'visiting firemen' from HQ, but as we were delighted to have him staying as our house guest for the whole week we benefited from the addition of personal gossip. He touched base with HMA and the President of the university, and then called on all four of the institutions where our KELT project colleagues worked, plus the medical faculty and Comrade Wondmu, the regional administrator in City Hall. But his top priorities were to get to Asmara by air to size up our library there and to boost staff morale in an increasingly siege-like situation.

Alas, the third day of his visit was declared to be the Prophet's birthday, and on the following day he and Ato Mulugeta waited at the airport for five hours, at the end of which the aircraft allocated to the Asmara flight was declared unfit. (This experience of failure to fly was a valuable lesson for us in planning for the visit of the director-general two months later.) More happily, on the same day my youngest sister Antonia arrived for a short stay *en route* to Malawi to resume teaching with Peter Tolhurst, her husband, who had also stopped over three weeks earlier. So for several evenings we were a happy foursome. We saw Colin off on Sunday morning, but what we did not know until much later was that ill luck had dogged him again in that he found his UK ticket to Cairo was only accepted after a long argument. Colin has since risen to the highest overseas post in the organization, as Minister (Cultural Affairs) in charge of our work in India.

Professor Sir Phillip Randle of Oxford is certainly the tallest visitor we have ever fielded. He came to give a Leithead memorial lecture at the invitation of Professor Asrat, the dean of the medical faculty. He was also asked to deliver it at the Institute of Health Science in Jimma, so, despite our doubts about his ability to be at all comfortable in a landrover seat, we took him on the 350-kilometre journey to the southwest. While he was taken to a district health centre next day, we made useful calls on the Junior College of Agriculture and on the Teacher Training Institute — both typical of a provincial centre.

About this time news came of the Berlin wall coming down. The subsequent events in eastern Europe were to have a profound effect on the fate of Mengistu's regime, even if it had been showing signs of moderating its ideology all through the year since our arrival. At our earliest official functions all Ethiopian men in responsible positions, including office holders in the academic world, wore the obligatory party members' uniform in either blue or khaki. Within a few months these were abandoned, except by a few who found it too costly to re-equip with jacket and tie. Addressing each other as 'comrade', however, survived until the collapse. The resuscitation of private property began, too, so that some occupiers could consider renting out for income; more political prisoners were released; and the price of petrol raised far enough to undermine the black market.

One more medical visitor was Sir John Golding, with Lady Pamela, from Jamaica under the auspices of WOC, so it was our orthopaedic consultant, Ginger Wilson's job to programme him. We helped by arranging a weekend in Langano, which satisfied Ginger's long-held desire to see the lake just before he handed over to Brian Madden. Both our guests were keen bird watchers who revelled in the long list of observable species.

To be receiving the director-general for a second time after only 18 months was a rare privilege. Instead of chartering a yacht for Sir Richard Francis, this time it would have to be an aircraft. The priority task was to get him to Asmara, so we were able to convince London without much difficulty, in the light of Colin Perchard's recent experience, that £2500 would be well spent on the private hire of a Twin Otter. The embassy's deputy head of Mission, Alan Collins, was able to advise me in detail, based on his frequent use of the Relief and Rehabilitation Commission's aircraft for VIP visitors; and the cost was comparable with an Ethiopian Airlines first-class return fare when multiplied by the number of passengers we intended to take.

On his first evening the director-general was entertained by the chief administrator of Addis Ababa, Comrade Gizaw Negussie, to a traditional display of Ethiopian music and dancing with supper, and during his second day we called on the Ministers of Education and (because of his former BBC service) of Information. We gave a lunch-time reception for 50 and HMA gave a dinner for 24 'key contacts', as the inescapable jargon has it. Then, on the third day we flew. A Boeing 737 does the flight to Asmara in one hour; our Twin Otter took two and a half hours, flying just under the cloud base at 14,000 feet, with much of the rugged terrain only a few thousand feet below us. Seated behind the pilot with a series of American maps borrowed from the embassy, my navigational compulsion took hold and enabled me to follow the whole route on our 360 degree course, spot on due north. It was unexpectedly cold in the unheated cabin; by the afternoon the sun warmed our return, but not enough to forestall my streaming nose two days later. We were in Asmara from 10.00 a.m. until 3.00 p.m. — just five hours on the ground for five hours flying — but every moment was useful. We had brought 400 kilograms of books for the library (using up spare passenger capacity), which was the first consignment for many months; the director-general made a book presentation to the University of Asmara, being thanked by Dr Tewolde Berhan with characteristic charm; and he saw the building in Lorenzo Ta'azaz Street we subsequently obtained as enormously improved premises. When he left for Khartoum the next day we were able, with embassy assistance, to employ the VIP facilities, so there could be no repetition of Colin's problem getting to Cairo.

1990: the calm before the storm, but much travelling
Over Christmas we had Nigel and Sarah to stay, together with two of Sarah's Durham friends, so we had a heavily laden land-rover with a party of six going to Langano for the New Year weekend. Almost as soon as they had gone we set off for six weeks of postponed home leave, beginning with an Alitalia flight to Rome and on to Malta the following day for a second visit, but this time as guests of Brian and Margot Hitch in their British High Commissioner's residence. For three days music and walking took most of our time and included a trip to the old walled city of Mdina in the centre of the island, where Brian practised on the cathedral organ and we introduced Margot to the remarkable mosaic floor of the preserved Roman villa.

After the obligatory couple of days in London we reached Totnes just in time to entertain Abate Mekuria who was visiting the Northcott Studio theatre in Exeter. Thereafter, we made a couple of memorable excursions. One was to Birmingham and Solihull to go with Elnora Ferguson to a CBSO concert (thanks to our previous connection with them in Finland) and to lunch with Nigel's parents, Frank and Joy Clark. Another was to see Paul and Karen Docherty with her mother, Mrs Leithead, near Gloucester, and staying with Reggie and Patsy Merryweather in Paradise near Painswick.

Meanwhile, we had collected some rather bizarre luggage to take back to Addis Ababa. Diana had decided to buy a saddle in Newton Abbot and Lufthansa kindly agreed to include it in our hand-luggage (it was actually given a vacant first-class seat). Unknown to anybody, however, was the presence of a skeleton, named George, placed diagonally across a specially large suitcase. Louise had helped us get a discounted price from medical suppliers for this plastic teaching aid requested by the orthopaedic department and, although he arrived with a dislocated neck and one broken finger, he was duly presented for remedial treatment to the Black Lion Hospital doctors in training. Ginger Wilson had left some money in an orthopaedic equipment fund for such purposes. Booked into the Steigenberger Hotel at Frankfurt airport, for the reasons already explained, we took the opportunity to telephone our old Bucharest friends, Ivan and Marianne Kauntz-Jacobovitz who, despite being surprised to hear from us, came the short distance from their home in Wiesbaden to see us.

In addition to an entitlement to take leave annually, as a so-called 'hardship post', Ethiopia was one of only 12 countries designated by the FCO as deserving provision for 'breather visits'. We noticed that a new route via Lilongwe to Windhoek was being advertised by Ethiopian Airlines in the light of Namibia's impending independence, so we decided to go and see Jessica in May. The route was actually no more than some sanguine wishful thinking by the airline's management; it never got beyond an inaugural flight, so we had to go indirectly, a change which became an advantage. Just before embarking on this adventure we gave a big party to introduce our most useful contacts to our new Ambassador, James Glaze and Rosemary his wife, who had arrived six weeks earlier. James quickly showed strong support for our work, and became a co-belligerent in our struggles with London, as had his predecessor, H. B. ('Hookey') Walker, who has been Sir Harold since his period in Bagdhad during the Gulf War.

A night stop in Nairobi enabled us to entertain to dinner John and Barbara Gardner, whom we had known as colleagues in Kuala Lumpur, and next day to be met at Lilongwe's new international airport by Stanley Msusa, the British Council driver who had been recruited by me in the late-1960s and whose ear-to-ear smile lives on to this day. Stuart and Joan Newton were kindness itself, putting us up in his newish Representative's house and showing us the custom-built offices and library where we met a handful of Malawian staff who had bridged the 20 years since we had left. Then, with a car hired on favourable terms, we sped down the tarmac highway to Blantyre in only a few hours (it had taken all day by landrover in our time) to join my sister Antonia and Peter Tolhurst for a four-night stay in their house on the campus of St Patrick's Mzedi Catholic Boys' School near Limbe.

In the next few days we indulged in much nostalgia. We saw the changed surroundings of the houses we had lived in, met Elias Sanudi the driver–projectionist who had stayed in Blantyre when the British Council moved to Lilongwe, spent a Saturday walking on Zomba mountain, sought out our singing immigration officer, Edson Lamya, and met the retired police bandmaster, Matt Numero, who had trumpeted for us so energetically. It was very gratifying to learn that the music society we had started some 25 years earlier not only continued to flourish but had grown branches in Zomba and Lilongwe. Generally, too, it was uplifting to return to a country that had not declined through misgovernment since independence, where the people were still as open and friendly as ever and, despite problems with food shortages and Mozambican refugees in uncomfortable numbers, continued to live peacefully together.

Another night stop in Johannesburg and we were telephoning Jessica from Windhoek airport's car-hire desk to get directions for finding her. The Helmut Bleks Foundation's farm school was 40 kilometres west of Windhoek, and the Project Trust volunteers were assigned to teaching and supervising the pupils with an age range of 7 to 22, all farmers' children who would not otherwise get any education. The environment was arid rolling scrubland as far as could be seen in any direction, but the altitude ensured cool nights. Jessica and her paired volunteer lived in one end of a classroom block and were constantly exposed to close scrutiny. The pupils' living conditions were pretty primitive and ill-supervised, so the girls set up dormitory tidiness and cleanliness competitions, which amounted to a revolution in their lifestyle. With independence the Namibian government decreed that English should replace Afrikaans as the medium of instruction, but as the teachers had hitherto taught in Afrikaans they needed much coaching in English, which Jessica found more rewarding to offer than many other duties. The celebrations to mark the end of UN trusteeship over what had been South West Africa, and originally a German colony, meant longer school holidays than in a normal year, so Jessica was able to travel throughout most of southern Africa and up to Zimbabwe before returning home and going up to Edinburgh.

We met David Godfrey of the Rossing Foundation (money from uranium mining) who was retained as Project Trust's local representative; we called on Jasper Utley in his newly established British Council centre; we thanked Peter Wallis, the newly established British high commissioner for his interest; and we took tea with Dr and Mrs Bleks at their own farm, set at a discreet distance from the school. Then we flew back to Johannesburg for a long weekend with John and Veda Carver, known since Malawi days. John's Management Selection and Training enterprise, which aimed to improve the prospects of black South Africans in all fields of business, was flourishing and expanding fast. For similar reasons the British Council had moved from its old Pretoria premises (where Richard Watkins had been working during my visit in 1984) and Bill Radford now reigned over fine new premises in central Johannesburg, which, as can be imagined, we viewed with envy. We enjoyed an all-day walk and picnic with John and Veda in the hills, bought some paint for the Mirror dinghy and, after a short night again in Nairobi, were back in Addis Ababa feeling much enlightened.

The 'summer' months in the Ethiopian highlands brought very heavy rains and several weekends huddling over log fires. Most expatriates working to the academic year contrived to evade the worst of the season; we concentrated on low-profile, internal 'house-keeping' matters. About this time London began to ask for quarterly reports to provide a flavour of what was going on, so a few short quotations are offered as indicative — 'It took six months for our fax machine to be installed by Telecoms following its clearance through customs;' 'Slippage [in negotiations for a World Bank contract] has been continuous and cumulative, so that what should have begun last August has no hope of beginning until next January;' and 'A new project vehicle (Ford Fiesta) for our orthopaedic consultant was ordered and air freighted but sat at the airport from 8 May, while two and a half months of tortuous paperwork was negotiated, until 24 July when we were able to hand it over to Professor Geoffrey Walker.'

But the general outlook showed signs of movement. Mengistu had made a U-turn speech in which he said, in effect, 'We cannot ignore what is happening in eastern Europe; we have tried communism for 15 years and it has failed us; we shall now develop an open market political economy.' He may have persuaded the central committee and some members of the National Shengo, but so many years of indoctrination cannot be reversed overnight. The Soviet withdrawal from Afghanistan had been followed by Gorbachev's refusal of any more military aid, and Mengistu had returned empty-handed from a begging trip to North Korea. So the government army was on the defensive, especially in Eritrea where Asmara was being shelled with impunity.

A special commission 'set about calling up experienced and trained old soldiers, and there was concern by the parents of teenage boys over the hazards of underage impressment'. Nevertheless, there was 'a much improved atmosphere among the intelligentsia, and less fear of the regime, as the turn away from Marxist–Leninist doctrines began to gather pace'. Indeed, in the university both teachers and students abandoned the study of 'party doctrine' quite precipitately, leaving a vacuum in the curriculum of the philosophy department, such that we were asked to find a British academic who would come and redesign the applied philosophy course, in the interests of 'rejoining the mainstream of thinking in the world'.

In August Diana flew home three weeks ahead of me to help Jessica settle in after her Namibian gap year and prepare for Edinburgh. Left behind, my job was the DIY renovation of the kitchen with a large consignment of flat-packed Hygiena units. The assembly instructions were so complex that we could be sure no one else would be able to follow them, so over several months a total of 50 hours were put in as a relaxation at the end of an office day. Once assembled, Ato Hailu and his willing son helped me install them.

Our autumn leave was largely taken up with three excursions. The first was by air to Bordeaux where Peter and Pat Harrison met us and took us north to spend a week in Le Perou, their home in the Charente valley midway between Saintes and Cognac, a visit which has since become an annual fixture. The second was by air from Plymouth to Cork to explore Ireland for the first time, taking Potty Granny with us to satisfy her long-held desire to see her Irish grandmother's birthplace, and to see our ex-Khartoum colleagues, Patrick and Stephanie Early in Lahinch near Burren in County Clare. And the third was to take a rented estate car by motor-rail overnight to Scotland to convey Jessica and all her possessions for her first year in Edinburgh, calling on Peter and Kay Orr in Guisborough and my sister Phillida and David Shipp in Delph on the return journey southwards. Another Lufthansa flight via Frankfurt took us back to work in Addis Ababa.

Fiddling while Rome burns: keeping the show on the road
Bill and Jenny Collings of Helsinki days had written to propose celebrating their twenty-fifth wedding anniversary by coming to stay with us and, by judicious juggling of dates, we managed to ensure that there would be plenty going on to amuse them. Two events had been in gestation for several months. First was our 'Britain and Sport' exhibition, which came to us with two of the 13 crates missing, had a very awkward mounting system and required all of five days to construct in the National Museum, which was the only available space with the required 300 square metres. It also needed constant invigilation by a rota of our staff, but the response was very gratifying as it attracted 18,000 visitors and required an extension of its showing from two to three and a half weeks. Bill Collings enjoyed a stint of stewarding one morning.

Second was Paul Archibald's English Brass Quintet. Almost by chance one of its demonstration cassettes had landed on my desk earlier in the year, but since our computerized budget printout contained precisely £10 for music, it was obvious that only through commercial sponsorship could we hope to receive them. On hearing the tape our Lufthansa friends offered us the five business-class return fares required, so negotiations over dates were begun by my visiting Putney where the Archibalds lived during my autumn leave. We did have some money in the drama kitty, but since nothing was currently on offer from London we diverted that for their fee; and it was satisfactory to be able to tell Music Department what excellent value for money we had obtained — six days and five performances for only four and a half fees! They gave one concert in the City Hall Theatre, another in the Italian Cultural Institute and a third in the garden of the Ambassador's residence within the embassy compound. James Glaze and his (or rather my) trumpet, Bill Collings with a triangle and me on my cello joined the professionals in *The Elastic Band* for a grand finale. The quintet also ran two morning workshops, one for the students of the Yared Music School and another for the Ethiopian police bandsmen. Shallow breathing was diagnosed and amply demonstrated as the all-pervasive shortcoming of the locals' technique. By agreement in advance, no hotel costs arose because hospitality was provided in the embassy by James Glaze and by Matthew Kidd, who had by then replaced Alan Collins as deputy head of Mission.

With Matthew we would before long be discussing Gulf War jitters, security measures and contingency plans, but meanwhile there was little to prevent the Motley Singers and Players rehearsing under my direction for the usual two church performances, this time of Berlioz's *L'Enfance du Christ* in a slightly truncated form since we lacked trombones for the first part. Little to prevent, one might say, other than the work of many incoming visitors, a summons to fly to Cairo for a four-day management planning seminar, a bad patch of bereavements and illnesses among our librarians and office staff, and my third time round the cycle of book presentation visits and speech making.

We had also by this time decided that in the short term we should maximize the use of our existing premises and, in particular, that we should replace the leaking roof of the room where we held regular screenings of the 'film of the month'. For this mezzanine area we consulted a local architect from the Building

College who provided an excellent design and called for tenders. No sooner had the winning contractor signed than he said that of course he could not obtain the materials without our help, so we had to back up his requests to the authorities and generally supervise what was, in the end, a very good job. Emboldened by the success of this operation, we later created a staff refectory in a previously dismal kitchen area. (The reader may query these undertakings by us as tenants, but it has to be realized that landlords in communist countries do not have any incentive and certainly no inclination at all to spend money — even if they have any. The same applied to any improvements made in the staff houses we rented — until the change of regime confirmed the restoration of property rights.)

Our team of ELTO colleagues in the KELT project were funded by the ODA and, consequently, were very dependent on the good esteem of Dr Digby Swift, one of the ODA's education advisers resident in London. Fielding him was an experience fraught with strong emotions and it was occasionally my failing to keep these firmly controlled that led to difficulties. After his November 1990 visit, however, his report 'vindicated our past activities and future intentions' and 'paid tribute to the tight and effective programme we arranged for him'. A year later he came again into a very different political context, but we knew him better and were able to extract many more positive recommendations.

Raising money for local charities took two main forms — either selling tickets for a variety of musical entertainments, with or without meals, or sponsored walks or rides, such as the annual one in aid of the Cheshire Homes. We both enjoyed the 12-mile walk in the Ambo direction, but in 1989 there had been a strong tendency to argue about the route among the participants, on account of fading memories of the previous year; so in 1991 we decided to use the embassy horses and to rely more on navigation (or rather, orienteering perhaps) with my pocket compass. We got there rather more directly that time. Diana was active both with the International Women's Group, which did very well each year with a concert in the Italian Institute, and with similar events in our embassy. The proceeds from the retiring collections at our Motley concerts normally went to charity; for example, the two

Solomon performances attracted 230 people who contributed 2000 birr, or about £600 at that time.

It may be remarked that we managed to escape to Lake Langano rather frequently, even if (as was usual) work came with me. The reason was the very large number of public holidays, rivalled only by those in Japan. The Orthodox Church was to some extent (as in Romania) collaborationist, and certainly the regime made no attempt to take it on. The Ethiopian calendar was based on the church year, with Orthodox Christmas usually two weeks after the Western one and the two Easters sometimes as much as a month apart (26 March and 30 April in 1989, for example). *Timkat* (Epiphany) was celebrated in mid-January with big cere- monial processions and *Maskal* (Finding of the True Cross) in September, together with the Ethiopian New Year later in the same month. But the calendar also enabled the national airline and tourism offices to proclaim a land offering 'thirteen months of sunshine' — a technical half-truth! All the Islamic holidays were also observed, so the disruption to office routines was almost a habit.

One Friday afternoon a few months after his arrival, James Glaze 'phoned me asking 'Why is it that Ethiopians are far and away the brightest people in Africa [he had previously been HMA in Cameroon and Angola, and had served earlier in Lesotho] and yet have made such a mess of their country? Do you think you could let me have a think-piece by Monday morning?'

He must have known that my weekend was not otherwise bespoke: in any case the request had to be taken as an order. No text survives, but my memory suggests a couple of pages in which blame was laid primarily on topography, followed by an optimis- tic assessment for the future, provided the system did not destroy the cadre of very competent bureaucrats still surviving since before the revolution, but without adequate successors in sight.

The outlook deteriorates: obedient foreigners leave first
The map on the wall of Matthew Kidd's office plotted the steady encroachment southwards of the guerrilla forces from the north and, in the light of the best (but very sparse) information avail- able, there was no immediate threat within range. Of greater con-

cern was the risk of Arab terrorists attempting to attack Western people and installations as the Gulf War deadline for action passed on 15 January 1991. Embassies tended to have their own security guards, but foreign cultural centres such as ours were sitting ducks, and the Ethiopian police were eventually persuaded to provide minimal protection for us in the form of a 'uniformed deterrent' outside. London instructed us to institute bag searching of our library clientele.

None of this deterred Mrs (now Baroness) Linda Chalker, Minister of Overseas Development, from visiting Ethiopia to review aid strategy. At a working lunch James Glaze had invited me to join, a stage whisper to my neighbour and embassy colleague, Andrew Barber, asking 'How about an extension of the Know How Fund to Ethiopia?' was overheard by the Minister who pounced on the idea, saying 'Just what I was thinking.'

Sadly, however, in spite of the constant search for new ways of funding worthwhile development projects, anything of that sort had to await the political upheaval, although that was not then long in coming. Similarly, Keith Burd's recommendation that our budget for supporting the higher education sector should be doubled, found no favour owing to the distasteful nature of the regime; yet the case was a non-political one.

The sight of taxis queuing for petrol brought to mind the events that had triggered the downfall of the Haile Selassie regime in the mid-1970s. The fuel shortage developed this time, not because of an oil price rise or the Gulf War, but because of the bankruptcy of the government which had allowed the Assab refinery to run out of crude oil. Two of our own three vehicles were dry for a day, despite queuing, and some travel plans had to be abandoned, though fortunately some books had got through to Gondar and Bahar Dar just before the towns 'fell to opposition forces' or — more accurately in most cases — 'changed hands peacefully'. The demoralization of the government army was such that tactical disengagement normally preceded the arrival of the EPRDF — castigated by Mengistu's tottering regime as 'bandits'.

Personal health had seldom been a serious problem for us, but it was accepted that Ethiopia harboured some specially virulent strains of tummy bugs and respiratory infections and, although the climate was generally invigorating, the combination of altitude and dryness seemed to have exacerbated my own problem with nasal congestion and sinus pains. On a previous visit to London an ENT consultant had recommended a thorough clearout under general anaesthetic, so it happened that my absence from Addis Ababa for this purpose coincided with a sudden increase in EPRDF activity. This caused the embassy to stop families receiving children for the Easter holidays and to arrange for spouses to go home for 'reverse holiday visits'. This meant that Rosemary Arnott, my extremely efficient and charming assistant director, had to drop everything to sort out the air bookings.

It also meant that our five ELTO colleagues were deprived of their wives, in some cases for longer than was expected at that stage. Diana, too, had flown home to join me after my few days in hospital and, after a little time recuperating in Totnes, we went with Jessica for a second rather short visit (by train, ferry and hired car this time) to the Harrisons in Le Perou. Ordeal by nosebleed afflicted me twice, but thereafter the general improvement even extended to the feeling of having a new voice, consequent on 'opening the pipes' which, as William Byrd had said, was the chief benefit of 'all men learning to sing'.

Disregarding any official reservations about travel to a disturbed area, an impressive delegation of no fewer that ten British academics came for the first half of April to take part in the eleventh International Ethiopian Studies Conference at the university, including Christopher Clapham, author of a standard work *Transformation and Continuity in Revolutionary Ethiopia*, and Anthony Mockler, author of *Haile Selassie's War*. The latter was particularly relevant since the conference included a special session to commemorate the fiftieth anniversary of the liberation of Addis Ababa on 5 April 1941.

Several 'evacuated dependants' trickled back to post and all four international community schools reopened. Diana used her return ticket to rejoin me after a one-week delay, but others who took too much notice of 'advice' suffered from spouse separation for many uncomfortable months. My quarterly report summarized the atmosphere in this way:

While admitting that the current working environment is one of considerable nervousness on all sides, it is necessary to discourage the belief that a feeling of insecurity is an excuse to down tools. We have to continue to plan for the future, and to execute those plans, until a moment (which may or may not come) when it becomes patently obvious that we are forced to abandon them. Such a judgement is likely to be based on extremely slender evidence, since hard information is almost impossible to obtain.

It had been agreed between the embassy and the FCO several months earlier that there should be no question of leaving the embassy compound open to the threat of looting. The investment in housing, offices and equipment on an 80-acre site was not difficult to defend (other than from a deliberate military attack which was hardly expected from either side in the civil war) and the compound had its own water supply, electricity and food for many months. So a very small contingent of British 'soldiers' (a close protection team) took up residence and formed a very effective deterrent until the emergency was over. The British Council's staff houses, however, were spread all over the city, and the office and library could not have withstood any determined looters, so we drafted and redrafted contingency plans, taking care to keep in step with Matthew Kidd. Security reports went regularly from the embassy to the FCO and my London masters began to demand 'sitreps' every few days. Before long it seemed more sensible to read what the embassy had sent and then quote the references for my bosses to get from the FCO, but sometimes we could short-circuit the whole system by faxing material directly — only if (rarely) unclassified, of course.

Meanwhile, normal activity continued. The annual Eurofilm screenings were planned; the Motley Singers and Players began rehearsing *Noye's Fludde* (abortively); riding, sailing and tennis went on; and, in a capital with so many embassies all giving national day receptions, one exceptionally beautiful afternoon ended with the Swedish King's day and The Netherlands Queen's day parties in quick succession. We chatted to all our usual Ethiopian friends, yet the incongruity between this relaxed enjoyment

288

and the desperation of the regime was not lost on us. A few days later our entire staff attended the wedding ceremony of Dereje, one of our drivers, and a final 'rehearsed reading' of *Macbeth* in our garden promised well. Did we detect a slight parallel between us and Olivia Manning's 'Spirit of Guy Pringle'?

As the EPRDF's net closed round Addis Ababa, interpreting advice became a neurotic preoccupation. The Americans had been the first to evacuate dependants at a time when Matthew's wall map showed little cause for panic. There were twice-weekly meetings of the European Community representatives in an attempt at a coordinated response to the perceived risk, but in practice each country took its own decision. In mid-May events began to speed up. In a month since Mengistu's final televised appeal for unity and patriotism had registered only bored indifference in a war-weary country, there had been a commission for an interim government and a reshuffle of the Council of Ministers; but without warning one quiet Tuesday morning the rumour spread that Mengistu had fled to Zimbabwe. Disbelief was widespread, but confirmation soon came from an acting head of state who decreed a 9.00 p.m. curfew. That put a stop to Eurofilm. The Italian Institute and Alliance Française closed and, within a few days, the French summoned their entire community one evening to be at the airport by 6.00 a.m. for a special evacuation flight. We were not quite so obedient. By the end of the week the last flights had gone and the airport was closed for a fortnight, so the arguments for and against evacuation became hypothetical.

Living through a counter-revolution

A three times life-size statue of Lenin stood in a prominent position near Revolution Square, but a taxi driver's comment on his stance to visitors on their way in to town was 'You can see he has begun his walk to the airport!'

Two days after Mengistu's departure Rosemary phoned Diana with the news that Lenin was being removed, so she rushed to the scene and found that he was already on his side. The Ethiopians had made a much quicker job of it than the Romanians, who needed a crane and took three days.

On the same day there was a general release of political and

289

military prisoners, and on the next day came news of the 'fall', or more accurately the handover, of Asmara to the victorious Eritrean People's Liberation Front (EPLF), of which more later. Not until mid-July did we get Gebrehiwot's account of this remarkably peaceful changeover; communications with the north took time to recover. Then, over the weekend, an American-sponsored conference was convened in London, with Ethiopia's prime minister (formerly foreign minister) negotiating from a position of abject weakness with the EPRDF leadership.

These developments, seen from the point of view of our London colleagues, gave rise to concern lest we should be caught up in the sort of chaos from which Liberia and Mogadishu had suffered, and by a curious coincidence the weekend duty officer in our HQ was Paul Docherty. It was easier for me to reassure him by telephone than anyone else; it seemed that no one had really understood the fall-back position of safety in the embassy compound that we had available to us. Furthermore, the EPRDF forces were not the undisciplined rabble of popular imagination. Although largely consisting of teenagers armed with kalashnikovs, they were very strictly trained and under radio control in small groups. The greater risk for us, though short-lived, was the straggling lines of government soldiers walking back from the front (to which they had been taken by bus) carrying over their shoulders weapons they tried to sell in the market for food. Fortunately for everyone, the few people left who were able to exercise authority and influence in the army made an excellent job of enticing these demoralized men back into their barracks with the promise of a square meal. In short, any threat of disorder rapidly became minimal. The remaining question was how much damage might arise from last-ditch defenders of the now surrounded capital.

Some weeks earlier we had agreed to hold our annual staff lunch party on the Monday and, despite a vague feeling that morning that postponement might be wise, we were domestically geared up for it and knew it would be difficult to reinstate. As it was about to begin, a call came through to Diana from my mother to check that we were all right; she could hardly believe Diana's explanation. The party progressed normally until the early afternoon and the taking of the official photograph, when a group of prudently thoughtful colleagues decided to take the landrover to the bank and withdraw the cash required to pay everyone. It was 27 May, and it was a very wise move (see photograph).

The peace talks in London were stalled, so the Americans sensibly advised the EPRDF to take over the capital as swiftly as possible. Unaware of this on the ground, we went back to our desks after lunch, but my journey home lay via the embassy to which Diana and our ELTO colleagues had already been summoned by radio. Only very reluctantly would they allow me to go (at high speed and with an escort) to my house to fetch food and my ready-prepared emergency office, and to give instructions to our cook, gardener, housemaid and gatekeepers/watchmen to sleep inside the house, not in their own quarters.

It was a noisy night but relatively quiet by the morning. The dying agony of Mengistu's regime consisted of a tank battle outside what had been his palace, over which, visible from the embassy, hung a pall of smoke, later supplemented by that of an ammunition dump going up. That Tuesday my 'camping office' served to make and receive calls from London and to check in turn the safety of each one of our local staff who had telephones in their houses. A 7.00 p.m. to 6.00 a.m. curfew was decreed — a welcome measure at first, but increasingly inconvenient as time went on. Next day our military friends made a recce and by lunch time it was deemed safe for us to go home where we found all in order, including water and telephone, although the electricity was a little intermittent for a while. On the Thursday most of my staff got into the office and, although the library clientele was slightly abnormal for a while — a few curiosity-driven strangers came in off the street — we were proud to have closed for only two days.

An incidental story must be told concerning the remnants of Haile Selassie's imperial family. Many had perished in one way or another and some were abroad, but a handful of survivors from prison conditions had been allowed to live in a house very near ours. They were not allowed to leave the country, but were otherwise living quietly, and, for fear of possible recriminations from any future rulers, our embassy had undertaken to shelter them in the event of disorder. Diana was the go-between, so on that fateful Tuesday she was instructed to tell them to get ready to come, with

291

only one suitcase each. Thus it was that on each of the two nights we spent kindly accommodated by James Glaze in his residence, we enjoyed the bizarre experience of dining with assorted princesses and younger princes, first in Matthew's house (he had been planning a dinner party that night anyway) and then with HMA. It could be suggested that in the real world outside all hell was being let loose, but that would be quite untrue.

A power vacuum gives rise to speculation, but one attempt to fill it was made before the weekend by the vice-chairman of the EPRDF who invited all donor and relief agencies to meet in the Hilton Hotel. Playing a John the Baptist role, he sought to assure the assembled representatives that their work would be respected and, so far as the bankrupt economy would allow, contracts honoured. Then, on the 'Glorious First of June' (known since my prep school days as a victory of Lord Howe, but where and when?), Melis Zenawi flew in from London and we quickly came to recognize him as the brains behind the successful campaign and as the head of the new regime.

Scarcely had we begun to relax, feeling that things might get trickier but that movement was in the right direction, when a third fateful Tuesday morning started earlier than usual. Rumbling and flashes, which were not thunder, penetrated our bedroom at 4.15 a.m. and, at 4.23, a big explosion with smaller ones to follow, about a mile away somewhere in the southern suburbs, proved later to have been a massive ammunition store on fire. As dawn broke a mushroom cloud grew high in the sky. Dramatic pictures were shown on breakfast TV at home and, at 8.10, Renate Hunt was asking me by telephone whether Oliver was safe. He had fortunately answered my enquiry at 5.30 saying yes, but all his windows were shattered.

This event gave a completely false impression, dramatized by the media, of the degree of violence associated with this counter-revolution, and it reinforced suggestions from London that we should evacuate our ELTO colleagues and then come ourselves. None of us felt threatened and each of the four ELTOs (Norman Pritchard having left already on the last Lufthansa flight out) wrote separate appeals to be allowed to continue their teaching, writing and administrative work. At the end of that week we arranged for Oliver Hunt to take the first flight out of the reopened airport to London and offer a first-hand account of the situation. Incredibly, it seems there was no one free to listen to him, which gave me the chance to point out that of the four London colleagues at various levels who had sought to give me instructions in recent weeks, not one had visited Ethiopia. No one's fault, of course; just too many countries to supervise: but John Lawrence made sure of a visit pretty soon.

The following Saturday, with the teenage warriors camped around strategic points all over the city, we had an embassy wedding. Sue Owen married an Australian aid worker, Paul Schlunke, in the City Hall registry office (we were honoured witnesses), followed by a blessing service in the English church (during which Colin Battell pointedly said that embassy staff should not only come for weddings) and a feast in the residence, which Diana had helped to prepare in the absence of Rosemary Glaze.

Then we got news that our lecturer at the Alemaya University of Agriculture, Dr Hill, supplied at last under the World Bank contract, had found that his flat was in the firing line between the EPRDF and some recalcitrant Oromo irregulars operating in the Harar region. He expected us to rescue him — an eventuality which was precisely why we had doubted the wisdom of the contract in the first place — and we could not send the landrover with a lone driver, so both had to go.

A personal sting in the tail of this whole episode was the humiliation of Rosemary Arnott at Frankfurt airport (nothing at all to do with the Germans), treatment which made me more angry and distressed than anything within memory. Rosemary had gone to Prague for a well-earned spot of leave on the last flight out in May, but on her way back in mid-June she was intercepted with a message from London saying she should not go on to Addis Ababa but return to London. She phoned me for advice, but it was impossible to advise her to disregard the instruction for fear of the noose of disciplinary action for either or both of us. She flew straight home to Leeds in disgust, but with encouragement from me to fight tooth and nail and to insist on being allowed to return where a mountain of work was (hardly surprisingly) in arrears. The point was that the FCO had agreed to allow the few embassy staff who had left back to their posts a week earlier, but another week elapsed before we saw her again, with much relief.

In the aftermath, my statement on 'The Lessons of the Emergency' did get a reasonable reception in London. For me the blame for the unnecessary differences of opinion lay with modern communications. The use of telex, fax and telephone gives people at a distance the illusion of thinking they know what is going on, so they cannot resist underestimating the views of the man on the spot. Furthermore, our London colleagues were not able at all times to distinguish between the advice being given by the FCO to the public and the FCO's thoughts about its own staff.

The dust settles and the EPRDF consolidates

Keeping his public promise, Melis Zenawi opened a national conference on 1 July, exactly one month after taking over. It was televised live for all to see everyone represented except the discredited Derg — a pejorative word used to refer to the former ruling military clique. At the usual 4 July party my American friends introduced me for a brief conversation with the EPLF leader, Isaias Afeworki, in which he readily sympathized with my concern for our staff in the Asmara library. Let no one decry the usefulness of such diplomatic functions!

Throughout the emergency, the plight of the Sandford School was acute. My ex-officio membership of its board put me in the front line at the frequent meetings to discuss how to advise the expatriate teachers, whether to keep open when pupils had difficulty attending and coping with the financial consequences. As the English community school, its policy had always been an equal balance of Ethiopian and foreign pupils, but the Central Bank retained the hard currency fees paid by its international parents and only rarely and after long delays would grant exchange control permission to make payments from it. Teachers were paid in local currency and it was impossible to pay for the import of books, supplies and vehicles — all in strong contrast to the support available from the French, Italian and US embassies for 'their' schools.

James Glaze, as ex-officio president of the school, was determined to improve matters and, with ammunition provided by me, lost no time in approaching the newly appointed Minister of Education to put the case for granting a truly international status to the school. This was eventually achieved, after my time, and made a radical difference; hard currency earnings could be used to ensure the recruitment of well-qualified teachers from Britain and necessary equipment could now be obtained normally.

With the knowledge that this was in train, we took off for our long-anticipated holiday in Finland and home leave. Our ELTOs also took summer leave, happy in the completion of their academic year against all odds. Three years since leaving Helsinki, we managed to renew friendships by accepting the Moorhouse's kind offer of their Puistokatu flat as a base, and then hiring a dormobile for excursions west and east. We saw most of those mentioned throughout Chapter 13, and a catalogue would mean nothing, but the whole fortnight was immensely enjoyable and we resolved that next time, if ever possible, we would make a similar series of two-night stops by boat — to the Sells in Raisio, the Gräsbecks in Bromarv, the Koivulas near them, and the Enkvists in the Porvoo direction.

Friends and relations in London, Totnes and Bosham were duly brought up to date; there were concerts in Dartington, a river trip and a one-day skippered charter from Salcombe; our flat required a new gas boiler — not a simple procedure; Potty Granny 'had a turn' (not fully diagnosed) and required ten days of TLC to get her right again; news of the unsuccessful coup against Gorbachev came in; and a party to celebrate Tim Bridgman's marriage to Christine was memorable for a rare evening (preserved in photographs) with all five family couples present with Potty Granny, 'the matriarch', at the Old Schools in Bosham. Then a night train to Inverness and a hire car took us to Culloden, Cawdor and finally Dunvegan on Skye to visit Donald and Rosemary MacLeod of Bucharest days. On the southward return we stayed with Isobel Duncan (ex-Malawi) in Linwood, Glasgow, and met Jessica for a concert by the Edinburgh University chamber orchestra in which she was playing during her first summer vacation. The final halfway stopover was a weekend with Nigel and Sarah in their rented bungalow in Stockport, necessary while he finished his MBA at Manchester Business School.

Back in Addis Ababa we found that, independently of any civil war damage, a hydroelectric generator had suffered flood damage and this resulted in intermittent electricity rationing. Because our typewriters, telex and fax machines were disabled by cuts, the telephone switchboard batteries went flat after so many hours, and our computers needed an uninterrupted power supply, we made enquiries about the availability of portable generators with enough capacity to keep our equipment going in the hub of the office. By happy coincidence we were able to take technical advice from an FCO visitor to the embassy. The Justesens catalogue offered exactly what was needed and, using telex to order and our newly authorized sterling cheque account to pay, we got it in three weeks, air freighted of course. My friends in the embassy could not believe such speed possible.

The rest of our time in Ethiopia was dominated by tussles with the ODA and feeding the embassy with the required drafts. First, however, was the reward of achieving a long-cherished ambition — an overland journey to Asmara. Relative peace now reigned throughout the northern parts, which had been inaccessible (and impassable except by air) for many years, so we applied to the Eritrean representative in Addis Ababa for permission to do the journey, pleading the long overdue replenishing of our library, the urgent need to bolster the morale of our staff and, above all, a desire to mark the twentieth anniversary of the British Council's presence in Asmara. Ato Haile Merkarios accepted my plan to spend only two days on the road, invite EPLF officials to a party on the Saturday, for which Rosemary Arnott would have flown up, fly myself back to Addis Ababa and have Rosemary return at leisure in the empty landrover the following week. It worked beautifully. Our excellent driver–mechanic, Teklehaimanot, shared the driving with me and we covered the 1100 kilometres by doing 12 hours on the first and 16 hours on the second day. We saw many burnt-out tanks and rocket launchers, many UN food lorries, two British-built Bailey bridges (without which the road would not have been open) and delivered some books *en route* in Woldiya, our night stop. Very uplifting to our spirits on the drive north was the sight of crops ready for harvesting in Tigray, indicating that there had been decent rains at last — much-needed encouragement in a war-torn landscape.

In Asmara we called on a series of departmental heads in the new provisional government, most of them sitting behind a desk still wearing their khaki EPLF fighter jackets. We met people who had run schools, libraries and hospitals in underground hide-outs for many years, and it was obvious that Gebrehiwot had hedged his bets very effectively in ensuring the goodwill of both sides towards our library service, which for so many had been a lone source of information over 20 years. My speech of welcome at the party in the library for Ato Assefa, the EPLF member in charge of Eritrean libraries, surveyed the chequered history of ours since 1971, with at least two periods when closure was only staved off by the determination of our staff to maintain the service. It was especially gratifying that the new authorities were prepared to let us move into really spacious new premises in Lorenzo Ta'azaz Street, at an affordable rent.

My report on this visit, which was quickly followed by one from the FCO's deputy undersecretary Patrick Fairweather, accompanied by James Glaze, said *inter alia* 'It is sobering to appreciate our degree of ignorance of the last 18 years of what has been 30 years of civil war, and I think it is fair to say that most people living in the south of Ethiopia have preferred on the whole not to know too much about it.'

Countdown to the end of official employment

Of several projects initiated in our last few months, but which came to fruition later, the most interesting was undoubtedly the request received from the new leadership. Melis Zenawi and his friends had abandoned their university studies in the mid-1970s. They had learnt how to run a guerrilla army and had effectively conquered the country, but they recognized that they did not know how to run a government. They said they wanted some sort of correspondence course to resume and make respectable their academic studies of political economy and history, and they also wanted 'a crash course in decision-making'. Clearly the best source of distance learning for VIPs was the Open University (OU) and, within a few weeks, we secured a visit from David Mercer of the OU's business school. He was impressed by the high quality of the potential students, and they in turn liked the materials he showed them, consisting of an MBA programme modified for emphasis on public administration rather than commercial business. In due course a costed scheme was put to the ODA for funding, and much pushing was required to get it through in time for the beginning of the OU's academic year in February. Some two years later it was reported that the president of Ethiopia had been awarded a first-class degree.

Another project at a less exalted level was the ODA-funded teaching of remedial English to the staff of Ethiopia's Ministry of Foreign Affairs. The Colchester English Studies Centre had done a formal needs analysis and was prepared to assign two teachers to the full-time task for an initial six weeks. Again, much pushing was required to get a contract signed in July so that materials could be prepared in August, teachers selected and nominated in September, and the course could begin in October.

While phase two of the KELT project, employing ELTOs up to 1995, was eventually given the green light, another idea connected with it failed to make progress. We knew that a reasonable standard of English had only been achieved in the 1960s through the employment of enough native speakers to provide at least one in each secondary school, and it seemed that much of our ELTOs' efforts would be wasted unless their methods and textbooks were backed up and practised not only by trained Ethiopian teachers of English but by a minimal number of native speakers. VSO was not interested in supplying volunteers on this scale in one country, but a scheme had operated for the Sudan whereby its embassy in London did the recruitment of 'junior contract' teachers with a volunteering spirit. We hoped in vain for this system to be applied for Ethiopia.

Macbeth had been presented in our garden just ten days before Mengistu had fled. We thought that a comedy should be next on the list and chose *Two Gentlemen of Verona*, which was differently enjoyed. The Motleys did Britten's *St Nicholas* and one of the Mozart *Vespers* in the German and the English churches. Diana distinguished herself once again in comic turns for the theatre club's cabaret, and Jessica arrived from Edinburgh in time to celebrate her twentieth birthday. Her boyfriend, Simon Mays-

ETHIOPIA and ERITREA: Civil War and Counter-Revolution

Smith, joined us and the Hicks family for a long Christmas mid-week in Langano. Early in the new year we were involved in a charity concert in James Glaze's residence, raising money for a mobile unit for street children, a very worthwhile cause in the interests of reducing the vast population of young victims of the years of civil disturbance. The Russian (no longer Soviet) Ambassador was present and asked for it to be repeated in his fine octagonal auditorium a few weeks later. So it happened that our swan song was a Russian one, breaking new ground by performing in what had been the heavily guarded facilities designed for the 5000 Soviet 'advisers', just inside the now welcoming gates of the embassy of the Russian Federation.

A year or more earlier my question put to the Ethiopian Film Corporation had been 'Granted that you cannot afford the rights payable for decent British films, if you were given the chance what would you like best?' Without hesitation they had said *A Passage to India*, which was, of course, the one film my contacts should be able to exert influence to obtain. After much chasing of elusive distributors, long silences and help from my former colleagues in Films Department, we were surprised to receive a consignment of 35-millimetre cans containing a print in mint condition with permission to keep it for as long as we wanted. So almost my last official duty was to organize a gala screening of this fine production in the Ambassador Cinema in the centre of Addis Ababa, and then to send it on circuit round Ethiopia.

A valedictory holiday in Kenya
The British Council rule is that retirement has to be precisely on one's sixtieth birthday and that any leave due must be taken before that date (in my case 14 March 1992), so it had been arranged that Michael and Patsy Sargent, our successors, would arrive in early February and we would leave in the middle of the month. We had met Michael in Devon the previous summer, and felt very happy to be handing over to someone whose heart was clearly in the right place. It can be a devastating experience if that confidence is lacking. After a plethora of very generous farewell parties we flew to Nairobi on the first leg of our final journey home.

299

So many years in Africa and we had never done any game viewing on the tourist trail; we thought we should take this possibly final chance. John and Barbara Gardner allowed us to use their house as a base and, after a pleasantly relaxed weekend, we hired a Suzuki 4WD and drove up to our Nightingale cousins' farm in Naivasha, last visited on leave from Malaysia 15 years before. Charles, my second cousin, was away on holiday, so we were able to be useful helping his parents, Ted and Billy, with the turkeys, and in a few days we learnt all the stages in the process, from hatching to slaughter. Then we had an adventurous journey in unexpectedly wet conditions through the Aberdare National Park to its country club near Mweiga, and had a night in the Ark, a place specially designed for watching nocturnal animal activity. Our next stop was the ultra-luxurious Mount Kenya Safari Club, from which we did much walking and riding, and then returned to Nairobi round the north and east side of the mountain.

A flight by Lufthansa via yet another night stop in Frankfurt took us to Malaga to use, for the last time, a self-catering flat under the Holiday Property Bond, which we had decided to sell. A week there, out of season, included trips to Gibraltar and Ronda; then we were ready to face London and the unknown prospects ahead.

The Director-General, Sir Richard Francis, invited me with Diana for a farewell sherry and said 'Ethiopia *will* get its new building', but if it had we would have heard by now.

Part III
The Third Age:
On Home Ground

15
Coda:
Pensioned But Not Yet Retired

I t would be unwise to attempt any sort of summary of an already very condensed narrative, yet a brief retrospect is needed to round it off. Some people prefer to make a clean break when leaving full-time gainful employment, but for us our affection for so many British Council and other colleagues has made that an unreal option; and the main purpose of this book lies in the hope that some of them will be stimulated to set down their own anecdotes, doubtless with far greater literary skill.

The BBC series *True Brits* gave a very fair view of life in the diplomatic service; so far nothing comparable has been written about life in the British Council's service, and only the small minority of the public having a personal orientation to the wider world is able to imagine what is involved.

The transition from one post to another, whether abroad or at home, will be seen to have been sometimes rough and sometimes smooth. The common network of operations, however, normally ensured that any unique features of a new job could be mastered within about three months. It has taken us three years to reach the same stage of feeling at home in the local community in which we have 'posted' ourselves. It is much harder going, even with threads of friendship and family connections ready to pick up from the past. On the other hand there is the feeling of having acquired a professional understanding of the art of doing just that.

It is not so much habit as a belief in its validity that makes me go on doing voluntarily so much of what was previously the vehicle for earning a living; and it has been rightly said that to stop using a talent you are fortunate enough to possess is an impoverishment of others as well as yourself. So the compulsion is there — to conduct concerts of choral and instrumental music, to navigate sailing boats whenever possible, to maintain friendships in the far-away homes of the past, and to build new ones around us in the West Country. Some of the questions that are most frequently asked — especially by those who have lived and worked in the same environment all their lives — may have been answered in this book.

The world is not kind to late-developers, but music enabled me to enter the higher education system by the back door and to leave it by the front. The fruits of that education gave me the key to a short-term beginning in the British Council which opened into a career. Maybe my writing suffers from the zeal of the convert; if so, may it be judged accordingly.

Select Bibliography

Windsor
Wridgway, Neville, *The Choristers of St George's Chapel*, Chas. Luff & Co Ltd, Slough, 1980

Clifton
Winterbottom, Derek, *Clifton after Percival: A Public School in the Twentieth Century*, Redcliffe Press, Bristol, 1990

Cambridge
Morris, Christopher, *King's College: A Short History*, Cambridge, 1989
Robinson, B. W., *An Amateur in Music*, Countryside Books, Newbury, 1985

Dartington
Bonham-Carter, Victor, *Dartington Hall: The History of an Experiment*, Phoenix House, London, 1958
Young, Michael, *The Elmhirsts of Dartington: The Creation of a Utopian Community*, Routledge & Kegan Paul, London 1982

Nigeria and Cameroons
Heussler, Robert, *The British in Northern Nigeria*, Oxford University Press, Oxford, 1968
Mahood, M. M., *Joyce Cary's Africa*, Methuen & Company, London, 1964
Morley, John, *Colonial Postscript: The Diary of a District Officer 1935–1956*, Radcliffe Press, London, 1992

Select Bibliography

Malawi

Adams, Michael, *Voluntary Service Overseas: The Story of the First Ten Years*, Faber & Faber, London, 1968

Ransford, Oliver, *Livingstone's Lake*, John Murray, London, 1966

Roseveare, Sir Martin, *Joys, Jobs and Jaunts*, Blantyre Print, Blantyre, 1984

Japan

Boger, H. Batterson, *The Traditional Arts of Japan*, Doubleday, New York, 1964

Tomlin, E. W. F., *Tokyo Essays*, Hokuseido Press, Tokyo, 1967

Malaysia

Ross-Larson, B. (ed.) *Issues in Contemporary Malaysia*, Heinemann Educational Books, London, 1977

Ryan, N. J., *The Cultural Heritage of Malaya*, Longman, Malaysia, 1971

Romania

Domitriu, Petru, *Incognito*, William Collins, London, 1962 (reprint 1978)

Manning, Olivia, *The Balkan Trilogy: The Great Fortune*, Heinemann, London, 1960

Ratiu, Ion, *Contemporary Romania*, Foreign Affairs Publications Company, London, 1975

Finland

Jagerskiold, Stig, *Mannerheim Marshal of Finland*, Christopher Hurst & Company, London, 1986

Mead, W. R., *An Experience of Finland*, Christopher Hurst & Company, London, 1993

Richards, J. M., *A Guide to Finnish Architecture*, Hugh Evelyn Limited, London, 1966

Siikala, Kalervo, *Finnish Reflections: Space, Time, Objects*, Kirjayhtyma, Helsinki, 1981

Select Bibliography

Ethiopia

Clapham, Christopher, *Transformation and Continuity in Revolutionary Ethiopia*, Cambridge University Press, Cambridge, 1988

Mockler, Anthony, *Haile Selassie's War*, Oxford University Press, Oxford, 1984

Ullendorff, Edward, *The Ethiopians*, Oxford University Press, Oxford, 1973 (3rd edition)

General

Donaldson, Frances, *The British Council: The First Fifty Years*, Jonathan Cape Ltd, London, 1984

Eliot, T. S., *Notes Towards the Definition of Culture*, Faber & Faber, London, 1948 (reprint 1962)

Frost, Richard, *Race Against Time: Human Relations and Politics in Kenya Before Independence*, Rex Collings Ltd, London, 1978

Mitchell, J. M., *International Cultural Relations*, Allen & Unwin, London, 1986

Wallace, William, *The Foreign Policy Process in Britain*, George Allen & Unwin, London, 1976 (reprint 1977)

White, A. J. S., *The British Council: The First 25 Years*, British Council, London, 1965

Index

Index

Index

Bucharest, 116, 160, 166, 168–9, 172–4, 176, 178–81, 184–7, 189, 191, 193–6, 202, 218, 224, 230, 257–8, 278, 295
Buckinghamshire, 71
Budapest, 167, 186
Bukovina (Upper Moldavia), 183; *see also* Moldavia
Bulgaria, 34, 166, 195
Burd, Keith, 286
Bure river, 203
Burgess, Guy, 209
Burgh, Sir John, 199
Burnham-on-Sea, 123, 131
Burravoe, 31
Burren, 282
Bursledon, 25
Bute, 215
Butterworth, Jack, 155
Byön, 250
Byrd, William, 287

Cadbury family, 74
Cadby Hall, 32
Cadiz, 16
Caesarea, 194
Cairns, David, 31
Cairo, 87, 272, 275, 277, 283
Caius College, 25, 28
Calabar, TSS, 65
Calcutt, Sir David, 28, 73
Calcutta, 26, 142
Câldâruşani, 190
Cam river, 27
Cambridge, 10–11, 14, 24–6, 28, 30, 33, 35, 37, 56, 58, 67–8, 71, 73, 77–8, 80, 91, 104–5, 113, 118, 134, 153, 194, 216, 237, 241–3, 258
Cambridge and Oxford Society, 119
Cambridge University Music Society (CUMS), 27
Cambridge University Musical Club (CUMC), 26–7
Cambridge University United Nations Association, 32
Cameron family, 61
Cameron Highlands, 146
Cameroon, 45, 48, 53, 55, 58, 104, 256, 285
Cameroons Baptist Mission, 49, 53

Canada, 56, 58, 103, 257
Canadian University Service Overseas, 102
Canaries, 41
Cannes, 201–2, 207
Canterbury, 167
Cape Province, 133
Cape Town, 42, 106, 109, 133, 151, 166, 242
Capernaum, 194
Carcosa, 156, 158
Cardale, Commander, 222
Cardew, Michael, 47, 63
Cardiff, 71, 127, 129, 215
Cardiff Polyphonic Choir, 114
Carewe, John, 73
Carey, Hugh, 125, 129
Carhaix, 204
Caribbean, 172
Carisbrooke Castle, 31
Carnwath, Francis, 158
Carpathian Mountains, 174
Cartwright, John, 205
Carver, John and Veda, 109, 280
Cavaliero, Roddy, 238
Cawdor, 295
Ceauşescu, Nicolae, 168–9, 196
Central Bank, 294
Central Office of Information, 200
Central Policy Review Staff, 155
Central State Library, 190
CEPES, 185
Chadwick, Tom, 14
Chagall, Marc, 194
Chalker, Baroness Linda, 286
Chan, Esther, 149
Chancellor College, 95
Charente, 282
Charles, Prince, 114
Charolles, 180
Chartres, 202
Cheah, I. K., 155
Cheah, Winnie, 149
Cheek by Jowl Company, 241
Chelsea Opera Group, 25, 32, 37, 71, 73
Cheltenham, 129
Chenery, Brian, 210
Chenonceau, 180
Cherub Theatre Company, 267, 269

Index

Index

160, 167, 169, 173, 181, 199, 208, 225, 243, 246, 263, 278, 288, 293–4, 296–7
Forglen, 153, 179
Forsblom, Kai, 228, 237
Foumbam, 54
Fox, Douglas, 9–11, 58, 96
France, 34, 58, 89, 181, 202, 204
Francis, Sir Richard, 249, 276, 300
Frankfurt, 271, 278, 282, 293, 300
Fraser's Hill, 146, 148, 156
Frean, Dennis, 133
Freetown, 42, 66
French Equatorial Africa, 53
Friends of the Musicians' Chapel, 270
Frost, Richard, 156
Frost, Robert and Martina, 147, 156
Fugelsang, Dr Harald, 216
Fuji, 118
Fuller, David, 240
Fulton, Lord, 114

Gabrieli Brass Ensemble, 180
Gabrieli Quartet, 251
Gaddafi, Colonel, 196
Gafton, Lucian, 165
Galen Kalala, 227
Galilee, 194
Gandhi, Mahatma, 210
Gardiner family, 59
Gardner, John and Barbara, 144, 278, 300
Garland, Jenny, 172
Garnons-Williams, Mary-Jane, 126
Garoua, 54
Garstang, Elsie, 130
Garton, Rosemary, 56
Gashaka, 50
Gatineau Park, 258
Gatwick, 104, 153, 249
Gavrion, 179
Gboko, 55
Gebrehiwot, Ato, 263, 266, 290, 297
Gee, Tim, 148
Gembu, 40–1, 53–6
General Wingate School, 260
Geneva, 30, 185
Genoa, 87
Gent, Peter and Lucy, 65
Georgia, 258

German Democratic Republic, 166, 268
Germany, 68, 89
Gethsemane, Garden of, 193
Ghana, 42, 70, 144
Gherla, 192
Gibraltar, 16–18, 87, 300
Gielgud, Maina, 186
Gillate, Don, 113, 199
Ginever, Stuart, 100, 102
Girton College, Cambridge, 23, 30
Gizaw Negussie, Comrade, 276
Glanville, Provost, 32
Glasgow, 70, 94, 104, 154, 167, 240, 272, 295
Glason, Denis, 62–3, 65
Glason, Keturah, 62
Glastonbury, 77, 87, 96
Glaze, James, 278, 283, 285–6, 294, 297, 299
Glaze, Rosemary, 278, 293
Glock, William, 256
Gloucester, 277
Glyndebourne, 26, 56, 58, 71
Gobir, Amuda, 36
Godfrey, David, 280
Godstowe, 179, 188, 203
Goethe Institute, 139, 184, 218
Gold, Jack, 196
Golding, Sir John and Lady Pamela, 276
Gombak Hospital, 148
Gombe, 45
Gondar, 266, 286
Gongola river, 47
Goodman, Ken and June, 53, 57
Gorbachev, Mikhail, 281, 295
Goree, Bob, 75
Gosling, Bill and Jennifer, 56, 57
Goss, John, 5
Gozo, 241
Graham, Colin, 114
Granada, 232
Granna, 216
Grant, John, 170
Grantchester, 24
Gräsbeck, Gottfried and LaVonne, 223, 295
Graur, Dr Tiberiu, 183
Gravil, Richard, 120
Gray, Robin, 93
Graz, 37, 188

Index

Index

Hobsbawm, Eric, 29
Hockney, David, 237
Hodgkin, Howard, 150
Hoggart, Richard, 198
Holcome, 154
Holiday, Miss Florence, 4
Holmer, Paul, 172
Hong, 47
Hong Kong, 120, 151, 218, 259
Honkeranta, Inger, 219
Hook of Holland, 240
Horezu, 183
Horton, Robin, 42
Hudson, Bill, 195
Hudson, Nigel, 259
Hull, 70
Hungary, 166, 186
Hunt, Oliver, 264, 268, 292–3
Hunt, Renate, 292
Hunt, Rex and Mavis, 146
Hunter, Keith, 139
Hurding, Una, 205
Hurmuzescu, Dan, 168
Hurt, John, 196
Hydra, 162
Hyökki, Matti, 221
Hyslop, Graham, 104

Iaşi, 174, 194, 196
Ibadan, 44, 59–61, 65, 69–70, 154, 189
Iceland, 233
ICI, 74, 104, 237
Ignatius, Mary Ann, 175
Ilala, MV, 102
Iliffe, Barrie, 204
Ilorin, 36, 44, 56, 59–62
Imatra, 229, 235
Imperial College, 258
Imperial Household Agency, 114
Indefatigable, HMS, 14–16
India, 26, 121, 138, 146, 151, 201, 207, 239, 275
India Office, 181
Iniö, 251
Institut Pedagogic, 173
Institute of Development Studies, 135
Institute of Health Science, 275
Institute of Higher Education, 183
Institute of Language Studies, 264
Institute of Medicine and Pharmacy, 183

Institute of Personnel Management, 76
Institute of Public Administration, 54, 63
International Ethiopian Studies Conference, 287
International Federation for Vernacular Languages, 226
International Livestock Centre for Africa (ILCA), 255, 261
International Red Cross, 37
International School of Bucharest, 179
Inverness, 295
Ionescu, Cornelia, 172, 185
Ipoh, 142, 151
Ipswich, 214
Ireland, 282
Iron Gates, 180, 189
Isaias Afeworki, 294
Isepp, Martin, 180
Iseyin, 61–2
Isherwood, John, 91
Ishibashi, Hiro, 118
Isleworth, 126
Israel, 193
Istanbul, 148, 189, 195, 272
Italian Cultural Institute, 184, 283
Italy, 34, 68, 166, 190
Iveagh, Lord, 32

Jacobs, Tony, 24
Jacques, Dr Reginald, 11
Jada, 48, 55
Jagoe, Robin, 41–2, 44
Jairos Jiri Rehabilitation Centre, 211
Jalan Ampang, 156
Jamaica, 276
Japan, 7, 106, 109–21, 129, 146–7, 151, 175, 179, 184, 198, 202, 214, 225, 238–9, 241–2, 256, 267, 285
Japan–British Society, 119
Jares, Terttu, 232
Jayawardena, Lal, 151, 242
Jean Sibelius Quartet, 226
Jebba, 44, 62, 75
Jedburgh, 26
Jeddah, 271
Jenkins, Peter and Waveney, 156
Jenkins, Sue, 105
Jericho, 194
Jerusalem, 193–4

318

Index

Index

Lahinch, 282
Lahti, 223–4, 236
Lake Club, 158
Lambert, Audrey, 120
Lambert, Ken, 127
Lambrook, 191, 195
Lamurde, Karfe, 44
Lamya, Edson, 98, 279
Langano, Lake, 268, 276–7, 285, 299
Lannion, 204
Laos, 127
Lapai, 63
Lappeenranta, 229
Las Palmas, 41
Lassa, 49
Last, Dr Rex, 79
Lautasaari, 226
Lavington, 3; *see also* Market
    Lavington; West Lavington
Lawrence, John, 146–7, 149, 154, 159,
    293
Lawrence, Mary-Ann and Peter, 158
Le Perche, 202
Le Perou, 282, 287
Leach, Bernard, 259
Leach, Diana, 93
League of Nations, 45
Leamington Spa, 244
Lean, David, 201
Lee, Rex, 182
Lee, Seton, 36, 110
Leeds, 11, 128, 293
Lehos, Peter and Aileen, 252
Lehtimaki family, 228
Leicester, University of, 228
Leithead, Dr Charles, 252, 275
Leithead, Mrs, 252, 277
Leningrad, 208, 224, 251
Lentiira, 246
Leow Siak Fah, 149
Leppard, Raymond, 114
Leprosy Relief Association (LEPRA),
    101, 105
Lerwick, 31
Lesotho, 210, 285
Levin, Bernard, 169
Liberia, 290
Libya, 259
Lieksa, 236, 246
Lighthill, Miss P., 131

Lille, 187, 201, 207
Lilongwe, 90, 91, 99–100, 278–9
Limbalo, Fly, 99
Limbe, 88–9, 91, 95–6, 98, 105, 279
Lincoln, 31
Lincoln Centre, 139
Lincoln's Inn, 73
Lindsay Quartet, 236, 251
Ling Ai Ee, 158
Linwood, 295
Linz, 37, 187
Lisbon, 19
Liston, Gerry, 144, 148
Little Cheverell, 3, 4
Littleton Panel, 3
Liverpool, 11, 38, 45, 66, 70
Livingstone, 92
Livingstonia, 102
Lloyd, John, 70
Loch Fyne, 167
Logan, Sir Donald, 189
Loire, 180, 202
London, 5, 17, 30, 32–3, 38, 41, 53, 56,
    58, 60, 66, 69–70, 72, 74, 80–1,
    91–5, 97, 99–100, 104–5, 110–14,
    116, 118–19, 121–3, 127–9, 131–3,
    141, 144, 147–8, 153, 155, 159–62,
    167, 169–70, 172–4, 177, 179–81,
    184–5, 187, 189–90, 193, 195, 197,
    198, 200–1, 205–11, 213, 216,
    218–19, 223, 225, 229–30, 236,
    239–40, 242–3, 245, 248, 252, 256,
    260, 263, 265, 267, 269–70, 272,
    283–4, 286–8, 290–5, 298, 300
London Baroque, 227
London City Ballet, 196, 223
London Chamber of Commerce, 242
London Film Festival (LFF), 209–10
London Multi Media Market (LMMM),
    209
London School of Economics, 76
London Symphony Orchestra, 119
London University, 73, 165, 246, 256
Longfield, Susan, 80
Lontano Ensemble, 186
Los Angeles, 53, 57
Louisiana Museum of Modern Art, 216
Lowe, Mark, 24, 68
Lübeck, 239, 252
Lugard, Lord, 36, 43, 52

320

Index

321

Index

Index

Numero, Matt, 97, 105, 279
Nunjoro, 152
Nupe, 64
Nurnburg, 187
Nyasa, Lake, 88
Nyasaland, 89

O'Hara, Jim, 144
Oby, 237
Office for Service to the Diplomatic
   Corps, 186
Ofjord, Audun, 185
Ogrezeanu, Stelian, 183
Okabe, Marie Lorenz, 119
Oktober Fest, 197
Oldham, 202, 240
Olive, John, 77, 80, 98, 104, 110, 123,
   126, 154, 202, 245
Olive, Phyllis, 77, 80, 123, 154
Oliver, Professor Roland, 274
Olives, Mount of, 193–4
Ong Teck Chin, Mr, 140
Ontario, 161, 257
Open University (OU), 297–8
Ord, Boris, 21–2, 25, 27, 29
Organization of African Unity (OAU),
   261
Organization for European Economic
   Cooperation, 32
Orkneys, 31
Ormerod, Nick, 241
Oromo, 293
Orpheus, 195
Orr, Peter and Kay, 153, 202, 270, 283
Orr, Tim, 79
Osaka, 111, 114
Oslo, 216, 233
Osman, Haji, 139, 147, 151
Osman, Hashim, 151
Osprey, HMS, 19, 31
Ostend, 167
Ottawa, 56, 257
Ottoman Empire, 35, 174, 191
Oulu, 223, 229
Outward Bound, 12, 48
Ouvry, David, 37
Overseas Development Administration
   (ODA), 125, 134–5, 139, 154, 160,
   243, 257, 259, 264–5, 274, 284, 296,
   298

Overseas Service Club, 35
Overseas Services Resettlement Bureau,
   72
Owen, David, 155
Owen, Sue, 293
Oxenbury, Bill, 22, 28
Oxfam, 30, 91, 259
Oxford, 4, 23, 25, 31, 33–5, 37–8,
   41–2, 56, 58, 65, 70–1, 73, 110, 119,
   127, 140, 144, 156, 188, 191, 236,
   255, 275
Oxford University Musical Club and
   Union, 37
Oyo, 62

Packard, Vance, 81
Padua, 180
Painswick, 278
Paisley, 241
Paivola, 224
Pakistan, 63
Palais de Chaillot, 32
Palmer, Kate, 34
Pangkor, 146
Papua New Guinea, 58, 91, 125, 129
Paradise, 278
Parador Golf, 232
Paris, 32, 81, 162, 201–2
Parsons, Robert, 91, 96, 105
Partidul Communist Roman, 168
Partridge, Ian, 256
Pathet Lao, 128
Patten, Chris, 259, 272
Patterson, Ken, 105
Pavlovsk Palace, 208
Payne, Andrew, 215
Peace Corps, 96, 101–2, 149
Pelly, Jane, 19, 24
Pelman Institute, 15
Pembrokeshire, 129
Penang, 139, 142–3, 151, 155, 157, 161
Penkridge, 134
Penzance, 73
Perchard, Colin, 90, 93, 146, 210–11,
   274, 276
Percival, Alan, 27
Perham, Dame Margery, 36
Perlman, Alvin and Ellen, 184, 258
Pescek, Jim, 77
Pest, 168

324

Index

Index

Rijeka, 180
Rimet, 192
Rimnicu Vilcea, Bishop of, 166
Riyadh, 228
Robb College, 78
Robe, 266
Roberts, David, 92
Robertson, Sir James, 43
Robinson, Alice Ann, 92
Robinson, Bernard, 25, 69
Robinson, Ed, 75
Rock Moor, 26
Rockies, 57
Rogers, David, 123
Rohia, 192
Roles, Nick and Wendy, 224
Romania, 28, 35, 103, 116, 121, 150, 156, 159, 162, 165–6, 168–73, 175–86, 188–91, 193, 195–8, 202, 209, 213, 215, 217–18, 220, 222, 239, 242, 261–2, 285, 289
Rombulow-Pearce, Avis and Christopher, 30
Rome, 116, 259, 271, 277
Ronda, 300
Roscoff, 204
Rose, Bernard, 37
Rose, Brian, 246
Roseveare, David, 33
Roseveare, Janet, 33, 57
Rossing Foundation, 280
Rotblatt, Professor, 161
Rotterdam, 241
Rounthwaite, Chris, 54
Roussel, Lyon, 204–5, 208
Routledge, Norman, 32, 195
Rovaniemi, 237
Rowntree, 74
Royal Air Force (RAF), 13, 76
Royal Artillery, 6
Royal College of Music, 4
Royal College of Physicians, 110
Royal Festival Hall, 25, 71, 133
Royal Malaysia Police Band, 144, 149
Royal Naval Air Service (RNAS), 13
Royal Navy, 14, 17, 222
Royal Northern College of Music, 130
Royal Shakespeare Company, 119
Royal Society, 173

Rubber Research Institute, 156
Ruissalo, 223
Rus, Alexandra, 183
Rus, Remus, 191
Rus Batin, Vasile, 183
Russell, Tris and Joan, 153, 179
Russia, 168, 209, 218, 229, 260, 264, 269, 299
Rutter, Trevor, 205
Rycroft, Judy, 92
Rymattylla, 227

Sabah, 127, 137, 160
Saddleworth, 240
Saimaa, Lake, 229, 235
St Andrew's University, 57
St Anne's School, 60
St Bartholemew's Hospital (Bart's), 202, 215, 258
St Christopher's, 123, 131, 146
St Claire, Marion, 196
St David's Society, 158
St Denis d'Authou, 202
St Donat's, 215
St Francis Xavier, 148
St George's Chapel, 5–6, 8, 93
St George's School, 5
St Ives, 150, 259
St Malo, 180
St Mark's, 258
St Mary's College, Durham, 202
St Nicholas Singers, 221, 233
St Patrick's Mzedi Catholic Boys' School, 279
St Sepulchre-without-Newgate, 270
Saintes, 282
Salakari, Tom, 221
Salaman, Clement, 42
Salcombe, 295
Salima, 88–9, 102
Salisbury, 71, 73
Salisbury, Zimbabwe, 104
Salisbury Plain, 3
Sallantaus, Olli, 237
Salmon, Hugh, 215
Salter, John, 189, 230
Saltmarsh, John, 22
Salzburg, 37
San Francisco, 57

326

Index

Index

Index